... And About Ti...

The next stumbling steps in the Baby Boomer saga.

Labelled as both feckless and gormless, a typical BB does his best to become groovy by topping up with a shedload of feck and a shovelful of gorm... not easy when perhaps only 4 minutes from nuclear oblivion!

Copyright © John Burden 2023

ISBN Number: 9798392376452

All rights Reserved

Covers by Archangel Design

Contents

Introduction ... 1

Two Tin Cans and a Piece of String ... 4

A Dedicated Follower of Fission ... 24

Sky Hooks and Elbow Grease ... 53

Two Thirds of Sex, Drugs and Rock 'n' Roll ... 79

Vertical Hold ... 119

Shell Suits, Vertical Artex & Other Mistakes ... 153

Acid Drops ... 183

So Far So Good ... 212

Hindsight's a Wonderful Thing ... 228

Postscript ... 231

What Next? ... 232

Acknowledgements ... 233

Charities supported:
Save the Children Fund; National Churches Trust; Bodmin and Wenford Railway Trust

Introduction

There's a saying:

'...if you can remember the sixties, then you weren't there'.

Well, I beg to differ. For a start, if that were true, then the next one hundred and twenty pages would be entirely blank, with just the odd *'er.... umm .... hold on a minute...'* to enlighten proceedings. So, in answer to the above assertion I would say:

'Don't include me matey! I was there, and like all of my ancient Baby Boomer pals, I certainly remember the whole decade in all its glorious detail - so there!

Of course, the implication of the saying is that those who experienced the sixties were…*like spaced out man... blowin' in the wind, hitting the positive vibes…and just soooo out of sight, baby… away with the fairies and other cool chicks…like wow, it was just one great and groovy love-in man.*
Oh really?

[1]

Well, for a start, the 1960's didn't start until the autumn of 1962… and if that seem a contradiction in terms, what I'm saying is that the first two years of the decade were like an undisciplined and chaotic dress rehearsal. We were all over the place as the curtain rose – props not in position, the scenery still being erected, make-up only half done, and many of us still hopping about on one leg trying to get the other into a tight-fitting pair of hipsters.

Without doubt, the late fifties had prepared us all with huge expectations, gleeful anticipation and most of the ingredients of the cultural volcano about to erupt. The discovery of an entirely new social group called teenagers, their emerging and novel fashion consciousness, the arrival of the iconic Mini, the invention of the transistor, access for many to some disposable income, *Emergency Ward Ten* on the telly and Y Front underpants are just a few which spring to mind. Bearing in mind the fact that the popular music scene was at the forefront of the enthralling blast-off to come, you get a better perspective on the decade's unpreparedness when looking at the eclectic and diverse range of well-loved entries appearing in the 1960 Top Twenty chart: Tommy Steele's *'Little White Bull'*, *'Itsy Bitsy Teenie Weenie Yellow Polka-Dot Bikini'* by Brian Hyland, Ken Dodd's *'Love Is Like A Violin'* plus Charlie Drake's *'My Boomerang Won't Come Back'* - all of them just about a ungroovy as you can get. But also in this mix were much more cutting edge entries, such as *'Take Five'* by Dave Brubeck, Elvis belting out *'It's Now Or Never'* and Billy Fury's *'Half Way to Paradise'*. So, it was a real odd mix, with family comedy, sticky pathos and trad jazz awkwardly rubbing shoulders with a growing surge of stuff which was emerging as being groovy, of being really *'with it'*… and all this at a time when most people were demonstrably *without it*.

For example, in the early sixties, fridges were still a rarity, very few people had an built-in shower and such basic tasks as keeping your house warm was still very unsophisticated. The majority of us still had to get coal delivered, and like many with no space for an external coal shed, our house was by no means unusual in that this very dirty commodity was stored in a great heap underneath the kitchen floorboards. Thus, to get a scuttle full for the open fire, you had to lift a large flap in the kitchen floor, and with shovel in hand descend a short flight of steps into the stygian darkness. That such a precarious operation was quite likely to catch an unwary family member by surprise, culminating in their own rapid and unplanned descent was hardly surprising. But never mind! The sixties were here! Something exciting was bound to happen soon...wasn't it?

If you were lucky enough to have a TV set, you might get just a whole half hour of pop music each week by watching *Juke Box Jury* every Saturday evening with the impeccably groomed David Jacobs in the chair. And if you didn't have a TV, well there was always an hour's worth of *'Pick of the Pops'* with Alan *'Fluff'* Freeman each Sunday on the radio, provided of course, your wireless was up to scratch. For the majority who still owned the old valve radios, this often presented as a problem. Instead of tuning in to crystal clear sound, many broadcasts were frequently punctuated with interference of the whistling, buzzing, humming and imaginative farting kind, which tended to get in the way.

Mind you, the only good thing about such interruption was that it might prevent you from hearing the radio news bulletins. Whereas things on the home front were looking pretty good, the same cannot be said of things abroad. International relations were becoming increasingly fraught, and there was a good deal of sabre rattling going on between US backed NATO and the Russian's Warsaw Pact. The cold war seemed to be slipping into a permafrost state. A popular – if tasteless - bit of black humour that went round at the time concerning *'Famous Last Words'* attributed one to the mayor of Hiroshima:
'What the hell was that bang?'... says much about lack of sensitivity at that time.

But did most teenagers care about international relations? Of course not. Our perspective gave us every reason to see ourselves sitting on the mat at the top of the helter skelter, and edging ever closer to the wild excitement that was certain to come!

1   Two Tin Cans and a Piece of String

I was reading a newspaper article last week which stated that tiny microchips, (whose wafer-like thinness goes down to just twelve nanometres - or just a modest smear of atoms) can have laser-imprinted on them anything from a few hundred to *millions* of tiny electronic circuits. Also, these itsy-bitsy miracles of technology are now present in just about every electrical gismo you can think of. All modern cars, for example, have thousands of the little beggars on board, all beavering away very efficiently. So, the fact that when you turn on any electrical appliance, it will usually behave itself exactly as stated in the glossy brochure, has pretty much become one of modern life's absolutes.

Well, such certainty, such reliable *invisibility* was unknown in the technologies which accompanied us in the post-war years. Despite the arrival of domestic TV sets during the fifties, these were still coveted, expensive and often temperamental items. Thus, the pinnacle of most people's technological prowess was still their radio set, – commonly called the *wireless*. Bearing in mind that virtually all of these had been constructed before the introduction of modern electronics, there lurked within their dusty interiors a number of delicate valves mounted in a surprisingly heavy and rigid metal frame. As a result, most of the radios we had at this time were anything but portable; not only were many of them large, furniture-like pieces of apparatus, they were quite often attached to a long and awkward aerial which had to be positioned *just so* if you wanted to get anything more than a prolonged fart from the speaker. They were also quite delicate. The valves that lay glowing mysteriously in their cobweb-laden interior didn't appreciate being moved at all, and were quite likely to blow, given half the chance. Like teenagers being coaxed out of bed, they also took a long time to get going, and in a manner that could well be described as sulky, they really *really* didn't like being turned on and off either.

One of my personal heroes of the era was a GPO engineer called Tommy Flowers. Never heard of him? Well, you might like to bear in mind that almost single-handedly, he built **'*Colossus*'** the world's first programmable computer at the top secret Bletchley Park during the darkest days of the Second World War. Inside this ground-breaking machine were about *two thousand* valves – an unprecedented number of such unreliable items in one device. His many scientific critics said that Colossus would never work because the valves would burn out, as they were so vulnerable to being continually switched on and off. Tommy agreed. So he didn't.... didn't switch them off, I mean. He just left them on...and *hey presto*. His consequent success played a significant part in unravelling the *Geheimschreiber** (secret writer) codes, so vital to winning the intelligence war in 1943. And the long-term consequences of the world's first programmable electronic computer? Well, provide your own description – but *incalculable* would be a good place to start.

So valves could be temperamental – but their post-war electronic replacement, the tiny transistor was stable and didn't mind a bit if you wanted to switch it on and off as many times as you liked. Invented mid-century, transistors were so successful that their name became synonymous with the little radio sets they spawned which were small, light and totally portable. All you needed was to bung in a tiny 9v battery and you were set up to listen in wherever and whenever you wanted. True, to start with they were just a little pricey, but as the manufacturers got into their stride, millions of the little marvels hit the worldwide market place in the sixties. The level of their success was, as one of my perceptive and intellectual classmates would have it - *'astro-bleedin'-nomical!'*

In an age where we all have mobile phones and instant global access to virtually everything as and when it happens, it is perhaps difficult to appreciate the impact that the arrival of the humble tranny had upon our generation. The technical innovation in itself was a massive step in the global access to what we now call 'social media', but the timing was also perfect, in that trannies hit the market at the exact same time as the revolution in pop music burst forth upon a desperately eager population.

* *The Geheimschreiber was the next step up from the better known Enigma code machine. Tom Flowers spent all of his time and quite a lot of his own money in developing Colossus. After the war, a grateful government gave him £1000 in token of his efforts. It barely covered his expenses. The quiet and unassuming Tommy's brilliant contribution to our modern world has never really been fully recognised. A truly great man.*

The third ingredient to this magic potion was the availability for the first time of disposable income. Thus, with the help of the many hire-purchase companies around, there were relatively few who could not afford to jump on the bandwagon: pop in an *Eveready* battery, and off you went. Without the tranny, the speed with which the roller coaster of Rock n' Roll and the social revolution that was the sixties gathered pace, would have been hampered and restricted. The cultural explosion which burst forth with such energy and dynamism was fuelled by the access the general public had to it – and for the young generation especially. Somewhat inevitably, many of the older folk viewed youngsters wandering around the streets with a tranny glued to their ear with disdain, and even more so when radios were played out in the open – *Rock n' Roll in the park? Good God, whatever next?!!'*

A typical 60's tranny: if the sound was a bit tinny, who cared? This was radio on demand, and some of it was pop music!

The only slight drawback at the beginning of the new decade was that as far as pop music was concerned, there were so few programmes to listen to. The only dedicated shows were *Pick of the Pops*, which at first was broadcast late on a Sunday night, and *Saturday Club*, which became the main part of the Rock n' Roll enthusiast's menu from the BBC, and was at least accessible to all with its two hour show being the *'must hear'* each Saturday morning. Other than that, it was really a matter of catching incidental pop music, usually part of a request programme and until the arrival of Radio One in 1967, there were really very few dedicated pop offerings on the old Light Programme. As a result, devotees of the genre – and by that I mean virtually the entire teenage population - turned their listening ear to Radio Luxembourg, which despite its very patchy coverage, developed an enthusiastic audience, mesmerised by the station's catchy presentation interspersed with commercials. To be frank, it left the BBC in the dust, and made the arrival of pirate radio by the mid sixties an inevitability.

So, the popularity of radio received a terrific shot in the arm with the introduction of the new technology, and gave the medium a much needed boost in its rivalry with television. And it was not just its portability and increasing affordability – the little transistor radio became part of the rapidly emerging teenage culture; it was modern looking, it was instant, it was reliable. The overall impression on a pliable youth market was that it was a world away from even the smallest of the old valve radios which were so firmly rooted in the world of fuddy duddy classical music, everyday tales of country folk and the shipping forecast.

The invention of the tiny electronic transistor and the radio it spawned became the foundation upon which all of our current technological wizardry was based. Since the early 1960's, the development of communications technology has been exponential – in fact *double exponential* if there is such a term. Nowadays many things which we considered state of the art in that era are now dead and forgotten: for the first time ever, technological innovation has been created, introduced to great acclaim... and then become entirely obsolete *within a generation*. For us well-hard baby boomers, the fact that our own grandchildren haven't the remotest idea what some of the things we considered the most indispensible pair of bee's knees ever is a matter of wonder. Such a state of affairs is, I think, new to the human condition; for something important and fairly essential to appear *and then vanish* is a unique feature of the modern age. Don't believe me?

Ask anyone born just post-1945 to picture in their mind a *telephone*, and as like as not, they will have this in mind:

For three decades after the war, the sole provider of all telecoms in the UK was the General Post Office, a department of the government. The model shown is the '*GPO 312L Black*' telephone, commonly installed in thousands of homes and businesses in the late fifties. It had a curly fabric-covered cord attached to the chunky handpiece which *always* got in a tangle. You rang another telephone by rotating the big round thing on the front in a clockwise direction, and after each number this dial would spin back to its starting place. Perhaps *spin* is too active a word – *'grind grudgingly anti-clockwise with a fair bit of clockwork type noise'* would probably be more accurate. After you had gone through this laborious business, you would, hear the ringing tone in the earpiece part of the receiver. Sometimes, however, you might hear someone else talking, and telling you to *'get off the bloody line'* as some of these phones were on *party lines* – i.e. you shared your pair of wires with other people who lived nearby, and had to take your turn to make a call - honest! At the bottom of your telephone was a little drawer which you pulled out, and in which were often kept the numbers of family and friends, but the centre of the dial itself was always reserved for the number to ring in case of emergency. Now this, of course was 999, a number no one could possibly forget. Unfortunately, it was also the number that took the longest time to dial. Imagine that the house is burning down around your ears – you rush to the phone and grab the receiver... the damned cord is all tangled up and you have to let the receiver spin round a few times to free itself. OK ... you dial the first nine; the dial takes an age to grind all the way back to the start; you do the second nine with the same interminable time lapse and finally get to the third... the dial sticks on its long anti-clockwise journey back! You give it a shove, but it WILL NOT BE HURRIED ... you put the receiver to your ear, and someone says *'Oi!! Get off the phone! This is a party line you know!'*

    Well, it wasn't always quite as bad as that, but you get the picture – we all had the old 312L Black, and knew exactly what they were like. *'And your point is?'* I hear you ask. Well, show any child a picture of this beast - *they won't even know what it is.* When you tell them they'll almost inevitably say: *'That's not a phone, Grandad! Where's the screen? Where's the buttons? Where's the camera?'*

    Get my point? OK, the dial type telephone started disappearing a good thirty years ago, but such examples of the increasing rate of technological change don't stop there. Have a glance at the next page,

and put your hand up if you've still got a load of these:

Plenty of you, I bet. More to the point, *have you still got anything to play them on?!* In many cases, the anwer is no... but we just can't bear to be parted with them, can we? They were state of the art in the late eighties and the nineties, but yet again, show these to anyone under the age of fourteen, and as like as not they won't have a clue what they are. Oh, by the way, if you're amongst this group, they are VHS Video Tapes – each one containing a spool of about a mile of very thin magnetic tape which often felt itself obliged to tangle up right in the very depths of your video player just at the point when the villain was about to be exposed on *Bergerac*.

OK, lesson over. You can put your hand down now and we can get back to the early sixties, when the newly transistorised tip of the massive communications iceberg had just broken the surface of our collective consciousness. Needless to say, several of my mates appeared at school glued to their new tranny status symbol and soaked up the rather tinny sound that such small speakers provided. It was just such a shame that more often than not, they had to put up with *'Housewives' Choice'* or *'Music While You Work'* when what we really craved after was some moody crooning from Billy Fury, or the latest from Marty Wilde or Cliff. Even so, we all wanted a tranny, and the old paper round money was hoarded week by week until the possibility of owning your own shiny red Philco became a reality. The word *'cool'* meant little more than being a tad on the freezing side in those days, but it would have been perfect for describing how utterly chuffed we tiny teenagers were to get our first tranny... they were shiny, they were small, and you could switch them on and off like anything, with no delay or nuffink!

Envious? You bet! Almost overnight they made the old valve radios look real dinosaurs, and even the mainstay argument of the traditionalists that the sound quality of their old valve radios was 'far superior' quickly disappeared as the new radio sets became larger and more sophisticated. Thus the old cabinet valve radios were swept aside in an amazingly short space of time The ones that were kept seemed to fulfill a need more as a piece of furniture than part of the information highway ... or footpath, as it was in those days.

This model, made by the Bush company was something of a 60's icon – a tranny that was classy and appealing to all age groups.

So what of other technologies at the dawn of this new electronic age? Just now we mentioned the fact that these days, all phones have a camera as an integral and indeed, essential constituent. As a result, we are now knee deep in photos, aren't we? I'm told that just last year alone, so many photos were taken that this one year's output alone comprised something like 90% of all the photos *ever taken.... ever.... since the world began!* If you happen to be looking for a gob that has been well and truly smacked, then look no further – I'm your man! And yet, how could you doubt it? Everywhere you go, there are people on their phones, talking incessantly, occasionally listening, taking photos, watching videos, *making videos,* checking their bank balances, buying a tumble drier from someone in Kuala Lumpur... the list is endless. If you can't do something on a phone these days, it probably isn't worth doing, so taking photos is a matter so normal, so uneventful that it receives no consideration at all. *Here we go again....***Not so in 1960!**

Cameras – or any that deserved the title – were expensive and precisionmade, and were out of the question as far as most ordinary folk were concerned. If your dad had a really nice camera, it was somehing of a status symbol. The rest of us had to put up with a range of cheapo stuff which (occasionally) took small black and white pictures that were frequently out of focus and more often than not had curious white smudges on them caused by the unwelcome ingress of light from god

Pre-war Box Brownie cameras were very common even a couple of decades later. Some got good results, but a lot didn't.

knows where. Added to that, the results often led to further dismay in that a resulting print would often end up with the decapitation of the subject, or the achievement of just getting the left half of someone - because these box shaped cameras were so difficult to aim. You'd think, wouldn't you, that with a part of your camera called the *viewfinder,* it might just be a slight clue that what you were seeing in the little glass prism might just possibly be what you might get to see in glorious black and white when you ripped open the packaging on your excited return from the chemist a couple of weeks later. And were you pleased? Was the result as eagerly anticipated? Was it hell. Disappointed comments such as *'Well, that half of your uncle Ronald looks quite nice – shame you missed the bit with him holding up the only fish he's ever caught in his life in the other hand'* were typical and legion.

And what's all this about the chemist? Well, cameras in those days were not electronic... they were mechanical in a Heath-Robinson* sort of way. In my opinion, most of them barely warranted the name camera - perhaps *'something which is going to cost you a fair bit of money and will almost certainly lead to disappointment'* might be more accurate, but it lacks that certain marketing cachet doesn't it?

What all cameras had in common was their need to be fed with film. This was sold by companies such as Kodak, and was really quite expensive. You couldn't afford to make a mistake, and given the total crappiness of most of the cameras we used, this was a vain hope if ever there was one. Most rolls of film would allow you just twelve shots. Yes, I did say **twelve** - and whereas these days most people take at least that number of selfies just having their breakfast alone, it puts the whole

*Heath Robinson inventions: difficult to describe but well worth a look on the net. The man was a genius, and set a fine example for those interested in string, pulleys, levers and springs.

thing in perspective. Another slight problem was that you had to get the film out of its packaging and into the camera without letting in any light- so loading your camera in the dark was something of a necessity.

Inevitably, the problems associated with this tricky manoeuvre led to a great deal of muffled cursing from within the confines of your eiderdown – and was made a lot worse when your mum came into the bedroom and switched on the light with a cry of *'John – whatever are you doing under there?!'* I suppose you can't blame her; the sight and sound of an infuriated son thrashing about and swearing in frustration under the bedcovers could easily be misconstrued, especially when accompanied by a scream: *'turn the bloody light out!'*

So, getting the film successfully engaged on the little sprockets was just the first step on this perilous journey. Bearing in mind you had so few shots to play with, choosing what you were going to take became a decision not to be undertaken lightly; after all, once the camera clicked, there was no going back, and if you were of an indecisive nature, this part of the process could well run into hours. Once all twelve exposures had been used up, it was now off to the chemist for the film to be developed. This too, was an expensive process, made even more painful when more often than not, you discovered that of the resulting dozen pictures, two were entirely black because you'd had your hand over the lens, another showed a large part of your thumb which in a moment of chance vindictiveness also happened to completely obscure the head and shoulders of the girl friend...and the remainder were a sad compendium of light ingress, out of focus countryside views, and one of your left knee when you pressed the button by mistake. *Hey ho.*

Maybe it was just that I was crap at taking photos. To be fair, the later Box Brownie cameras became more sophisticated, and some of my mates got some quite good results. Nevertheless, it came as a great relief to us all when in early 1963 Kodak introduced its brand new *Instamatic* camera. As the name implies, this was a camera designed to take the hassle out of photography: it would be *instant* and *automatic,* just perfect for a photographic moron like me. What's more, the film came in a cartridge, so loading the camera was easy - the only downside being if your mum came into the bedroom and witnessed a certain amount of muttering and writhing under the blankets, the old film-loading excuse was no longer viable. Another departure was the inclusion of a flash cube whose little bulbs could be used just once each. Such technology gave certain keen types the chance to extend their emerging photographic skills still further.

And once you had got your prints back from the chemist, what

Chic, compact, easy to load – and your very own flash: what's not to like?

then? Well, traditionally, family photographs were treated with some reverence, and stored in an album whose covers were always made of thick black cardboard, and whose pages were sometimes interspersed with a kind of thin semi-transparent paper. I was informed that the purpose of this inclusion was to protect the photographs, and stop them sticking together. Well, perhaps so, but in the dampish surroundings of our house, the thin paper itself did a fine job in adhering to the neighbouring photos in a manner which can only be described as 'enthusiastic'. Also, of course, you had these little triangular pieces of card which you used at the four corners of each snap, and were then stuck to the page to stop your photos sliding about. Truth to tell, they were not sticky enough, and woe-betide anyone foolish enough to open up the family album without first laying it flat; to do otherwise was to encounter an autumnal like leaf-fall of recently liberated photos, accompanied by a shower of tiny black triangles. Oh the joy!

You may have noticed that the word 'colour' has not crept into the narrative thus far. That's because colour film was rare and expensive in comparison with monochrome. Bearing in mind the poor black and white results achieved by yours truly and many like me, it's hardly surprising that investment in such new technology was not our first priority: we'd leave such sophistication to the professionals. Just getting a few snaps in focus, and of what you intended was enough - for now.

And other technologies in the early sixties? Bear with me for a mere moment or two if I whizz back to the old classroom. For kids like me, languishing in the bottom stream of a grammar school, the chance to continue studying the finer things in life that Art, Music an English Literature represented was abruptly axed at the beginning of our third year. In a first class example of the blunt social engineering for which the post-war decades were notorious, we not-quite-so-little chaps were deemed to be lowlier creatures most likely destined to become technical types, or perhaps able to make our way towards occupying a middle-ranking position in the Civil Service or a bank. As an example of a self-fulfilling prophecy it was pretty near perfect. Were we consulted? Were our parents asked for their views? I'll leave you to fill in the answer. But... did we protest? Did our parents demand an enquiry from the Local Education Authority? The same answer applies. This was the sixties, for heaven's sake! You did as you were told because SCHOOL KNOWS BEST... got it?

Mind you, it did leave us techie kids wondering what might replace the artistic void in our lives. With many of our voices going through that awkward transitional phase when the hormones dictate that you break into a most unexpected yodel in the middle of a perfectly ordinary word, we were attempting to voice our speculations on what the new subjects of *'Engineering Drawing'* and *'Workshop Practices and Processes'* might involve. That our curriculum was to be more heavily biased towards the sciences in general, and maths in particular was beyond doubt, and I for one, was grateful that Miss Grant at Highland Road Juniors had pummelled in the old twelve times table presumably in anticipation of such an outcome. So a burning question of the moment was *'what extra help and equipment would such a curricular shift merit?'* After all, the brainy kids in the top class would presumably all be given junior sized mortar boards, and be liberally entertained with soothing Elizabethan music from the school's very own Dansette whilst dashing off a quick soliloquy, so what about techie stuff for us? How about a bit of electronic assistance with all those sums we'll have to do … not too much to ask, surely?

Well, seems like it was, because when considering what emerging technologies there might be for the likes of us, the words *'all'* and *'bugger'* sprang to mind, but not necessarily in that order. There were no shiny bits of electronic machinery in sight, and unless you count access to a drawing board with accompanying T-square as something to be marvelled at, there was nothing. In fact the only good thing I can remember was that in the metalwork shop, we were introduced to a file which rejoiced in the name of *half-round bastard*. Well, what a gift! To a man, a mob of sniggering yobbos then spent the next few days identifying all their favourite HRB's on the school staff; who said schoolboy humour was dead?

Of course, the one thing we did get to assist us in our technical and mathematical studies was our own set of **log tables**. Now, it may well be that those of you under about fifty will be asking yourselves, *'Why would every thirteen year old schoolboy be given his own set of rustic furniture? Was it to do with catering, perhaps? Had the school the almost prophetic insight to foresee the arrival of wall to wall TV celebrity cookery programmes which were lurking over the distant entertainment horizon?'* Be still your beating hearts... it was nothing to do with any form of creativity or primitive furniture at all. The log tables were provided to help us do BIG SUMS.

At the beginning of the sixties, there were no electronic calculators, and so all calculations had to be done with pencil and paper. For those of us who were still having trouble with remembering whereabouts to leave the carrying number (*was it on the doorstep with the milkman, or up in the air with the Hundreds, Tens and Units?*), a book of log tables was supposed to be an aid. In this respect, the word *log* was short for *logarithm*, not a splinter or twig in sight - and although thumbing through the contents makes pretty tedious reading, the first couple of pages at least did help you to multiply 235.6 by 429.9.

Now, why on earth you should want to do such a thing is another matter; the point is, we had to be able to work it out... it was good for us...it was part of our preparation for the world beyond. Nowadays, technology is such that we can just reach for the calculator, press a few buttons and hey presto! How long would that take? A matter of a few seconds... provided you can find the damned thing down the back of the settee. Brace yourselves: in 1960, you had to look up the 'log' of each of the numbers in question then add them together. That done, you then flipped over the page...find the number you added up, run your finger along the appropriate line, go to the 'mean differences' table, make a best fit judgement, add that into the earlier answer... and then collapse in a heap in a darkened room for a couple of hours.

So what is a logarithm? Few of us had any idea, except that a bloke called Napier seemed to be the culprit, as posher volumes of such tables were blessed with the title *'Natural or Naperian Logarithms'* . Well, you can take it from me, the chances of page after page of columns of figures didn't strike us as being in any way natural. Reading a book like this would even have made *Titus Andronicus* seem like a walk in the park. Good job we were all well-hard.

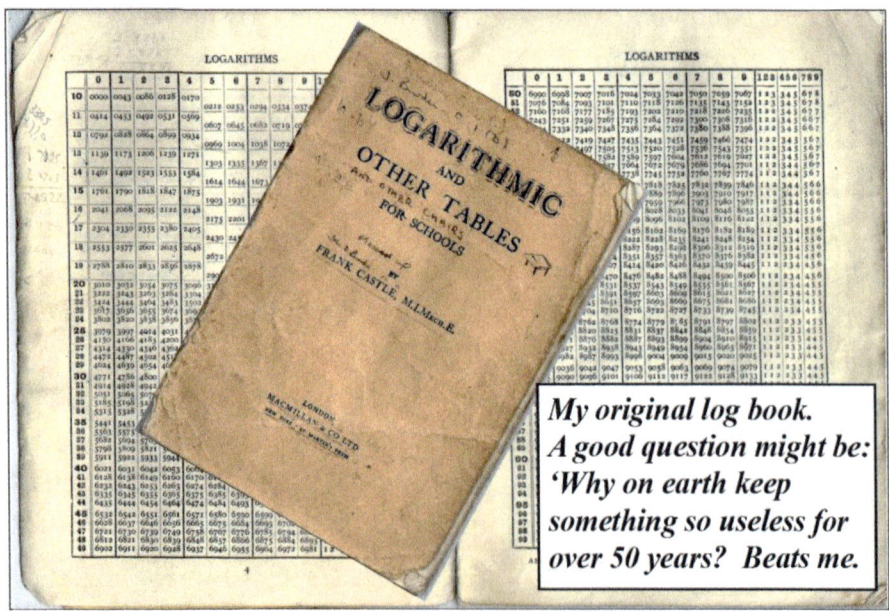

My original log book. A good question might be: 'Why on earth keep something so useless for over 50 years? Beats me.

And lack of technical wizardry didn't end there: the information highway was barely a muddy track fifty years ago. There was no reaching for the Iphone or tablet if you wanted to know something instantly, and acquiring information was a tedious and very manual process. If you needed to search for information and didn't have your own expensive set of encyclopaedias, then the only recourse was to get down to the local library. True, many of us had our own small collections of non-fiction, but the *'Boys Own Wonder Book of Trains'* was not much help if the biology bloke at school had demanded a three page analysis of 'the life and times of the amoeba'. So it was a trek to the library, which in my case was a good twenty minute walk away. And when you got there, the presence of your required area of study was by no means guaranteed. Science type books were a bit thin on the ground, and the lady librarian's response of '*... no dear, I don't think we've got anything on amoebas... how about this nice 'Observer's Book of Butterflies'? – I'm sure there'll be some creepy-crawlies in there somewhere*' was no doubt well meant, but as an aid to preventing me getting a detention next Monday was completely bloody useless.

Mind you, I did like the library. It was always warm and ever so slightly damp, but in a comfortable sort of way. There was an aroma of moist cardboard and ink in the air, and I was ever impressed with the solid and satisfying *ker-CHUNK-CHUNK* noise made by the inky date stamping machine just prior to the kindly soul presenting you with a fortnight's worth of borrowed butterfly books, need it or not. So, having failed dismally to further investigate the dull and frankly uninspiring life of one of the world's lowliest life forms – and I'm still talking about the amoeba here, not we lowly schoolboys - the only option was to hop on a trolley bus, and shove off down to the much larger Central Library.

So, getting information was difficult in that it was simply not readily available: many households had a newspaper delivered, and this kept you perhaps a shade better informed of current events than those who didn't, but as regards even a fairly light touch level of individual research, it was tricky, to say the least. There was much less printed matter around, and the daily onslaught of circulars, adverts and unwanted junk mail we get by the sack-load these days was totally unknown. Printing your own stuff was unheard of, and had you told us that within less than a generation, you'd be able to compose, type, and print your own stuff *in colour* and then, at the push of a button send a copy to the other side of the world, you'd have had us casting a glance at the sherry bottle, and wondering if you'd been enjoying a few secret swigs well short of Christmas.

If you wanted anything typed, you needed someone who had been to night school and had passed the necessary *Shorthand and Typing* exam. This was a qualification sought by thousands of girl school leavers as it provided access into the world of commerce and secretarial jobs – and

Whilst the big old 'sit up and beg' typewriters did a perfectly good job, they were not trendy like the models of the sixties. Plus the fact that the new ones were in colour...the case, I mean. And you could carry them without fear of a hernia.

to own a typewriter was quite a status symbol. Most of the machines available post-war were quite old and very heavy, but then along came companies like Olivetti with their compact portables, and any trendy young secretary would do her utmost to acquire the latest must-have. So reprographics took a small step towards being not only a little more fashionable, but the cost of such machines, though expensive by today's standards, made them a more economic proposition. There is little doubt that the purchase of such typewriters in the home saw the first timid flurry of snowflakes in what was to become the information avalanche we know so well today. Not that this made a lot immediate difference to us amoeba sleuths in 1960; if you could get your sister to type out a few bits and pieces, bully for you, but in the meantime it was down to the old Platignum fountain pen and blotting paper again.

Back at school, there was the establishment's own library, but that was really for reference on the premises only. Other than the well thumbed text books we were provided with in class, there were of course, the individual sets of information sheets produced by various members of staff and copied and distributed by the school secretary. The age of the dreaded worksheet was upon us. To be fair, these were usually welcomed, especially if they had been produced on the school's own Banda machine.

For those of you who have no idea what I'm talking about, the Banda was a spirit duplicator, and the secret lies in the first word: *spirit*. The teacher producing the handout would use a shiny master sheet on a coloured ink stencil simply by writing, typing or drawing on its glossy surface. He would then peel this off the ink backing, and give the resulting coloured negative to the school secretary who would clip it into the Banda machine in the duplicating room. This was usually a tiny windowless facility near the school office. The secretary would then fill the duplicator with the spirit, and then start cranking the machine round and round to produce the required copies.

Nothing to sniff at? The trusty Banda, much appreciated by school kids... and the school secretary. Happy daze!

The production of these became more and more erratic as the process continued: the spirit poured into the drum of the machine contained a fair amount of chemical alcohol, and in the close confines of the duplicating room, had an increasingly inebriating effect upon the operator. The very fact that, in order to spread the ink smoothly, the machine would deposit a thin film of the duplicating spirit over *each page produced*, will give you a clear idea as to how much of this volatile fluid made its way into the atmosphere. It will also provide you with an indication of just how much made its way up the nose of the school secretary. As a result, it would often be that the door of the Biology lab would be flung open mid lesson to reveal the good Mrs. Collins holding a whole year group's supply of duplicated Banda unnecessarily close to her nose. She would then enter the room following a curiously pin ball-like trajectory, having occasion to bounce off various doorposts, laboratory benches and eager pupils into whom she frequently bumped, and on being reminded by the teacher '**Over here, Mrs. Collins!**' would eventually – and somewhat reluctantly, it must be said - part company with her chemical friend.

And then, of course, it was our turn. The sooner the papers were distributed the better, because full evaporation had not yet taken place. I have little doubt that the teacher concerned must have been filled with pride to note how anxious his pupils were to avail themselves of his fascinating details of the life of an earthworm, and looked on benignly as each boy grabbed his sheet and buried his face in the valued paperwork with a deep and appreciative sigh. The smell of the fluid was indeed quite intoxicating, and was, I suppose the first bit of 'sniffing' we ever did, and we made it last as long as possible. True, it could be interrupted by the teacher saying something like:

'Oh, Burden, just retrieve Mrs. Collins from the store cupboard... she seems to have shut herself in there – be a good fellow and escort her back to the secretary's office, would you?'

As the years progressed, more elaborate reprographics took hold, and by the mid sixties electric typewriters and mass duplicating using *Roneo* ink duplicators had made significant inroads to the locally produced information sheets. Yes, they were good, they were efficient and all that, but they didn't give you the instant fix that the good old Banda did and were therefore seen as pretty dull by comparison.

It's a calculator .... Honest!

So, what else did the world of technology have for us as the new decade burst forth on an unsuspecting population? Well, not a lot really. The tranny was the big thing and presented a glimpse into the electronic future, but there was still a lot of really antiquated mechanical stuff around. Occasionally we would be let loose on mechanical adding machines: to put it bluntly anything less like their modern electronic equivalent is hard to imagine. Looking like a typewriter whose inventor has forgotten to install the essential letters, it was a cumbersome hand-cranked piece of kit, which was almost as much bother to work on as the old log tables. At best, it was something of a diversion. And what could it do? Well, the four rules of number, I suppose, but not much else. Square roots? Bit of basic trigonometry? You must be joking... and asking it to put anything in its *memory*, and leave it there for you to *retrieve* after you've returned from the delights of escorting the mildly inebriated Mrs. Collins back to her office and making her a nice cup of black coffee... well, you're having a laugh, aren't you?

The only other bits of technology available to the general public were the reel to reel tape recorder and the more refined – and expensive – world of home cine films. My family never had either, and to many such equipment seemed a bit extravagant when there were so many other things to spend your money on – like a desirable and oh-so-modern fourteen inch black and white telly, for a start. Tape recorders were seen as rather more specialist: the tapes themselves were very long, very thin, and - working on the reel-to-reel principle - very inclined to get in the most god-awful tangle the minute you turned your back. Friends of mine who had one seemed to spend most of their time *fast-forwarding* or *fast re-winding* in a vain effort to find a fifteen second recording of someone giggling inanely and saying things like: 'What?... Now? ... Shall I speak? ... Is it on? OK, OK, here goes... HELLO - THIS IS ME – TRACY, AND I'M GOING TO SING YOU 'PUFF THE MAGIC DR............' At this point, the tape usually decided to wrap itself around the spindle, and required three quarters of an hour unpicking, only to reveal that the eagerly anticipated song about the adventures of the said dragon had been entirely lost.

And cine film was even worse, because it was so expensive. Movie cameras were a no–no for most of us, and those who did invest in such technology got precious little for their money. A small reel of 8mm film, sufficient to give you just a few minutes of projection time could cost pounds to buy and develop, and there was no accompanying sound... unless you tried to use a separate tape recorder at the same time. Trying to synchronise the two machines, each prone to snarl-ups and entanglements on a truly epic scale, was beyond the reach and patience of nearly everyone. And of course, you had also to invest in a film projector. These too were expensive pieces of equipment, and your

Everything you need: 8mm projector, portable screen, movie camera, tripod, £££s and patience.

processed film had to be carefully threaded into this complex machine. An integral – indeed essential - part of the projector was its powerful built-in light bulb, but these had a tendency to blow just when everybody was gathered together, the screen was up, and everyone was looking forward to a full four minutes of jerky pictures showing the family acting super self-consciously. Nevertheless, movie making did have its adherents, and many's the wedding or family Christmas recorded in rather erratic fashion, when Dad, with perhaps one or two more sherries on board than was wise, thought that waving the camera about in order to catch the exact trajectory of the cork flying out of the Champagne bottle would be a good idea. Bearing in mind films were costly to develop at the local camera shop, the results were often a bitter disappointment. Remembering which way the on/off switch worked on the camera seemed to be a key issue. Many a film show was spoilt by the wrong choice, resulting in the filming of a knee, or the living room carpet. OK, I know that this happens these days too, but at least you can now see what you are videoing on the screen, and instantly delete your mistakes and try again five seconds later. So, techie problems with cine were a-plenty. You might as well have just stuck with two tin cans and a piece of string.

'Oh – and what's that all about?' I hear you ask. Well, it's technology at its most basic. As kids we always wanted to have our own phones or radios to be just like the Beano's *General Jumbo*. The only way you could get anywhere near it was to bash a hole in the

bottom of two [...] nd thread a long piece of string between them. Your se[cond partne]r would then take his can to as far as the string would st[retch, pulling i]t very taut. With one of you yelling into the can, and t[he other holding] his to his ear, the voice of the speaker could just abo[ut be heard by th]e listener. To be honest, as a radio-like communicatio[n device it was] not great. For a start, you had to yell so damn loud to s[tand any chance] of the vibrating string having the desired effect, you m[ight just as well ha]ve just chucked the thing away as the recipient coul[d hear you quit]e plainly anyway. Secondly, there was always an arg[ument as to who] should be speaking and who should be listening, and [the end result] of two sets of stringy vibrations meeting in the middle [and cancelling] each other out was as likely as you both standing at op[posite ends an]d listening to sod-all. The length of the string was also an issue: taking it around a corner was a no-no, as the requirement to keep it taut meant that your communication transmitter was now touching Mrs. Stephen's garden fence, and to be honest, informing her about your next raid up the bomb-site was not really part of the plan. Some enterprising kids even tried to have *two sets* of cans-and-string, in a vain bid to provide the operators with both receiver *and transmitter*. And the all too obvious outcome? Either you forgot which way round you were supposed to hold them and ended up with voice talking to voice and ear listening to ear, or the strings touched and the vibration maliciously turned around mid-string, and you found yourself talking to yourself.

So, the *tin cans / string* combo wasn't a particularly good example of early sixties' technology… but then, apart from the all-new trannies and the fourteen inch monochrome telly – not much else was either.

2 A Dedicated Follower [of Fashion]

You may be wondering - with all this co[ncern for do]mestic life, be it at home or at school, did the mome[ntous events un]folding in the outside world ever impinge upon our som[ewhat cocooned] existence?

Well not much, if truth be told, but [there were ex]ceptions. The previous decade hosted the Suez crisis o[f 1956 and th]e huge import of that event was largely lost on us kids ([although th]e invention of the bubblecar which it spawned was not[... ...so] you could say we scored about three out of ten in ter[ms of 'ju]dging current international events' in those primary sch[ool days].

Nevertheless what could not escape ou[r notice was th]at Portsmouth was, after all, a very large naval town, and as such made awareness of the outside world a little difficult to miss. For example, it would have taken monumental short-sightedness to have ignored the fact that there were loads of sailors wherever you went; indeed, quite a few of our collective dads were naval personnel of one sort or another and, like all servicemen of the time, were totally unmissable as they were obliged to wear their uniforms when out and about in the city. Not only our lot, of course, but also those from visiting navies, and we used to watch out, for instance, for any French sailors, because their naval headgear was surmounted by a red pom-pom. Laugh? How on earth could a fighting force be taken seriously wearing a red pom-pom for heaven's sake? Jolly Jacques Tar? Don't think so. And the Yanks were very popular because **a)** they were Yanks, and therefore came from a land with a glamorous lifestyle which we all wanted to copy and **b)** they spoke with Yank accents which we all wanted to imitate…and occasionally tried to lapse into, because it seemed so cool. In reality such a ploy was so totally transparent and bogus that it was, even to me, embarrassing, e.g. *'Hey baby, gimme a candy bar and make it snappy'* really didn't go down too well on a wet Thursday lunchtime when you were asking the harassed dinner lady to hurry up with that day's delicious spadeful of semolina. But it was worth a try.

The Yanks also wore funny hats which looked just a bit like a rather knocked-about nurse's bonnet, but we didn't take the piss because... well, they were Yanks, and they had chewing gum, and lots of chocolate – oh, and they also had some really, really big ships.

But in this at least, they were not alone. I can remember in 1953 being taken by my dad on a boat trip to see the Coronation Spithead Naval Review. That the Coronation was a really big deal did, I'm sorry to say, rather pass me by, but in my defence, I was still at Bramble Road Infants at the time, and there was still a lot of hard bits of clay to roll into worms prior to making a useful Stone Age pot. Nevertheless, we were all given a blue hard back book to commemorate Her Majesty's ascendance to the throne. I regret to say that as far as me and my tiny chums were concerned, this gift from our new sovereign was not given the level of appreciation it merited. As far as I was concerned, it was a thinnish book with a coat of arms **'EIIR'** on the front, had no coloured pictures inside - and of the several black and white ones, there was not a single one featuring a Vauxhall Velox, or even a Morris Oxford. We didn't have a TV in those days, but even if we had, the prospect of actually *seeing a TV* would have been the allure, not the fact that our new queen was taking up her regal duties. Sorry Ma'am, but that's the way it was. However, *'every cloud'*, as they say, because after the Queen and her hubby had dashed off on another visit somewhere or other, my mum decided to take my sister to London to see all the Coronation decorations. I wasn't included – a wise decision. Instead, and by way of compensation, my dad took me to see the afore-mentioned naval Review. These days you can, of course, Google the occasion, and although the footage I looked at recently follows the progress of the Royal visitors right around the fleet, it does not fully portray the immense size of the great grey warships, which from the deck of a small pleasure boat, and my wide-eyed perspective within it, made each of them truly massive. What's more, there were hundreds upon hundreds of the things; in 1953 our navy really was still mighty, and I was hugely impressed.

OK, so fast forward to 1956, and something scary happened in Portsmouth, which even I noticed. It was the occasion of a visit to the UK by those whacky fun-loving cheerful chappies, Messrs. Bulganin and Khrushchev, who were something IMPORTANT in the Kremlin. They didn't come by plane – oh no; if you wanted to flex your muscles you came in something big and grey and bristling with guns, and I don't mean John Wayne. So a big warship was just the ticket. You have to appreciate that at this time, the cold war was really hotting up… if you see what I mean. Mutual suspicion was massive, and the continual din from sabre-rattling across the international stage was deafening. Quite why these two cheerful chums were visiting was unclear, particularly to a ten year old whose only interest was whether the next Weetabix packet would have another cardboard cutout model of the latest exciting offering from the Vauxhall range. So, into the dockyard sailed the Russian cruiser *Ordzhonikidze*, a name no one in Portsmouth could pronounce, let alone spell. So far so good - and once the two sombre gents had been taken to London to carry out their diplomatic duties, the ship was left bobbing about in Portsmouth dockyard sort of twiddling its thumbs. Now, at this stage of the cold war, there was huge mutual interest and suspicion regarding technological developments, and apparently, someone on our side thought that the Russians had something attached to the hull of their ships which gave them a distinct advantage, and therefore, wouldn't it be a good idea to go and have a quick look?

Of course, we knew nothing of this at the time... but there was a growing air of speculation in the ensuing months, so much so that it became generally accepted that a frogman had been sent down to have just a little peep at the under parts of the Russian ship. And then the brown stuff really hit the fan the following year when it became known that **a)** the frogman, a certain Commander 'Buster' Crabb, had never returned from his mission, and **b)** in April 1957, a headless and handless corpse wearing a frogman's suit was dredged up by a passing fishing boat in nearby Chichester harbour.

Well, you can imagine the scandal, the intrigue, the sheer morbid excitement of it all: blimey! An international incident right on our doorstep! Nevertheless, for us it didn't take long for the dust to settle... there were still stones to throw, girls to think about, voices to suddenly crack mid sentence and chins to be scrutinised for the first appearance of anything that could be considered remotely beard-like. But the seed had been sown; a tiny part of my awareness was now occupied by a wider view, so that when big naval affairs were on the cards again, I felt a little more prepared. OK, it was three years later, but nonetheless, I felt myself to be something of a man about town when it came to things military, especially as by now, I was bringing a worthwhile shine to the toe caps of my newly issued CCF army boots. Thus it was that on a lazy summer afternoon in 1960, something else happened in Portsmouth which did prompt me to lift my gaze from the closely typed print of the Radio Times and cast a quick glimpse at the outside world.

On August 4th 1960, our last remaining battleship, the mighty HMS Vanguard, was to be towed out of Portsmouth dockyard at the beginning of her last – and very sad – voyage to the breaker's yard in Scotland. Now, whether you've been to Pompey or not, you have to understand that the harbour entrance between a narrow peninsula called Spice Island on the Portsmouth side and Gosport on the other is extremely narrow – no more than a couple of hundred yards or so. Because of this, the tidal flow at this point is particularly strong and dangerous. So, the scene was set: a number of powerful tugs began to pull the mighty ship slowly, slowly out of the inner harbour and at a speed of no more than three or four knots it approached the narrow entrance. At that point something of immense joy… or chilling fear happened: it really depended upon where you were standing. The huge ship, all forty five thousand tons of her, broke free from the tugs, and instead of making her sedate way out into the waters of the Solent, decided instead to head straight for Spice Island. Right on the harbour side at this, the narrowest point of the waterway, is a famous old pub called *'The Still and West'*. The hundreds of on-lookers standing at this point were suddenly aware that a bloody great big ship was coming straight towards them, and it was getting closer and closer and closer... and... RUN FOR IT!!

At almost the last moment, the keel of the Vanguard touched the muddy shingle of the seabed, and she veered a little to starboard, missing the pub by a few feet and coming to a complete halt towering above a little customs shed, whose occupants were no doubt wondering

OOPS! HMS Vanguard decides to go it alone. No doubt humorists who witnessed this event close up would have been quoting Lesley Phillips' comic catch-phrase from BBC's 'The Navy Lark' as the ship got ever closer: 'Right hand down a bit!'

if anyone would notice the sudden staining to their uniform trousers.

Well, it was exciting, and turned a fairly sad event into something much more memorable – even sufficient to break into our collective schoolboy consciousness, and a reminder that there was a world beyond the classroom door. Such pace! Such worldliness!

And that was not the only pointer. Sometime in the late fifties I was suddenly presented with a model boat. Nothing particularly special about that, you might think, but this was a beautifully crafted wooden outrigger canoe model, complete with elegant triangular lateen sail made out of woven reeds. It was, in fact, a genuine and hand-crafted model boat made by someone who lived on an island in the central Pacific. And why would I be getting such an exotic gift? Well, the fact was that one of my parents' friends was a naval officer who had just come back from Christmas Island. Those of you who were around at the time will know what's coming next - for this area of the Pacific was the site chosen by the British government for the atmospheric testing of its nuclear weapons. The first British hydrogen bomb was exploded there, and its fearful mushroom cloud sent a tremor of apprehension mixed with pride down our spines. The tests lasted for three years, and there were a lot of them, so it was not surprising that so many UK service personnel were involved in this massive military operation. But the receipt of this lovely model by an awestruck ten year old didn't affect me beyond the obvious gratitude such gift would generate, and it was not until about five years later that the connection hit me.

You see, during the post-war period, the UK continued to be armed to the teeth. As recorded above, we had a massive and powerful navy, and our large conscript enriched army had huge bases all over the world. Of particular interest to me was the RAF, and in the early sixties we possessed some of the best and most capable aircraft built to date – and that includes the Yanks and the Russians. I can hardly believe that you could ever be tempted to put this gripping book down for more than a moment or two, but should you do so, may I recommend a TV programme I came across just a year or so ago called *'Cold War, Hot Jets'?* Whether or not you are interested in militaria is not really important, for what the programme does is to show with brilliant clarity just how big the nuclear threat in the post-war years really was, and the enormous lengths both sides went to maintain the aggressive edge over the other. I found it both revealing and quite frightening; we Baby Boomers lived through this precarious time, and although the term '*life on a knife edge*' has been used far too many times, it actually was true. Bear in mind that in the early sixties, neither side of the great divide – NATO and the Warsaw Pact – had any direct communication with the other; there was no Washington – Moscow hotline, and as far as we were concerned in the UK, even two tin cans and a piece of string would have been better than nothing. So, where do all these elements lead us? To the Cuba Crisis of 1962, that's where.

Back at the old Southern Grammar, we were at last fairly hard at it. There was a hell of a lot going on. Transistorised pop music, girls, new teenage fashion for both sexes, girls, personal hygiene products to consider, girls, O level syllabus requirements, breaking voices, girls,

Titbits newspapers, the need to change socks rather more frequently... and to top it all, a bleedin' great big international crisis which threatened to wipe us all out! Yes, even the bottom stream of the fourth year at the old Southern Grammar, damned cheek!

Talk about conflicting pressures on our time: both the Beatles first hit single '*Love Me Do*', and the fact that we could all be vaporised in one blinding flash of nuclear fission occurred in the same month – October 1962.

Details of the crisis are well documented, and quite brilliantly dramatised in the film *'Thirteen Days'* which was released in 2000. The long and short of it was that the Russians were trying to put missiles capable of carrying nuclear weapons on the island of Cuba, which was under the control of a hard line communist regime headed up by Fidel Castro. Despite having a most extravagant beard, this chap was very popular with the Cubans, but not nearly so well liked by the Yanks who lived almost within spitting distance. Having the Ruskies armed with nuclear weaponry virtually on their doorstep didn't go down too well with Uncle Sam, and when it became clear that a fleet of Soviet ships was heading for Cuba filled with undesirable hardware, Mr. President – John F. Kennedy – felt he had to do something. The Russians were asked to turn back: they didn't. The Russians were *ordered* to turn back: they didn't. In the end, the US Navy imposed a blockade on the island of Cuba, and sent a massive naval flotilla to meet the Russians in the Atlantic. Shit! The world held its breath, and even I put down my copy of the Beezer and decided that perhaps now wouldn't be the best time to ask if I might have my own tranny, as they were coming down in price a bit, and anyway we might all be dead soon.

Fortunately, diplomacy won the day. The Russians turned back, and the world breathed a collective sigh of relief. But there was a cost: the Americans removed some aggressive weaponry from Turkey, and I had to go without a personal tranny, but if that's the cost of international peace and harmony, then I suppose my sacrifice was worth it.

It was a good job that I remained entirely calm throughout it all - a steady hand on the tiller, there to calm both school chums and teachers alike. My view was that I was sure *nothing would happen*... but I have to admit that this assertion was quite without logic or foundation, apart from my shrewd calculation that as Kruschev had visited my home town just a few years before, that would certainly count for something, wouldn't it? He obviously would now have mates in Pompey, and an affinity with its residents, surely? OK, we'd spied on his ship while he was there, but they'd got poor old Buster, so *Even-Stevens*, I'd say.

It was with this firm grasp of international politics that I then felt confident on advising my classmates that all would be well and used intellectual analysis and well considered arguments such as: '*Nah...they'll never do it! Old Kruschev was here a few years ago, wasn't he? Obviously likes the place, so it'll all be fine*'.

 I have to say that my confidence in a favourable outcome, being based as it was on almost total ignorance of the situation, was not shared by many; indeed, I can remember our history teacher making reference to the seriousness of the situation as he was dishing out that night's homework. Such grave forebodings were taken to heart by a number of boys, whereas others were wondering whether or not it was really worthwhile him setting the homework in the first place, if we were all very shortly to be the recipients of mankind's expertise with nuclear fission... which therefore begged the question '*Should we do the homework or not?*' Be a shame to spend our last four minutes on earth trying to coax the old Platignum into knocking out a few blotchy sentences about the *1906 Liberal Reforms* and the *Half-day Closing of Shops*, when we could be riding our bikes, looking at girls or re-adjusting the trendy blow wave for the nth time in front of the bath-room mirror whilst yelling out a personal version of '*Be Bop-a-Lula.*'

And so it was that the term '*four minutes*' acquired a new and sinister interpretation. Whereas it had formerly been the well noted – indeed famous - time required to boil an egg to an agreeable '*thoroughly cooked, but with the yolk still delightfully runny*' condition, it now became inextricably linked to nothing less than human annihilation. All over the country the government had installed secret communication centres to monitor the state of alert in case of attack. We were told that, should the enemy launch nuclear weapons, we would have just four minutes to take the proper precautions. These varied from:

a) If you happened to be in school, get under the desk, and in my case, hope that the person with whom you happened to be sharing this confined, and intimate space would be someone like Susan Watts;
b) Construct yourself an emergency shelter from large concrete blocks and any available thick sheets of lead which happened to be lying about
c) Stick your head in a paper bag and hope it would all go away.

Of these, the last was probably as practical as any, because unless you happened to be so important that you actually did have access to a nuclear shelter and it was within four minutes travel time, there was absolutely bugger-all you could do to avoid total obliteration. So there.

Thus it was that the pastime of speculating on what you would do when the four minute warning sounded became immensely popular. In a way, it was like a miniaturised bucket list, as four minutes isn't a lot, but the inventiveness of some was extraordinary, imaginative and frequently illegal. For most of us boys it involved sex, although even then, many of us still didn't have much of a clue as to what to do with what, where and when. I suppose our four minute fantasies depended upon a learning curve that was to all intents and purposes pretty damn vertical. Still, lascivious speculation is a wonderful thing, especially when you've just turned fifteen and there's no street-wise classmate handy to tell you just how things work.

So, the nuclear threat did have an effect; the Cuba Crisis of 1962 was very menacing, and left the world quite shaken especially as, unlike in previous conflicts, any life that survived such devastation would be subject to the appalling effects of radioactive fallout. Having seen what had happened in Japan in 1945 was enough to make your blood run cold, and those weapons were small in comparison with the H bomb. It didn't bear thinking about. Not when you were fifteen and the sixties were simply bursting at the seams with creative energy and the roller coaster of the pop scene was just tipping over the very summit of the slope and gathering pace with breathtaking speed. Music, miniskirts, hipster trousers, booze, telly, records – these were the explosions that we had – and they were welcomed with open arms. As far as fallout was concerned, the bawdy joke of the time was: *'If you're worried about fallout, change your underpants'.* Let me explain.

The Christmas Island nuclear tests made everyone very aware of the gathering pace of the arms race, and the vast amount of damage these weapons could do – not only at the target site itself, but afterwards as well, with the deadly clouds of radioactive fallout that followed. As a result, many people across the world were calling for a ban on nuclear weapons, and in this country an organisation called *'The Campaign for Nuclear Disarmament* (CND) was formed. Demonstrations followed, but really got going when it was decided that each Easter, CND demonstrators would march the fifty two miles from London to the town of Aldermaston in Buckinghamshire, the home of the government's Atomic Weapons Establishment. These annual marches became very popular, and were a yearly focus for those who wanted the UK to subscribe to unilateral nuclear disarmament.

'So, what's that got to do with underpants?' I hear you ask. Well, as you might expect, the 'ban the bomb' marchers had a logo which symbolised their cause and was prominently displayed on all their many banners thus:

At the same time, we young and increasingly swarthy young chaps were experiencing all sorts of growing pains, and some of these were related to the tender areas... need I say more?

As a result, the underwear commonly used was proving less than reliable in coping with sudden rushes of blood, so that an unexpected bid to see the outside world by a particular body part was increasingly common. Such involuntary expeditions were not only somewhat embarrassing, they were downright dangerous, as increasingly, trouser fronts were being equipped with particularly vicious zips, whose hasty application could cause a lot of grief. Disappearing quickly were the halcyon, but cumbersome days of the trusty button-up fly. Now, all this pain and embarrassment was caused by the inability of the old nineteen fifties style underpants to impose the necessary restrictions required to contain a member whose sudden and unexpected friskiness permitted a break-out. They were, after all, no more than boxer shorts, but without the all important restraining buttons. But help was at hand: just in time *Y Front Underpants* hit the market in large numbers. I'm sure you can't have failed to notice the similarity in design to the 'ban the bomb' emblem. What you may not recall so clearly was the almost inevitable

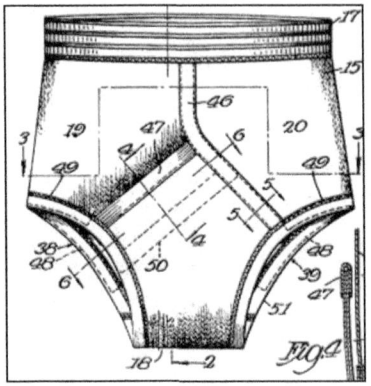

but witty schoolboy slogan that neatly brought together the anti-nuclear campaign, and the new remedy for unexpected bodily escape:

'Y-Fronts prevent fallout'

Pretty good eh? I suppose it's only contender in the pithy punch line stakes was the one to do with mobile ice-cream vans whose whirlwind spread was also a phenomena of the early sixties. As well as their customary musical chimes, many such vehicles advertised their willingness to sell by writing *'Stop me and buy one'* in large and colourful letters all over any part of the van large enough to take it. When a bit later, we discovered what on earth 'johnnies' were for (as far as I'm aware, the term 'condom' was largely unknown and certainly never used at the time), the witticism *'Buy me and stop one'* scrawled across prophylactic vending machines brought much mirth.

So, there we were, schoolboy Boomers getting nearer and nearer to the time when we would have to make important decisions about what life would hold for us post-school in just a year or so's time when we would be eligible to leave. In the meantime, there was loads of work to

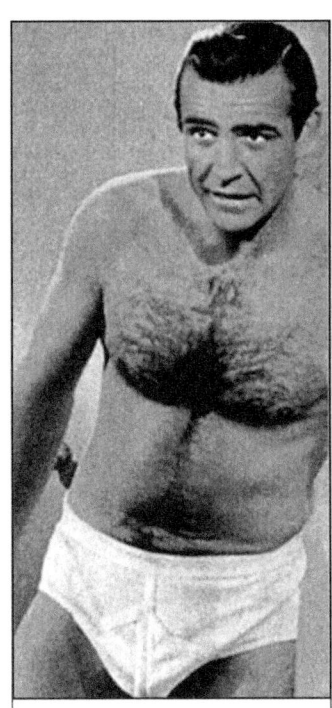
All present and correct

do, because the old mock GCE's were looming, and all those lessons wasted listening in gleeful anticipation of one of our classmate's timely disruption with his next on-demand fart were starting to have an effect; *it was time for us to buckle down.*

But it was all so inconvenient. The teenage world was going like crazy with pop music, fashion and girls, so brushing up on Avogadro's Hypothesis in chemistry, or fighting with a quadratic equation in Maths didn't hold a candle to listening to Radio Luxembourg.

And then, along came James Bond. The first film of the genre, *Dr. No* was released in 1962, and was an immediate sensation with all teenagers everywhere. It was violent, it was fast, it was exciting... and most of all, it was sexy! Bond got the girl, disposed of the villains in a properly dynamic fashion, and to cap it all, the film ad showed him wearing Y-Fronts! What more could you want? All teenage boys wanted to be James Bond and countrywide, many fifteen year-olds could be seen leaning nonchalantly on the doorpost next to the Maths room holding their 30/60/90 set square-cum-Beretta automatic in a Bond like pose, and muttering:

'I'll catch you later Moneypenny – if I'm late, start without me'.

I have to say that the first Bond film had a big effect on our reading habits. Bearing in mind we had been denied access to, or instruction in English Literature, we made our own, and when one or two boys brought copies of the James Bond books into school to show the juicy bits to their goggle-eyed mates, the queue for borrowing expanded at the same rate as the associated need for underwear that provided a firm measure of restraint.

And especially so, as most of us had at last found out a thing or two about sex. In case you are confused about this, let me assure you that, perhaps contrary to an alternative interpretation of its title, *'Dick and Dora'* was NOT an early sex-ed manual – although on reflection perhaps it might have been rather more useful had that been the case. *(Here is Dora. Dora sees Dick. Dick is big. Run, Dora, run!!)*

No. Although our sex ed could be described as 'look and say', it was not through anything formal via the school of course, but by talking in hushed and conspiratorial tones to other kids who had eavesdropped on older brothers, and so on. In my case, some degree of clarification came at the age of about thirteen, when my cousin Steve and I had been dragged out for what my Aunt liked to call *'a brisk and invigorating walk'* in the local woods. Had she and my mum bothered to have paused their endless nattering to glance over their shoulders for a second or two, they would have been pleased to see their respective offspring deep in earnest discussion, with the younger of the two in goggle-eyed concentration. It was probably just as well that they were too far away to catch snatches of conversation which would have been along the lines of *'..What, when it goes all... you know...and then you put it ... where? ... I did wonder what that's for...'* and so on.

And so it was that the process of ensuring the future of the human race took one miniscule and faltering step forward when, along with whole heap of misinformation, most of the bottom stream at the old Southern Grammar found out more or less what bits do what and, more to the point, how you do it. Just how you got to that desirable point with a real live girl was, of course, another matter entirely, but it didn't escape our notice that *personal presentation* was pretty much a key element, and one in which all of us were sadly lacking. OK, we used a certain amount of Brylcreem to produce a blow-wave and complementary duck's arse hair style, but many clearly needed to look to personal hygiene and overall grooming as a matter of some urgency.

As you might expect acne was a major problem; no-one bothered to tell us why we were getting it, and the unfortunate appearance of some of our worst affected comrades made our Geography teacher's relief map model of the Himalayas look almost two dimensional by comparison. Added to this was the twofold need to start shaving: one because you were getting just a little bit hairy, and more importantly the second, because it was seen as a rite of passage. If you came to school with a few bits of bloodied fag paper stuck to your face where the old Gillette had attempted to dismantle some acne-clad peaks, then you were growing up...*you were a teenager!* Naturally, this came at a cost, the most immediate being the growing trend to administer after shave lotion. Until the early sixties, cosmetics for men were virtually unknown. The only stuff I'd ever come across was the orange lotion dispensed from a rubber bulb powered atomiser and sprayed about with so much gusto by Mr. Ransom when he had finished cutting my hair. Now, however, there were aftershaves which Henry Cooper, a well known heavyweight boxer, invited all men to *'splash on all over'*. So we did... and spent the next three minutes hopping around the bathroom clutching a towel to the face and going *'Aaaaah...shit....ouch... bloody hell....'* and other such pain-borne expressions.

But, man up! We did it because that's what the new youth culture demanded, and provided you only burst into tears in the privacy of your own bathroom, there was manly stature in wafting around the place smelling like the cosmetics counter at Boots. And a good job too, for about this time, the spectre of being labelled as someone who had body odour (B O) reached levels of anxiety far beyond the simple name calling. A highly successful TV advert of the time turned its fairly unwelcome spotlight on the sensitive subject of men's personal freshness, and went something like this:

A social gathering is well under way, and people are moving around, drinks and snacks in hand and making cheerful conversation... except for one poor bloke, who every time he gets near to *anyone* seems to trigger an immediate need in that person to scoot off somewhere else. After a number of attempts meet with such an outcome, he is clearly downhearted, and has to make do with a cup of Tizer and a half eaten sausage roll. That is, until the kindly hostess of the party sidles up to him, and in a moment of tenderness whispers in his ear:

'B ....O.....'

Now, as an opening gambit to the fruitful liaison our sad hero is no doubt looking for, such a short presentation lacks merit; indeed he at first seems a little puzzled, and perhaps it is only when he notices that the good lady's eyes are watering, and that she is about to pass out from holding her breath too long, that he remembers the brief communication is simply an abbreviation for '**Body Odour**'. It seems that our hero takes the message to heart, as the next social occasion reveals him surrounded by admiring ladies all eager to catch the alluring aroma of his newly acquired spray-on wafting from freshly treated armpits.

And so we teenagers were introduced to the world of deodorants, and of equal importance, where - and where not - to put them. As far as the boys were concerned, the liberal application of such products sometimes went a shade over the top, and it was not unusual to find half the class gasping for breath when some clown had just emptied nearly all of a bottle of a pungent alcohol-and-something-or-other-else liquid all over his torso following a particularly sweaty game of football.

It was increasingly noticeable throughout the early sixties that commercial organisations were targeting the young as never before, and the world of cosmetics was just one element of this. Fashion and styling also played a major part, and being more conscious than ever of our image, we adolescents were putty in the hands of the marketing men. Bearing in mind there was not a lot you could do within the parameters of the strict uniform regime at school, we nevertheless did our best to look a bit trendy. First and foremost was to get your trousers tapered. Standard school grey trousers had seventeen or eighteen inch bottoms, complete with turn-ups. Naturally these unglamorous items flapped about your spindly ankles in a most unappealing way. In 1960, the current fashion demanded something almost as close fitting and narrow legged as the male version of tights, and so getting your pair of school trousers tapered down to fourteen inches was a must, provided you also got your mum to cut off the reviled turn-ups. The result was that as well as being thus identified as a '*with-it kid,*' such tapering allowed you to show off to greater advantage your newly acquired winklepicker shoes. These were, of course, anything but school uniform, but boys wouldn't be boys if they didn't push the limits, and see what they could get away with. To be honest, most winklepickers were a bit on the uncomfortable side, and the pointy bits were inclined to get a bit dented when playing football in the playground – but such is the cost of being trendy.

Clearly, there was a limit beyond which Uncle Stan, our less than revered deputy headmaster, would not allow the more adventurous boys to go and these brave frontier-pushers ran the risk of being condemned to wearing plimsolls for the rest of the day. These were the exact opposite of what had been intended, and so wearing such pointy items to school was therefore something of a Pyrrhic victory. Of even greater daring was to slip on a pair of the newly available *'day-glow'* socks, whose luminosity in orange, green or pink drew many an admiring glance from classmates. Inevitably, this also merited severe reprimand and perhaps a detention or two from the powers that be. Still, if you can't be a martyr for your art, what's the point? And of course, the prowess of such noble and daring teenagers could only be enhanced by such bravado. What an oversight of ours it was not to have invented the term *'street cred'* right there and then.

Pointy they were, and definitely unacceptable at the old SGS – even though the points were soon blunted.

So, with increasing confidence in our fashion expertise, the ability to at least mask the dreaded *'B O'*, the little know-how we had acquired about sex, and the fact that we weren't going to be zapped by the Russians for a while at least, we were fast approaching the age when we could be launched upon an unsuspecting adult world.

For many of us, this was viewed with apprehension. True, being able to earn some money to buy your own tranny and a plentiful supply of brightly coloured socks was one thing, but having to get a job? To actually do some work and earn a living? Strewth! The ominous prospect of having to martial the little grey cells into a semblance of order sufficient to pass the necessary exams was enough to make you to turn up Radio Luxembourg as loud as it would go, and to think about just about anything else.

Surely there must be something out there worthy of your interest? And there was. For this was the age of *the Youth Club*.

Places for teenagers to congregate in the late fifties and sixties were limited, and devolved around coffee bars, dance halls and youth clubs. Pubs were a no–no, especially for younger adolescents, as the age limit even for entry was strictly adhered to by most landlords - and anyway, the interior of a standard pub in those days was not a location likely to energise the young and lively. Coffee bars were the alternative, and were attractive to many as they often housed a juke box, and getting to hear the latest record releases in the company of other youngsters was a magnet to aspiring groovers. The only problem was, you had to be solvent enough to be able to buy at least a few cups of coffee if you were to spend the evening there, and besides the music and general banter, there was not a lot more on offer.

The youth club therefore filled an important gap in the market: it was cheap, there was a wide range of activities on offer, there was music in abundance and best of all – and remember, most teenagers went to a single sex school – it was a place to meet those of the opposite gender. Consequently, they were very popular; it is estimated that 70% of youngsters attended one, and although most only met weekly on a Friday or Saturday, they were for many *the* social highlight. Bearing in mind the grinding necessity of daily homework and in the case of those like me who chose to keep the nation safe by attending CCF activities of an evening, there was precious little time to spare during the week anyhow … I mean, you never knew what the Russians might be up to next, and if polishing the old army boots to a mirror-like shine did in some small way deter Ivan from launching a nuclear attack, then it was time worth sacrificing, wasn't it?

Many youth clubs were run by churches, and the one I attended was part of a much larger and quite sophisticated organisation, the Methodist Association of Youth Clubs. Thus not only were we able to meet other clubs within the city that were similarly constituted, we also joined in sporting competitions on a national basis, and this did quite a lot to widen our horizons. I recall that on one particularly noteworthy occasion, our club five-a-aside footie team was drawn to play a club in

Guernsey. Yes, *Guernsey*... overseas, for heaven's sake! Thus it was that quite a sizeable group of young and not so young assembled one grey morning at the old grass airfield in Portsmouth and with a mixture of excitement and terror surveyed our awaiting Channel Airways airliner. Now, just going on a plane in those days was quite extraordinary, and the view held by the less confident was that if the aircraft got in to trouble we were ALL GOING TO DIE. So with such cheerful thoughts we clambered aboard the tiny, old and probably fairly well-worn Douglas DC3 Dakota - an aircraft that might well have been left over from the Berlin Airlift of 1948. Nevertheless, it looked smart, as did the air hostess, but as far as in-flight facilities were concerned, you can forget overhead stowage lockers, forget in-flight entertainment, forget packaged meals and duty-free ... forget even a safety announcement, as far as I can remember. One recollection that has stayed with me from that memorable hop across the channel, was looking out of the window and noticing oil streaming back over the wing when the piston engines were revved up to screaming pitch just

A Channel Airways Dakota at Portsmouth, and youth club members embarking on our ground-breaking visit. Given our nervousness and the longevity of the aeroplane, perhaps that's an unfortunate turn of phrase. To be fair, we all really enjoyed what was for many a first ever flight – and Channel Airways went on to become quite a large and successful company... but the world had to wait another six years for the Jumbo Jet.

before take-off. I'm proud to say that, through magnificent and timely self control, the engine oil was the only dark brown fluid on the move over the next five minutes.

That this sort of youth club trip was exceptional is beyond question, and although small beer by comparison with today, it does illustrate the degree of organisation and commitment shown by those in charge.

Back on the ground, the youth club diet comprised mainly records and dancing, table tennis, darts, snooker and the like. But above all, it was a place to meet and socialise. Keeping up with trends was as important as it is today, but then it was not so easy – we didn't have 24/7 access to the media because it just wasn't there, and our lack of affordable TV and trannies further limited our knowledge of the big wide world.

Needless to say, adolescents forever push the boundaries, and the smuggling into the club of underage booze to enhance and invigorate the evening was not unknown, but usually dealt with quickly and efficiently when an inordinate amount of instability and giggling was spotted amongst the happy revellers. Mind you, getting alcohol was pretty difficult for *everyone* in those days. Booze was only available via licenced premises, where it was consumed on site or via an Off Licence. Although there were several of these around, they were not common, and the range of alcoholic beverage on sale was very limited. Moreover, the custodians of such businesses seemed to treat any young person who dared to intrude as – well, just that, really – an intruder. So, snaffling a half bottle of something or other found in a cupboard at home was about as far as it went for the average fourteen year old.

What was far more important to teenagers was keeping up with the latest in the pop world, and now you were on show to girls, dressing and grooming as groovily as possible. Such attempts, I have to say, were often doomed, and should have been seen as 'exploratory efforts' at best. Take for example, my mum's insistence that she was going to knit me a jumper for Christmas. Well, you can imagine how thrilled I was at the prospect: when nearly all of my trendy mates were getting stuff from *C&A* and *Burtons*, I was going to get something woolly, ill-fitting and brown. So the first battle was to get the brown changed to black, and the next to convince her that the neck band part of the garment could be *a different colour altogether*. Now this was dangerous country: you didn't mess with jumpers. If God had intended jumpers to have different colour neck bands, it would have said so in the scriptures without doubt. So, a high degree of subtle persuasion was required, not easy for someone whose level of gorm was still need of considerable improvement. But, necessity, as they say, is the mother of invention, and the pressure of not wanting to be a laughing stock resulted in an unexpected and psychologically penetrative master-stroke thus:

'But the minister wears a dog collar which is different to the black other bit, innit?' I said. Always a woman to be influenced by a sound ecclesiastical argument, for about the only time in my life it was game, set and match to yours truly. And what's more, I got my mother to complete the neck band part of the woolly ensemble in mauve. *Mauve,* for heaven's sake! One can only assume that she might have come across the remains of last year's Christmas sherry lurking in the back of a cupboard, and decided to reward her efforts at casting-on or locating dropped stitches with a brief restorative. And the result? Well, I thought it was good... until I wore it to the youth club the next Friday night. Teenagers can be very cruel.

The offending item* Just thank your lucky stars we only had monochrome film.

* The jumper, I mean

By the beginning of the decade, more and more pop records were flooding on to the market, and being soaked up by an adoring teenage audience. Yet still, there was a lack of dedicated TV and radio to exploit such interest: if you wanted to hear Billy Fury, or Marty Wilde, Bobby Vee or Cliff, you had to wait for someone to fork out the necessary at their local record shop, and then bring it to the club in their hot little hand. Otherwise, there was *Saturday Club* on the radio, or *Juke Box Jury* on the TV. Both were Saturday programmes, and therefore popular, but it did leave an enormous gap until the following weekend. *Juke Box Jury* was hosted by the impeccable David Jacobs, a thoroughly nice man, always perfectly turned out in smart suit and well groomed hair. Fine... but not the rebellious, pouting sort of idol we all craved. Nevertheless, the programme was watched by huge audiences, and although it would be unkind to add *'because there was nothing else'* I have to say that there would be an element of truth in so doing. The programme consisted of David playing that week's new releases on the studio Juke Box. Four guest panellists would form the jury, and they would judge each new release played to be either a HIT or a MISS. This would be accorded a bell for the former, or a claxon horn for the latter. In the event of a tie, three members of the audience were asked to give their own verdict. Usually, one of the artistes whose record had been included in the programme would make a surprise appearance, which gave rise to some embarrassment to those on the panel who had just judged his or her rendition to be crap. What excitement! The majority of the show just had views of the panellists tapping their fingers, or the audience sat in rapt attention, so to be honest, it didn't make the most riveting viewing – but at least it was pop music and gladly received.

Although *Pick of The Pops* had been going since 1955, (when it was introduced by Franklin Engelmann as *'a selection from the top shelf of current popular gramophone records'*) it was mid-week and clashed with *'The Archers',* so for many of us with only one radio, inaccessible!

Saturday Club, hosted by Brian Matthew was a bit more 'hip' in that there were pop news items and interviews between the music. Its slight downside was that, the music was live, and more often than not, a cover rendition by resident singers. This inevitably meant that one's favourite stars were replaced with a well-meaning and no doubt talented singer, but NOT THE ONE YOU REALLY WANTED TO HEAR. If Elvis had taken the trouble to put a monumental amount of doe-eyed pouting and moody looks into providing the world with *'Love Me Tender'* then I'm sure the audience wanted to hear him sing it, not some warbling bloke no one had ever heard of. It was a bit like having your Dad sing *'Heartbreak Hotel'* - not very reminiscent of the original, and more than slightly embarrassing. But, as with *Juke Box Jury,* it was at least a step in the right direction.

The other alternative was, of course, to go and buy the record yourself. The problem here was twofold, the first being the need to have access to a reasonable 45rpm playing record player – and many of the old gramophone types would only play at 78rpm. The result of mis-matching the one with the other was to get your heart-felt rendition of *'Love Me Tender'* transformed into something which lasted only a fraction of the time expected, and worse still, sounded very much like Woody Woodpecker on a bad day. The second problem was that records were relatively expensive, (6/8d old money*) and for those of us not yet earning, getting the necessary together from paper rounds and pocket money was not so easy.

There were economies to be made however, and a gap in the burgeoning pop market was spotted by none other than that stalwart of the high street, good old Woollies. There can have been few communities in the country who were further away from one of F.W. Woolworth's stores than a short bus ride. The store's cheerful presence in just about every shopping street was synonymous with a massive range of cheap goods, from floor mops to ice-creams, from *Liquorice All-Sorts* to tin soldiers, Woollies had the lot. The company was also alert to opportunity, and in the late fifties recognised that there was a market in cut-price pop music. Thus it was that it introduced its own record label – *Embassy Records,* and sold the little 45rpm discs at about half the price of those available via the dedicated record shops. It also made sure that its releases were up to date, so you would be unlucky not to find a recording of your heart's desire within a week or two of its release date. So, what's the problem? Well, in order to keep costs down, Woollies employed their own session singers to record the *Embassy* label renditions – so although not quite as bad as having your Dad singing, the product was only part way to being 'with it'.

Still, never mind; it was after all, a disc to add to your collection, and once on the old record player, the artiste had to compete with your own in-front-of-mirror-with-hairbrush-microphone rendition anyhow. There is little doubt that the copying of the original was therefore frequently overwhelmed by a cacophony of teenage excess. Well, it was in our house anyway. In any case, whether or not you could afford the latest waxing there was always the youth club, where a copy would be put on

*Equals 33p, but this at a time when a good average weekly wage for a man was a mere £15 a week. My family's first transistor radio bought for £13 was therefore a considerable outlay

at full blast of a Friday night. Such renditions added mightily to the club's cheerful background noise of furious games of table tennis, the rumble of snooker balls rolling across a wooden floor after being hit with an amount of enthusiasm destined to pitch them right over the perimeter cushion, the *thwack* of the very many darts that ended up in the adjoining scoreboard rather than the cork playing surface and the general shrieking, banter and slamming of doors which were so much a part of teenage life.

Just occasionally, this end of week mayhem would quieten down for a few minutes when club leaders would give out notices on forthcoming events and so on. If it was a church club, there might even be a minute or two of what was supposed to be quiet reflection into the deeper meanings of life. To be honest, self-analytical meditation was just about the last thing testosterone filled *yoofs* had on their minds of a Friday night. After five whole days of being knocked about by the loonies at school, and five whole nights of gazing at the homework sheet and wondering just what the hell the *1906 Liberal Reform Bill* was really about, a little light relief was what was called for.

By 1963 there was a very clear view that the new decade was a big step up from the fifties, that the days of the Teds, the Rockers and skiffle groups were firmly behind us. The future lay with the Liverpool Sound, with Carnaby Street fashion, with scooters and the Mods. It was therefore very much a youth culture, and a *young* youth culture at that. Little wonder, therefore, that the spotty devotees of the local youth club all of a sudden saw themselves as the centre of the world. There was also a discernible sense of excitement in the air... a growing feeling that youth culture was now driving the way forward, and for perhaps the first time ever, bringing some of the older generation with it. Of particular note was the way mainstream (i.e. adult) entertainment started acknowledging – and later actively following - the more obvious elements of pop culture, often with embarrassing results.

This became particularly apparent when, in the mid sixties, *the Twist* became a sudden dance craze, and the likes of Frank Sinatra, no less, gave the new dance some gravitas by releasing 'Everybody's *Twistin'*. This single record alone seemed to give our parents' generation the right to get in on the act and suddenly, to the acute embarrassment of just about everyone, your mums and dads could be seen swivelling their hips and bending their knees in an excruciating parody of the dance. How awful – but how indicative of the massive change in popular perception. Only a generation before, it had been the earnest wish of most teenagers to simply *'grow up'* - a term which meant emulating as quickly as possible the habits, dress and life-style of their parents… to wear flannel trousers and jacket, to acquire a pipe and a pair of slippers … and that was only the girls! Now the boot was firmly lodged on the other foot: the young generation revelled in being as different as possible from their 'square' elders, and the kids just teetering on the edge of the adult world, if not yet completely occupying the driving seat, were at least the essential market upon which the new movers and shakers of the sixties depended. If the *yoofs* at the *yoof* club weren't buying their records or copying their fashion ideas, they'd be quickly up the well-known creek, knee-deep in the brown stuff.

It's therefore surprising to reflect that a lot of the support for such a social revolution came – quite inadvertently – from that most staid bastion of traditional values and guardian of the status quo, the established church. Of the many organisations that provided a convivial meeting place for young people, a sizeable proportion of youth clubs were church based. In the days when the church played a much greater part in the lives of the community, the provision of specific venues for teenagers was, for the ecclesiastical authorities, just a step up from Sunday School, surely?

And for many, it was. Like lots of Baby Boomers, I had been brought up to go to church, and so had a sizeable proportion of my mates. Now, I'm not saying that we were especially holy – far from it - but the church provided a lot more than its obvious *raison d'être*. It was an important element of the social round, and one that was the perfect complement to family life. After all, If you were *'hatched, matched and dispatched'* by the church, why not go to the Beetle Drive as well? Many churches had additional meeting rooms suitable for social purposes, a caretaker to open up and a well-meaning group of adults willing and able to provide an endless stream of bloater paste sandwiches and butterfly cakes. Added to that, the vicar or minister was usually at hand to reassure you that your just reward would be in heaven - so what's not to like? I mean, fish-paste sandwiches, the latest pop music, girls to mix with, table tennis *and eternal salvation* – not a bad combo, eh? Not that concern for our mortal souls was necessarily the prime mover in making our weekly visit.

Of more immediate importance were the myriad of doubts, muddled thinking, uncertainties and general misconceptions which inhabit 99% of the teenage mind … not to mention trying to be hip by joining in with the latest song lyrics and getting them totally wrong. OK, it's a common human failing: just about everyone I've ever known has been guilty of yelling out a pop song at the top of their voices believing their lyrics to be entirely as recorded by the artiste. One of my many personal sources of such embarrassment came from Elvis Presley's hit *'Hound Dog'* when I used to belt out:

'…well you ain't never fought the habit, and you ain't no friend of mine…' Regrettably, this did in fact turn out to be:

'…well you ain't never caught a rabbit and you ain't no friend of mine'.

Rabbits? I mean…RABBITS?! To be honest, I thought my lyrics were a distinct improvement upon the original – but did my mates at the yoof club agree? Like I said before: teenagers can be very cruel.

And the oddest thing – sometimes the misinterpreted words didn't make sense to you either. Take for example, the song *'Rocket Man'* by Elton John. I know it's from a much later era than the one under discussion, but it illustrates the point entirely. At one stage Elton sings:

'I'm a rocket m-a –a- a-aan
Burning up the fuel up here alone'

Now, for the life of me, I simply couldn't make out what the second line said. To me it sounded like:

'Burning up the tool of parazone'

… so for me, that's what it became. Whenever I sang along with Eltie, and despite all logic, I was convinced that part of his spaceman's kit included a tool whose essential ingredient was a measure of a thick bleachy type product. Did seem a little odd, I must say, but who was I to argue with the likes of Elton John? Besides, I must admit that my track record in transposing and mutilating the compositions of many a great writer into something entirely different had a history: at primary school my *'Hark the Herald Angels'* deviation into the world of vegetarianism with *'Peas on Earth and Mercy Mild'* left me red-faced. And that's not all by a long chalk. Another embarrassing occasion came at the start of Grammar School when we little first years were having a wider and more sophisticated range of carols beaten into us. One such bore the cumbersome title of *'The Angel Gabriel from Heaven Came'*. Had I but paid attention rather than spent my time wondering if our resident *'fart on demand'* colleague was going to let rip again, I might have gathered that this quite tuneful and appealing carol dealt with what the church calls *'The Annunciation'* – i.e. Mary is given some rather startling news by an angel. So far so good. But, one of the subsequent lines – in fact, the most important and oft repeated lines go:

'*… **Most highly favoured lady,***
***Gloria!**'*

The second line of this pair, the *Gloria* bit, is extended over several notes for both musical and dramatic effect, and does give each verse a fitting climax. By now you will have gathered that if there is a wrong end of the stick to get hold of, yours truly is in possession of enough to build the second Little Pig a quite substantial mansion. Thus the hymn writer's intention of using the word *Gloria* as a means of purveying due verbal adulation of the forthcoming nativity - and especially Mary's unexpected but essential part in it - was entirely lost on me. As far as I was concerned, another lady – one Gloria - had come into the story. Perhaps she was Joseph's third cousin, or one of Gabriel's heavenly chums? I was not really sure - but I was certainly sure that Gloria was a girl's name; we had one at Highland Road Juniors, a chirpy kid and she now went to the youth club, so that must be it!

And worse still, my interpretation of the third word of the stanza – ***'favoured'*** - was also a corruption. In my defence I would say that:
a) Like most young teenagers, learning a new and difficult-to-sing carol was not at the top of my must-do list;
b) I always sat at the back of the class, because I wanted to be as far as

as possible from the slipper-wielding bloke who taught us music, and so words on the displayed hymn sheet were not always easy to see;

c) I was at this time the lucky recipient of a pair of National Health wire framed glasses, prescribed to correct a slight squint. Although they were not as opaque as those snot-smeared encumbrances adorning many other kids' noses, mine also lacked a good deal of the sparkling clarity that the NHS felt necessary. So the fact that I misinterpreted the word in question and added an unfortunate extra letter was not really my fault at all: that this Gloria person should become a most '***highly flavoured lady***' seemed perfectly logical to me.

We have strayed, have we not, from the early sixties somewhat? - but perhaps the lessons learned from my highly illogical interpretation of earlier lyrics made me a lot more attentive to those churned out by the wordsmiths of the new decade. For a year or two either side of the turn of the decade, there seemed to be a constant theme in pop lyrics which centred around *ownership*... not ownership of articles of any particular note, but of people – and mainly girls. Take for example, Cliff's hit '*Livin' Doll*', where the lyrics indicate that he has attracted a young lady whose principle attributes seem to be that she frequently resorts to '***crying, walking, sleeping, and talking***', though presumably not all at the same time. Undaunted however, Cliff determines to make this object of his affection his very own by confirming that he is '***...gonna lock her up in a trunk, so no big hunk can steal her away from me***'.

Well, whatever views we might have on kidnapping, I think it must be assumed that Cliff was being metaphorical in his plans for the new girlfriend. Nonetheless, such possessive sentiments were by no means uncommon. The pop song that really confirms this idea of the *ownership* of the object of male desire is Bobby Vee's hit of 1962 '*Take Good Care of My Baby*' which tells the soulful tale of the singer's regret for a love lost to another. He implores the new boyfriend (which might as well read '*new owner*') to show considerable solicitude towards the recently lost girl. The ownership crunch comes towards the end of this heart-rending account when, in an appeal to the new boyfriend's better sense he cries:

**'And if you should discover, that you don't really love her,
Just send my baby back home to me'**.

Now, I liked Bobby Vee a lot. After all, he did have a serious blow-wave haircut and was very good looking – but even then, I thought that the lyrics were a bit rich. It does make the young lady in question seem little more than a package to be handed around, and implies that she has little say in the matter, does it not? OK, I wasn't familiar with that many girls (and not for the want of trying, let me add) but of those I did know I'm pretty damn sure they would have had one hell of a lot to say. Had I known the word *presumptuous* I would probably have applied it in a moderately vigorous way, but that was always pretty unlikely as my levels of gorm were still a tad on the low side. Bobby Vee also released a record called *'The Night has a Thousand Eyes'* which robustly reminds any girlfriend of his who might consider responding to the amorous approaches of another bloke, that **there is always someone watching!** How creepy is that? I suppose that continual surveillance was a bit better than being '*locked up in a trunk',* and thus well out of the reach of any passing and overtly lecherous '*big hunk'* - but really!

At fourteen years of age, and still not knowing much about girls and their needs, just the slightest encouragement of a smile or a coy giggle would have sent our little pubescent hearts a-flutter, and perhaps be the only encouragement one might need to rush off to Boots to buy the girl in question a couple of lurid green bath cubes wrapped in shiny pink cellophane. Love? Well, as you can judge, most of us had a hell of a long way to go yet. To be honest, the girls of our acquaintance always seemed to be so much more knowledgeable concerning just about everything - except, perhaps, *Three in One* oil and how to replace the studs in your football boots. So listening to the success of pop idols, and trying to use mis-heard song lyrics for pointers as to how to *get the girl* was always going to be something of a long shot.

Mind you, unless your name was Roy Orbison*, it wasn't all gloom; there was always the chance that some songs might have an unintended

* *Roy was a truly great singer, but his songs were what one might at best term 'moody'. Titles included* '**I'm Hurtin' 'Crying', 'Running Scared' 'Love Hurts', 'It's Over'**, and the superb **'Only the Lonely'**. *There was a kind of feeling at school that his mates might have liked to have whispered in his ear- 'Hey, Roy, lighten up a little, huh?'*

double entendre to amuse the likes of us, and one such that came a little later and caused great mirth was *'It's My Party'* by Lesley Gore. The song is really a lamentation by the poor soul over the fact that her boyfriend Johnny had cleared off out of a party that she has been at considerable pains to organise. Well, OK, perhaps he's nipped out for a quick fag, or to re-arrange his blow-wave…. But no! Lesley notices that his disappearance is not the only one: gone too is an apparently acquisitive competitor called Judy. Is this a coincidence? Can they both have heard what they mistakenly interpreted as a four minute nuclear warning and made for the local fall-out shelter? It seems not. Noticing the absence from the party of both her boyfriend *and* the villainous Judy, the lyrics state: **'Nobody knows where my Johnny has gone…'** Bingo! What a gift! Bearing in mind that a Johnny was the much-used term for a condom, you can imagine with what glee these words were sung – and for a change, no one got the words wrong.

OK, we were not sophisticated, but don't forget, we had only just survived the very real threat of nuclear annihilation, so a little forbearance is called for, isn't it?

An original 45rpm copy of Lesley Gore's 1965 hit ***'It's My Party'***

3 Sky Hooks and Elbow Grease

All of a sudden, things at school started to get a bit serious; we were now in the year when BIG decisions had to be made. At the end of our fourth year, the results of the mock GCE O Level exams had given us a good indication of what to expect the following year and consequently the world beyond school hove into view… and a bit like the lookouts on the Titanic when they first noticed a large white lumpy thing getting closer and closer, many of us thought *'Blimey – better do something about that!'*

Apart from our ever popular-but-irascible classmate Bandy who had mysteriously disappeared when he was a mere fifteen, (claiming he was going to get a job *'…on the vans with the Co-op'*) hardly any of us had given much thought as to future careers in the world beyond school. Until now that is, when quite a few pigeons started to come home to roost. Our 'flatulence on demand' colleague Mick for example, found that job opportunities for those skilled in farting were a bit thin on the ground despite his near perfect timing and wide range of audio effects developed over several years of painstaking refinement. Others amongst us began to regret spending so much time gazing vacantly out of the classroom window and wondering if a lucky fire drill might save us from punishment when it was discovered that rather than doing last night's homework, the time had been spent on remodelling one's blow-wave and squeezing the latest crop of spots in front of the bathroom mirror.

Even more sinister, the attitude of the teachers underwent a subtle change in that there was now a very slight recognition that the spotty Herberts of class 5S were getting close to exam time, and would soon represent twenty per cent of those who would sustain the school's reputation as a centre of all academic excellence. Perhaps as a result of this growing recognition of how our class performed *actually mattered*, we started to get some grown-up stuff type equipment which was deemed as essential for our transition into the world of work. We techie types got newish T squares and a wider selection of sharper and more aggressive tools in the school workshops. What joy. Presumably, the kids in the top stream got fresh quills and their own personalised pot of ink – I dunno. Nevertheless, there we were, soon-to-be sixteen year olds, quickly approaching the time when a big decision would have to be made... whether to leave school and get a job, or to stay on into the sixth form and do A levels.

Now, we need to step back a bit from all this heady excitement and take a quick look at how things stood vis-à-vis post sixteen opportunities as they were in the 1960's. First and foremost it needs to be understood that only a small proportion of sixteen year olds stayed on into the sixth form, and of those that did, only a similarly small proportion went on to university*. In the sixties the number of universities was again, very much smaller than it is today, and the expectation of a university education was not within the remit of the vast majority of adolescents – and often quite regardless of how clever they might be. What was a far more common route into further (post-sixteen) education was to enroll for one of the many vocational courses offered by Technical Colleges or their senior partners, the Colleges of Technology. Whereas the former required a reasonable achievement at O Level and were therefore accessed by many when just sixteen, the latter provided for those who had some achievement at A Level, and provided courses that could, in the fullness of time (and often a *very* long time) provide vocational degrees or degree equivalents.

For those not entering the world of technology, there were any number of post-sixteen institutions offering vocation-specific courses. Of these, many provided opportunities to study for nationally recognised awards, and so young people might be studying commerce or banking, and many youngsters (mainly girls) went on to get secretarial qualifications through their attendance at Pitman's colleges and the like, where skills in shorthand and typing were taught.

So, back to the old SGS, where the Sword of Damocles in the form of the dreaded O Level exams was now positioned in a most threatening overhead location. The reaction to the need to get a large dollop of feck

*Nationally, only 4% of school leavers went to university in the 1960's. Compare this with the statistic of well over 40% today.

[54]

was two-fold: you could turn up the tranny, learn all the words and compulsory hip gyrations associated with Elvis' *'Devil in Disguise'* in order to provide a sensational impersonation in front of the bathroom mirror complete with handy hairbrush microphone … or you could wearily drag out the old school books. On doing so you might well reflect that drawing cartoons all over the title pages and colouring in each letter O, P, R and B hadn't been such a bright idea after all, and didn't help one bit with all this bleeding revision.

I suppose for most of us, it was a combination of the two, and there was a lot of pressure from both sides – the teachers in demanding the best results ever achieved by a bunch of teenage morons, and the world of pop culture, where the pressure to conform with all the latest trends was equally ferocious. Mind you, the fact that quite a high proportion of our class had done really pretty well in the GCE mock exams was one in the eye for those who had more or less written us off in the early days as mere 'workshop fodder'.

I'd like to think that those responsible for the social engineering manifested in the decision to remove from us lowly mortals the finer things of life represented by the Classics, the Arts and English Literature, might have been given pause for thought - but I somehow doubt it. In those days such curricular manipulation was very common and has to be viewed in the context of the time. It was still very much a case of *'the establishment knows best… just do as you're told!'* Although apparently brutal, it did work for most of the kids most of the time; whether or not some might have developed other skills is a moot point. In addition, it needs to be borne in mind that it was about a zillion times better that the ad-hoc procedures that were current before the 1944 Education Act. Even a decade or so on, post-war education was still in its early stages, and was proving to be a big step in the right direction… so think yourself lucky, you stroppy little bottom stream gits!

And anyway, who needed traditional 'culture' when we were immersed in, and very much part of the seismic and sparkling teenage social revolution that at that moment was bursting forth? For was it not true that our very own generation was well into the process of hijacking what people did, thought, wore, watched, listened to and ogled at? OK, Alan Breeze singing *'Bless This House'* on the *Billy Cotton Band Show* might be a turn-on for some, but it somehow lacked the explosive force of *'How Do You Do It?'* from Gerry and the Pacemakers, or indeed the literary merit of *'Da Doo Ron-Ron'* from the Crystals. And in the world of fine literature, whereas Gray's *'Elegy in a Country Churchyard'* still had, no doubt, a number of devotees, it somehow lacked the assertive punchy memorability of some of the chirpier bits of poetry and prose now available via song lyrics.

Even the new blizzard of advertisements possessed some literary merit which many overlooked... but not the culture hungry denizens of class 5S who knew an elegant stanza when they saw one. Consider if you will this exquisite verse of the time which captures not only the needs and aspirations of pubescent youth but combines it with perceptive health and grooming advice at the same time:

Max Factor
Knacker lacquer
Adds lustre
To your cluster

I think you will agree that this fine example of contemporary poetry shows that just because we had been banned from doing English Lit, it didn't mean we couldn't appreciate a good poem, albeit from an unexpected source. Clearly, in the absence of any formal support from the school, we not-so-little chaps of 5S had piloted our own course through the subject, and came up with some works of quite astonishing perception and relevance to our own time and age. Even such sophistications as haiku were meat and drink to us, and we commented upon it to each other as we quoted these curiously hypnotic lines and noted the compulsory seventeen syllables:

You'll wonder where the yellow went
When you brush your teeth
With Pepsodent*

You'll need a moment or two to dash a tear from your eye I have no

* *Don't bother. I've already counted them.*

doubt, so whilst you regain your composure, let me further emphasise the point by stating that our quest to fill the cultural gap didn't just restrict itself to TV jingles. Even in the unlikeliest of places, a haiku could leap out and grab you by the throat. Take, for example, the shimmering eloquence of the following two found by eagle-eyed class 5S culture fanatics scratched in the paintwork of a local public toilet:

The painter's paint was all in vain-
The crap-house poets
Are back again!*

And again: **Here I sit with a broken heart**
Paid my penny
But could only fart*

But let me remind you that it wasn't all literary appreciation and scanning the bawdier bits of Tit-Bits newspapers, I can assure you. There was serious stuff to be getting on with, principal amongst which was the need to find out if somebody – ANYBODY- would be likely to offer you a job.

For those in the process of leaving school in the early sixties, the perceived wisdom was that there existed a huge range of employment prospects for the fresh-faced adolescent. Some of these required no qualifications at all – but many more did, and were supported by courses of further education. The reason for this rosier prospect for work seekers was mainly because of the improved economic prospects of the country as a whole - and the fact that many industries were still very labour intensive, and thus required a larger workforce than is the case today. As the new decade got underway, the availability of work was increasingly fuelled through response to the consumer demands of the baby boomer generation itself. There was a kind of circularity: those who secured work enjoyed a growing measure of disposable income and keenly sought the products becoming available - which meant that more production was needed to meet the need in both … and so on. The post-war generation was eager to spend its newly acquired wealth on the huge quantity of goods and services flooding on to the market. Such

* Oh ye of little faith! Like I said, I've already counted them!

opportunity, when coupled with the brand new and powerful influence of television advertising, produced a heady cocktail of consumerism.

So where did this leave the spotty youths of class 5S? Well, worrying themselves sick that they would fail all their GCE O Levels, that's where. And suddenly, revising for the exams became something of a necessity: the realisation that you could be out on your ear with no prospect of anything like a promising future in just a few months had much the same effect as jumping from a warm bed into a frozen pond, and no amount of excuses such as learning the words of the Beatles' *'She Loves You!'* could dispel the fact that THE FUTURE IS HERE: DO SOMETHING! So we did. And in addition to revision, many also started to look much harder of what the options were for a sixteen year old.

One of these, of course, was to stay on at school for another two years, and try to get a couple of A Levels. But as noted previously, this was a path taken by relatively few, and of those that did, university entrance was far from being the obvious next move. I cannot recall a single member of my class even *mentioning* the word *'university'*. As a possible option it was barely – if at all – considered. More to the point was the fact that the successful attainment of A Levels would allow you to enter many of the same jobs as post-sixteen, but at a higher level. Thus for job-seekers, it was a kind of race: leave now, get a job with some kind of future, or stay on in the sixth form and hope for good A level results to provide a springboard into higher levels of employment.

Of course, the immediate attraction of leaving at sixteen was the thought of having a wage – and to a lesser extent - knowledge that most employers provided further education opportunities. This way you could still beat the alternative of staying for A Level study, and you'd have money in your pocket. OK, some would join higher up the scale later on... but A Levels were hard, and there were no guarantees. Shallow thinking? Perhaps. *'And what did your own school suggest?'* I hear you ask. *'What about careers advice?'*

Good question. If the experience of the teenagers in my class was anything to go by, there was precious little. Despite the fact that a goodly proportion of us had done well at the GCE mocks and were due to sit a whole bunch of O Levels, there seemed to be little interest in our career prospects. I can recall my Careers Guidance interview almost word for word – mainly because there were so few of them to remember. 'Uncle Joe' was an English teacher who seemed to have been pressed into the additional duty of Careers Advice Bloke for the week, and appeared as reluctant as – I suspect - he was unqualified to give expert advice to fresh faced kids about to launch into the world of work. To the best of my recollection, my interview went like this:

Uncle Joe: *Ah, Burden... Have you applied for anything yet?*

Me: *Yes Sir – I'm thinking of going into the GPO Engineers as an apprentice.*

Uncle Joe: *Oh, right... NEXT!!*

That was it. A shame really, since it would not have taken much to twist my arm to give serious consideration to the benefits of staying on and doing A Levels – but I never gave it much thought because, well, the sixth form was out of the ordinary. No one in my family, or those of most of my friends had stayed on - let alone gone to university, or even thought of it. I suppose a few might have considered Teacher Training College, but at the time, the thought of ending up like Uncle Joe or any of the other loonies we'd been subjected to over the last five years was not immediately appealing in the Spring of 1963 ... especially when there was so much else going on in the big wide world. So why an apprenticeship? And why the GPO?

The point was made earlier on about the social engineering inflicted upon us at the age of thirteen, and this in turn meant that choosing to leave school at sixteen was in many respects pre-ordained; we were the technical class, and thus no more was either anticipated or expected of us. There is little doubt that this ambition became almost as well ingrained in us as it was in the school staff. It was the law of the self fulfilling prophecy, no less. As far as most of us were concerned, there was little encouragement to have higher aspirations, although some of the braver (or perhaps bewildered) souls in the class did take that unknown step into the sixth form, but they were by comparison a minority. Also, the number of apprenticeships available for the sixteen year olds was large, and within that category offered a wide range from the trade-based manual occupations at one end, to those which saw the award of a degree, if you chose to persevere that far at the other.

Portsmouth, being a naval town, took a vast number of youngsters each year to go in to the Royal Dockyard, where there were any number of trades offering worthwhile apprenticeships, from careers as diverse as boiler making to naval architecture. The 'Yard' even had its own school in which apprentices were required to pursue the more academic side of their vocation on a weekly basis. Bearing in mind that nationalisation was still a relatively new concept, there were also a large number of apprenticeships and other job opportunities available in these recently established organisations. Thus the Southern Electricity Board, the Gas Board and the Water Board soaked up a good many*. The GPO, (General Post Office), was another. Originally created to reconcile the Royal Mail postal system with the technical innovations in telecommunications, it took on a wider role and became the government department responsible for all aspects of the new technologies. As far as I was concerned, the GPO had a certain cachet to it: after all, everyone wanted a telephone, didn't they? And you could now get them in green and dark blue! Also, Douglas Bader and the other fighter boys of WW2 had depended on blokes on the phone to tell the girls in the plotting room at Biggin Hill where Jerry was, so that was good too! The fact that my cousin Steve had taken the same career path the previous year also had a part to play. He was a sensible chap, and his reliability in remaining at the top of the information highway was beyond doubt. For example, his sex education advice had been particularly sound, and so I was sure he could be trusted to make a good career choice as well. Also, he now had a motor bike. You'll have noted that despite my best efforts over the previous five years, there was still a need for that final top up in the gorm department in the Burden psyche.

* *No pun intended, and please don't associate the term 'water board' with the less than pleasant application it has these days. All the public utilities were run by publicly owned 'Boards', and there was no choice for consumers as to where you obtained your electricity, water and gas. People of the sixties therefore had a great deal more spare time as they didn't have to spend about 40% of their adult life chasing cost comparison websites, as we do today. Sorry to sound so bitter... but really!!*

And so it was, with that level of sophisticated thinking, I took the plunge and decided to leave school. At the time it seemed a wise choice: the GPO required a good handful of GCE's and provided a well trodden path of further education. What's more, GPO apprentices, at a princely £5–3/6d (£5-17) a week, were better paid than dockyard apprentices. The GPO also had green vans with a ladder on the top and *'Post Office Telephones'* written on the side in white, so what more could anyone ask?

And yet, come the month, come the week, come the day, there *was* genuine regret at leaving school. I think many of us were surprised at the affection we felt for the place. With all its eccentric teachers, arbitrary violence, bonkers rules and regulations, it was still *our* school, and I think many of us were surprised at the very mixed feelings we had about our final departure from the dear old SGS. Like many of my fellow leavers, I took the opportunity to go round to various teachers to bid a fond farewell, and one of these was the irascible Wilf who you might recall from the first book in this series, had *not* taught me Art for the last three years. I am certain he had no idea that I had not darkened the door of the art room since 1960, and greeted me with as much warmth as he always had towards every boy – guarded suspicion and barely suppressed venom ready to explode at any moment… until he was sure I hadn't come to take the piss. Once that was established, he was all affability and even offered me a brand new art book with the words *'There you are old man – earn yourself a bit of cash over the summer!'* This only underlined the fact that he had no recollection of the last time we had met in class. On that occasion he had regarded my sketch of a Hawker Hurricane aeroplane with something approaching apoplexy and yelled *'There's nothing there! Take it away and shade it up!!!'* Perhaps the ensuing three year absence had made his heart grow fonder… but with dear old Wilf, I somehow doubt it. Nevertheless, we parted amicably, and this was true too with almost all of my teachers … and certainly with my classmates, many of whom had become good friends over the years.

As far as I can recall, there was no particular school occasion to mark our departure, other than an end of term assembly for all boys, when a brief mention of good wishes to all who were leaving was made – as well as … *'and don't forget to hand in your text books '*. There was absolutely no end of school party, discos had yet to be invented, and as regards a *prom...* good grief, if someone had told us that in a generation's time you might have expected to have donned a formal dress suit prior to being picked up by a stretched limo and taken to a location already crammed with sensationally dressed adolescent girls, we would have thought you had spent too long assisting Mrs. Collins in the Banda cupboard. Had the prom option been available, it might just have been enough to have ensured that Bandy would have at last cleaned the accumulated snot off his glasses, and that Mick might exercise a modicum of restraint when he realised that comedy farting would do little to impress a gathering of pretty teenage girls.

But we were the well-hard Baby Boomer kids of class 5S, and as such squared our shoulders, cast doubt aside and to all outward appearances went our separate ways with little immediate regret, and hardly a look back over the shoulder. No more homework! No more school dinners! We were young! We were free! We were almost clear of acne! The only slight cloud on the horizon being that the O Level results were not expected until August and so, for the likes of me, there was a little nail biting still to do. But in the meantime, there were six whole weeks of glorious idling before earning an honest living – and this was 1963 – it was exciting, there was so much going on in the big wide world, and the youth club had loads of things organised including all-night hikes, a visit to London and various sports competitions. So, all in all, a good deal to take your mind off the approach of the serious matter of earning a living.

Being a member of a non school-based youth group did confirm for many of us the imbalance of opportunity which was implicit in the Eleven Plus system, as club members came from a whole range of schools. A number of teenagers I knew left school with no recognisable qualifications at all, and although there were plenty of jobs around, the longer term prospects of the employment opportunities on offer to such youngsters were limited. As you might expect, such concerns were inevitably lost in the heady expectation of real wages at the end of the week, and the chance to buy records, fags, clothes, cosmetics – even deodorant, for heaven's sake!

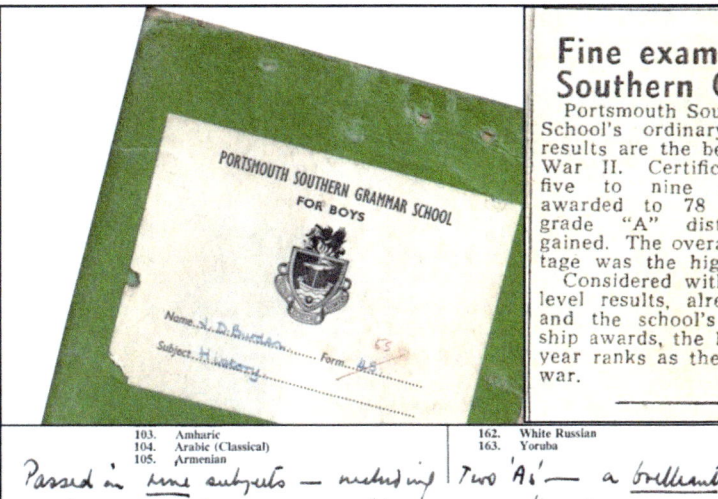

All original 1963 stuff: Ye olde History exercise book containing page upon page of teenage wisdom and a terrific analysis of the 1906 Liberal Reform Bill: Half Day Closing for Shops. Also, it is interesting to note that despite being such an utterly gormless mob of Baby Boomers, the whole year group had done really pretty well. Interesting too, that in his post-result euphoria, the Head had entirely forgotten that he had signed my leaving form just prior to the end of term, and thus his assertion that 'a splendid future' awaited me in the sixth form was a little ambitious, wouldn't you say?

It was only later, when the initial excitement had worn off, that the realisation that a future of largely unrewarding and sometimes precarious work did not necessarily equate with a happy long term future. That a goodly proportion of young people in this situation did go on to have happy and successful working lives says much for the resilience of the human spirit: with determination, there were still useful opportunities for the resourceful.

As noted before, educational opportunity seemed to be biased against girls, the excuse being - even at the beginning of the sixties - public opinion maintained that *'a woman's place is in the home'*. Therefore, girls didn't need long term job prospects... they'd be busy at home bringing up babies, and getting hubby's tea ready. Oh yeah? If you want any confirmation of this viewpoint, just Google the words of the song '***Wives and Lovers'*** recorded and made very popular by the gorgeous American singer Jack Jones in 1963.

The whole song is advice to wives about being attractively made up and in felicitous mood when welcoming home the husband from his 'day at the office'. Housewives are reminded to:

'***Comb your hair, fix your make-up,***
Soon he will open the door...'

and later:

'**Hey, little girl**
Better wear something pretty'

The song then takes on a somewhat sinister turn as it reminds these ladies that should they choose to ignore such timely advice then they run a real risk in the sense that:

'**Don't think because**
There's a ring on your finger,
You needn't try any more'

And just to ensure there is absolutely no doubt about their duty to be welcoming and perfect in every respect, wives are reminded that:

'***Day after day there are girls at the office***
And men will always be men –
Don't stand him up with your hair still in curlers
<u>***You may not see him again***</u>*...'*

Blimey. So despite the fact that baby's thrown up all over the washing, the Vesta *Chou Mein* has boiled dry while the puke was being cleaned up, the telly's not working despite frequently bashing the cabinet and next door's dog has shat all over the lawn ... the wife has to be ready to greet her returning hero with a coquettish and alluring smile, a fragrant kiss and a glass of the finest chilled Muscadet.

The thing was though - outrageous as such lyrics might seem now - they were completely acceptable then; Jack Jones was adored by many women, and was seen as a glamorous role model by men. What's more, this song was probably the one most associated with this famous singer, and am I right in anticipating that a good number of those of you who were around at that time have its catchy tune in your head right now? So, the fact that opportunities for girls were more limited is hardly surprising when viewed against such a background.

Nevertheless, as the decade gained momentum, there were rather more encouraging signs of better things to come. For a start, many of the new Technical Colleges were increasingly providing accredited courses aimed at an audience which was mainly female, and the numbers of girls who studied for qualifications in secretarial, book-keeping and hotel management type courses was large. The Civil Service and other large publicly owned organisations also offered a whole range of opportunities which were popular with girls, and more often than not provided an improved career path to boot.

There was also a group of really determined youngsters – both girls and boys – who looked to increase their employment opportunities by augmenting an apparently modest level of qualifications by enrolling on O and A level courses at the local Tech. Financial support for such a move would often come from quite generous Local Authority grants, bolstered no doubt by supportive parents and Saturday jobs. Although a tough path to follow, a good number did achieve their aims, and so were able to access a far wider choice of occupation; it wasn't easy, and required a lot of dedication and noses to the grind-stone – always a difficult thing to do, but especially so when you were newly released from school discipline and subject to the myriad of tempting distractions the early sixties provided.

As the summer holidays 1963 frittered away in a kaleidoscope of new record releases, chatting up the opposite sex, trying not to decapitate too many spots when using the safety razor, working on where exactly you should *'splash it all over'*, and still resorting to a bit of nostalgic stone throwing, the world of work was suddenly and uncompromisingly here and now. I guess most teenagers were anticipating that, like at school, they would be hand-held in their first few weeks and months, and I suppose this was true – up to a point. The realisation that you were expected to actually *work* for your crust was something that filtered through quite slowly for some – me included -

plus the fact that we were now independent, and had to take on a degree of personal responsibility. Luckily for me, I had some training in this as it was my job to put the milk bottles out most evenings (except Fridays as it was youth club... and Sundays of course... oh, and the odd Tuesday and more often than not Wednesday as well) so I was pretty well hardened in the personal responsibility stakes as you can see.

But now I had to get myself to work by 8.00 am at a location twice as far away as school... with no bus pass or nuffink! Strewth. Also, like thousands of other apprentices, I found I was signed up to further education at the local Technical College ('...*five miles away, no single bus journey mate... hard luck ... on yer bike!'*) under the slightly misleading title of the 'Day Release Scheme'. Well, yes, OK, we did have a day off per week to go to the Tech... but the GPO, along with the majority of other course providers also required us to attend technical College **two nights a week as well!** This was a feature that had largely passed me by – the fact that on two days of each week, after working for a full day (leaving home around 7.00am and getting back at 5pm) I had then to get to the Tech for the evening session which stretched from 6.30 – 9.00 pm. And, what's more, we also got homework! Good grief!

And it really was, in a way. Only the fact that everyone else was in the same boat made it even remotely acceptable, and it is not surprising that, at the end of a long week, we were pretty knackered and spent even longer in bed of a Saturday morning. So, going to work for me and a good few thousand others was something of a steep learning curve. But hey! We were young, we were full of vitality and an excess of hormones all bursting at the seams to do exciting stuff. What's more, I was out and about in one of the GPO Engineer's vans with our very own ladder on the top.

OK I had little idea what I was supposed to do, but I was given a huge blue overcoat with large black buttons with the letters G-P-O embossed in grand manner upon them, leaving no one in any doubt that I was now *an engineer.* And to prove it, I could do complicated things like get the ladder down from the van and stand around looking confident and knowledgeable while the fitter installed Mrs.

Whitworth's sexy new *'706L Green'* telephone which toned in so well with her dual tone Artexing and woodchip wallpaper.

Added to all this newness was the fact that we apprentices had also to go on courses to the GPO Engineering centre in Buckinghamshire. To put this in context, you need to understand that in the 1960's hardly anyone went *anywhere.* Travel out of the local area was still considered quite adventurous, and to have to do it as part of your work was something of a bonus. At least, I took it as such... travelling over Portsdown Hill to fit a party line was a new experience... but to be given a railway warrant and being told to get yourself off for a week to Bletchley Park for a week's intensive training was something else again. And yes, I did say **Bletchley Park**... *the* Bletchley Park.

In Chapter 1, I mentioned the amazing Tom Flowers and his brilliant construction of the world's first programmable computer. And where was it built and installed? – Well in Bletchley Park of course. During the war years, the site was one of the most secret locations in the country and home to some of the finest brains. The great Alan Turing worked there on breaking the Enigma code and as part of that, his famous analytical bombes could be found clicking around in their unstoppable search for a solution within the dusty confines of the 'huts' at Bletchley. So, did I or any of my fellow apprentice buddies know any of this when we piled out of the coach and gazed uncomprehendingly at the eclectic mix of architecture that constituted Bletchley House? Was I aware of the momentous part this location had

One of the analytical bombes built at Bletchley Park during the dark days of the war.

[67]

played in winning the war and providing us all with the freedoms and blessings of the welfare state that I – and just about everyone else – was now taking for granted?

Well of course not! Our only concerns related to the whereabouts of the dining hall and whether or not there were any girl trainees who might care for a dance or two in the evening. To be fair, it should be mentioned that it wasn't just our collective under-provision of gorm that was to blame; what went on at Bletchley during the war was still *very* secret at that time, and it was only in the following decade that a trickle of information started to reveal the Park's magnificent wartime contribution… so I do have an excuse. Nevertheless, and even to this day, it is still thrilling to think that next door to the training hut we were allocated, there may well still have been one of the analytical bombes, or even evidence of the first Colossus itself.

I have to say that, hard-going and rigorous though it was, the technical education we got at the hands of the old GPO was pretty good. The training package on offer to apprentices did provide for those able, willing and talented enough, a real chance to progress to senior positions. None of us – and by that I mean society in general, - had even the remotest idea that within the space of a generation, communications technology would be transformed into something totally unrecognisable. The prospect of being able to phone *anyone* around the world *at any time* from *any location*, let alone *see them in motion and colour on something the size of a fag packet with no wires attached*, was still in the realms of General Jumbo and his inventive Lenin lookalike professor pal in the Beano.

In 1963, we still thought it pretty cool when Subscriber Trunk Dialling was introduced, and instead of the familiar '**Number please**' or '**Just trying to connect you**' from the operator, you could actually dial the number of someone in another town and speak to them from the comfort of your own draughty hallway. At that time, phones were anything but mobile, and were therefore often installed in a neutral location in the house which provided access for everyone. Thus it afforded no privacy for those who didn't want to share their inner-most secrets with anyone other than the girl at the other end of the line - and especially mum or dad who were trying to listen to *'The Archers'*. Needless to say, watching a film on your very own phone whilst simultaneously paying your electricity bill and ordering a new wardrobe from Sweden at the push of a button were never even *imagined*. Had we even the remotest idea of the sort of wizardry to become commonplace in telecoms before our due time of retirement, well then we young apprentices might have shown off our GPO buttons with even greater pride and deftly handled swagger.

But we didn't. A phone was a phone... you just talked to someone else, all plain and simple and our job was to learn how all the bits and pieces worked. For us apprentices, the weekly menu of work and college became our routine, only a little interrupted when we were sent to experience another department within the GPO Engineering department which was a requirement before moving on to the giddy heights of *'Technical Officer in Training'*. Wow! Also, of course, there were exams to pass, and new skills to master. Thinking that the pressurised regime of panicking, cramming and scraping through such tests was something we'd left behind at school proved to be a total misconception; internal training exams and the demands of Technical College were equally stressful, especially as there were new skills to be mastered. These could often crop up out of the blue, and from unexpected places.

Now you'd think doing Maths at college would be reasonably straightforward – in a *'slogging through it, remembering the formulae by heart and working out if it was a 'times' or' gozinta' sum'* sort of way, wouldn't you? Well, think again. You see, electronic calculators had yet to be invented, so punching in a bunch of numbers into your handy and brightly lit little chum wasn't an option... we had to do it the hard way, which meant the dreaded log tables again. But then along came our maths lecturer who said *'Forget log tables, boys*!' Phew! What a relief! Are we no longer required to do hard sums? And then he added those immortal words *'We'll use slide rules instead!'* And so for the first time since the heady days when we had opened up our little tin boxes full of useless geometry stuff in the first year at grammar school, we were shown a new and baffling piece of kit. Yes! The *slide rule.*

By now you will be too worldly-wise to even suspect that this particular instrument had even the remotest connection with a jolly day out at the local playground, or indeed, to have much to do with any winter sports. Of course not... but it did have a moving bit that, well, did some sliding up and down, or indeed, side to side. And the maths bloke explained to us that this weird contraption could do all sorts of hard sums without even going near a set of log tables. Exciting? We could hardly contain our indifference. Apart from being a pretty dull looking piece of kit, we were also informed that we had to get our own, and in those days, they were quite dear, and so inevitably, the second hand market was a place many turned to. I've still got mine... I don't know why really, but it's been living in the dusty recesses of an old brief case, along with other mathematical geriatrics for many a long year... well, you never know when you might be required to dash off a hasty calculation to four places of decimals, and all the batteries in your calculator are flat do you? Anyway, I've still got it, and like Archimedes' bath, it's a genuine piece of forgotten mathematical history. I can almost sense your growing excitement.

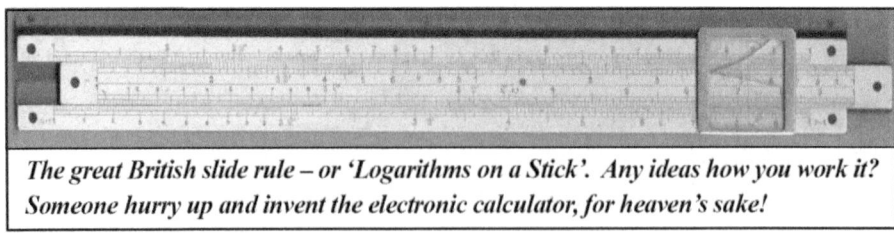

The great British slide rule – or 'Logarithms on a Stick'. Any ideas how you work it? Someone hurry up and invent the electronic calculator, for heaven's sake!

As you might just be able to see, my ancient and trusty slide rule, bears the scars of some hard fought calculations and is therefore a bit well worn. I have thoughtfully moved the slidy bit to the right to give you the idea of just how damn useful this instrument can be. I would also point out that there is not just one but TWO slidy bits, as the little metal framed window on the right, also slides along. As you can see, this slider on mine is so knocked about that it has two cracks in the tiny Perspex screen, making seeing through it about as optically efficient as Bandy's national health glasses. Nonetheless, I think the point is well made... this is a quality piece of kit whose second slidy bit was called *the cursor*. Yes! Years before the little flashing jobby appeared to light up your lives on the computer screen, its mechanical ancestor was zipping up and down the slide rules of the worthy mathematicians at Highbury Technical College. Progress? Huh!

Oh, and what was it used for? Well, the measurements along the top of the rule look like length measurement units don't they? But they're not... they are actually logarithmic lengths! Still not clear? Well, the slide rule is a handy multiplying (and dividing) tool for the practical teenage mathematician about town; it is really a set of 3D log tables….and you can imagine how chuffed we were to get them, I'll bet. Still, it was quite useful to be able to poke the bloke in front with the slidy bit at full reach, but I guess that was really a secondary purpose.

OK, hardly a life changing bit of kit, but it does illustrate how tedious and time-consuming mathematical tasks were in those days – and don't forget, we were still using the totally bonkers imperial system. So the teenagers who worked in shops still had to calculate customers' bills using their knowledge of the old twelve times table; no wonder the cumbersome mechanical adding machines we looked at in Chapter 1 were still popular.

And back at the day job, where settling into an entirely different work-based environment was the order of the day, there was the newness of working with adults who were a lot more expert than you. They, in their turn had also to come to terms with having a load of spotty *yoofs* to knock into shape, and the first step in this process was to put all new-comers through an *initiation ceremony.* I suppose such a procedure is something of a natural human reaction: the need to make sure the young whipper-snapper is firmly put in his or her place, and left in absolutely no doubt as to who's who in the hierarchy. Mind you, the most common forms were not unduly unkind, and served the secondary purpose of enlivening the day for those already part of the organisation – the vast majority of whom would have gone through these rites of passage themselves. Thus it was really little more threatening than being given the bumps on your birthday at school – although generally a little less bruising.

A favourite practice of older workmates in factories and other industrial settings, was to send hapless newcomers on pointless errands for things that were impossible to acquire. Thus sending the fresh-faced apprentice to a neighbouring building to ask the foreman in charge for *'a couple of sky hooks'* was a firm favourite. The rule was that on receiving the request, the foreman would claim that he was right out of sky-hooks... did the apprentice think they grew on trees, for heaven's sake?! They were like gold dust weren't they? *'... so what you could do, son, is go to the transport bay at the end of the factory yard where they might just have a couple left over... and better be quick about it, or they'll be gone!'* And so on and so on.

Another favourite was tracking down a large tin of elbow grease, because without it, the whole workshop would grind to a squeaky and unlubricated halt – *'so hurry up – we need it right now!'* Well, most newcomers would start to smell a rat after about two or three hours of these pointless perambulations and with a rueful smile become part of the family... and therefore be looking forward themselves to the ritual humiliation of the next intake of novices.

So, after the initial shock of entering the world of work, it is little wonder that the weekends were seen as such havens of familiarity and certainty, and therefore looked forward to with gleeful anticipation. If work was pretty much full-on each week, our two day's respite was something to exploit to the maximum effect, and now, for the first time, we had money in our pockets. OK, my meagre £5-3s 6d per week didn't go far, but even such small amounts gave teenagers the ability to get something much more expensive on Hire Purchase. Universally known as *the Never-Never* (because however much you paid, you seemed never any closer to owning the item outright) this was a popular way of impressing all and sundry with your new found wealth and wage earning prosperity. And the targets for such expenditure?

Well, record players were an obvious must-have, as were the posher types of trannies, but by far and away the most adventurous use of your cash was to get yourself some wheels. Although some got themselves better push bikes, to many it was the chance to get motorised and the cheapest way to do this was to buy a moped. As its name implies, the moped was a combination of motor and pedal power, and was the first step towards getting a powerful motor-bike. OK, it wasn't that sexy, but at least you didn't have to push, and the first ones available in the 1950's were pretty basic, comprising little more than just a tiny two-stroke engine cleverly installed within the back wheel itself.

As far as I can recall, it was bump-started by pedalling frantically along and then engaging the clutch, whereupon it would often emit a cloud of blue smoke and a large amount of noise. The one pictured has all the attributes of a standard push bike, so as a means of impressing the ladies, it was not a great start. However, the German firm NSU realised that if they could make the humble moped just a bit more motorbike-like in appearance, they could be on to a winner. Thus the *NSU Quickly* was born. And now you're talking ...

for a start it looks a lot more like a standard motor bike with its petrol tank between your knees and a proper chrome plated exhaust pipe extending rakishly alongside the back wheel. The tyres were a bit thicker than a standard push bike, and it had lights which really look the part. As far as the aspiring *ton-up kid* was concerned, however, its only drawback was that it still had pedals rather than the symmetrically placed footrests of a proper motorbike. This had something of a dampening effect upon the teenage Hell's Angel aspirant who was out to impress his lady friend in that his feet were always positioned in such a way that really REALLY underlined its complete *push-bikiness*. Nevertheless, it made a lot of noise, and you could still sweep past girls standing by the kerb at an impressive 20mph or so… just a shame she might not be able to see you too clearly through the accompanying cloud of blue smoke, or hear your manly greeting above the mad wasp type screech of the tiny engine.

Mopeds also really didn't cut the mustard when you came to a steep hill, as the sort of pretty clapped out ones we owned needed quite a lot of extra power to ascend, and this could only be provided by pedalling like fury…which was not sexy in any way, shape or form. Still, it was a start, and you could cut a dash by wearing a crash helmet (at that time not mandatory) and a silk scarf as you wandered into the coffee bar, and at least pretend the *Triumph Bonneville 650* twin parked outside was yours, and not the humble moped with the shopping basket on the front leaning up against the wall next to it.

But wider choices regarding self-propulsion were opening up. Those who really wanted to follow in the footsteps of the 1950's Teds with their greaser lifestyle could shell out on their first proper motorbike which would probably be a little *BSA Bantam*. The telegram was still in pretty regular use in the early sixties, and to deliver these, 'Telegraph Boys' were employed by the Post Office to whizz around on their noisy little *Bantams* which were

The chirpy BSA Bantam looking resplendent in its GPO telegram delivery finery.

painted bright red with large gold painted GPO letters down on each leg guard. Why BSA should want to name their smallest motor cycle after a chicken remains a mystery, but the humble *Bantam* was the entry point to the world of biking for many an aspirant Rocker.

As the decade really hit its stride, the alternative was to embrace the trendy world of the 'Mod'. Whereas Rockers liked to identify as the rough-tough leather jacket skull and crossbones type greasers, the Mods adopted an entirely different image which said: *We're smart, we're chic, we're incredibly with-it, a totally groovy creation of the sixties.*

Mod fashion was an integral part of the 'new scene' and complemented the deluge of innovative music which was taking the UK by storm. Of this more later, but the effect upon all aspects of teenage life was dramatic, and an increasingly essential element of this lifestyle was the *way* you got about. Well dressed and fashionably turned out Mod fashion simply did not mix with the macho and hard line greaser image of the motor bike.

And so an alternative and more sophisticated means of transport for the young Mod-about-town was sought, something that was trendy, colourful, attractive and utterly cool, something that wouldn't get elegant clothes smeared with grease and oil. And fitting the bill to absolute trendy perfection was the motor scooter.

This compact little machine was clean, it was colourful, it was chic and although still pretty noisy, it had huge potential for 'personalisation'. Even the names of the two most popular makes - *Vespa* and *Lambretta*, were enough to set many a teenage girl's heart a-flutter; they were so Italian, so continental, so *sophisticated!*

Quite modest by comparison with many, this 1957 twin seat Lambretta has added pannier storage. It shows how the scooter provided reasonable comfort for both driver and pillion.

Er, yes, OK. But they were still powered by noisy little two stroke engines which were pretty inaccessible and thus hard to work on. Also, with its high centre of gravity and small wheels, the motor scooter was inherently less stable than a motorbike. But in the early sixties, did any Mod worth the name give a damn? Of course not. Gone were the leather jackets and the drainpipe jeans – on with the fur lined hooded

Parkas, the flared trousers and the roll-neck sweaters. And more to the point, the possibilities of making your scooter just that bit different from everyone else's was an opportunity to spend loads more of your hard earned loot on chrome bars on which to mount an impressive array of headlamps and mirrors.

Just a tad OTT perhaps? Interesting to note that the driver is still a learner… at least when he takes his test he will be able to claim that the road ahead is well lit, and he has an excellent view of what's going on behind.

The other major innovation that this new smart and up-beat form of transport brought was that many girls also joined the craze, and quite soon there were modest but fast-growing numbers of female scooter owners. Unless I'm missing something here, and chariot riding in about AD 200 was popular with a greater number of ladies than just the fearsome Boadicea*, I suspect that scooter ownership became a transport emancipation for teenage girls. For the first time in history they could own and ride a colourful, clean and reasonably cheap form of transport that was not only very convenient, it was also one of the central elements of the sixties cultural revolution.

For those of us just starting out in the motor-powered world, the acquisition of such transport also meant you now had the opportunity to become a *people carrier* as well. Although riding as a pillion passenger was not everyone's cup of tea, nevertheless, being able to offer someone a lift was, for many, a new and empowering experience. As Mike Sarne's popular 1963 release *'Just for Kicks'* reminded us:

* *This was what Boudica used to be called. Quite when and why the famous warrior queen of the Iceni tribe changed her name I have no idea, but with a lady who delighted in duffing up Roman soldiers with her spiky-wheeled chariot, you don't argue, do you?*

[76]

If there's one thing that I like
It's a burn-up on my bike,
A burn-up with my bird
Up on my bike...

It would be wrong to say that the arrival of the other innovation of the motorcycling world, the Honda 50, went almost unnoticed, because that famous machine also made its debut at about the same time as the hullabaloo caused by the invasion of the Mod scooter-driven culture.

The big difference was that the Honda was a cross between a motorbike and a scooter. Like the latter it was a 'step through' mount and possessed in-built leg guards. It was also available in a range of colours, but it was blessed with motorbike diameter wheels, a motorbike type exhaust system and despite being of small capacity, the engine was a four stroke unit. This made the little Honda surprisingly quiet, and when other luxuries such as electric starters were introduced, it quickly became a popular machine which appealed to a wider range of owners than did the scooter or the motorbike.

The Honda 50 with its symmetrical footrests, colourful paintwork and a pillion seat was appealing, and a huge step up from a moped.

So there you are. Most of us Baby Boomer originals have left school, and are earning cash. The brand new word '*teenager*' has become an accepted and integral part of the dictionary and has transformed the status quo by shoe-horning in a raucous, punchy and above all *confident* section of society that really didn't exist before. Now its presence is unmissable and in many respects, it is in the driving seat. The images of older adults attempting to learn the Twist, and of politicians trying to wear fashionable clothing designed for young people - remain as exquisitely painful reminders of the fact that the culture and direction of domestic life in the early sixties has been taken over. As never before, it is the *emerging* generation that is in charge.

In retrospect, such a development might seem almost inevitable. We Baby Boomers were the first generation to benefit from the birth of the welfare state with its wrap-around provision. We had been provided with educational opportunity the like of which had never been experienced before, and despite having some experiences during the secondary phase which might well be described as 'interesting', most of us had emerged from it fairly cheerily, and with good job prospects thanks to the availability of work.

But equally, we had been in at the birth of new forms of communication which in turn drove and facilitated a popular revolution in music, resulting in the growth of a new culture at a time which cried out for creative expression. And there we were, confident, cocky little gits with our eyes aglow at the prospect of taking our place in the pantheon of pop icons, quite ready willing and able to do our bit.

Good job we had been brought up to be so well-hard.

4 Two Thirds of Sex, Drugs and Rock 'n' Roll

Now before you get all of a doo-dah concerning the title of his chapter, let me just remind you that as far as sex was concerned, most of us leaving school at the age of sixteen were far less well informed about the details of such intimacies as the average six year old is today.

Formal sex ed at grammar school was as near to non-existent as it's possible to be without disappearing altogether. Unless you can include the multiplication and division of cells within primitive life forms as part of a programme designed to help pubescent boys to learn about the facts of life, then it is possible you will see where we were coming from. Perhaps an unfortunate choice of phrase? Well, to be honest, the thought of a couple of amoeba shagging each other's brains out hardly peeped over the horizon of our collective consciousness, so we were left in a bewildered and confused state of sexual frustration populated with misinformation, innuendo and totally incorrect old wives' tales ('*you'll go blind if you keep doing that!* etc etc). Oh, and being at a single sex school helped not one jot. I suspect that had we been subject to the pleasure of female company during our formative school years, then even for boys as bereft of gorm as me might have realised that girls had other things to put up with, and I don't just mean records by Bobby Vee. Information about such things as the menstrual cycle were thin on the ground, and I'm certain I was not alone in only finding out about it when I had a girl friend of my own:

*'You mean **every** month? And you have to wear... And that's the reason you might be a bit tetchy before, during and after?... blimey!'*

Acquiring knowledge of the female form was usually limited to the adverts in women's magazines or the classified section of daily newspapers, and the one seen here

is pretty typical. As a stimulating example of the female form it certainly lacks the wow factor, but it does at least show a lady in some state of undress. Quite why she is opening a kind of trap door at the front of the garment is unclear, and the purpose of the small triangular object thus revealed remains the subject of idle speculation… a small Christmas tree or an umbrella perhaps? And the fact that within its folds this alluring article contained *elastic panels* and *spiral steels* did little to increase the casual observer's understanding of just what was needed in the underwear department.

As the sixties progressed, corsetry adverts became a lot more explicit – if not revealing - and showed that as far as female undergarments were concerned, you had to be careful not indulge in too close an embrace lest you end up with perforated lungs as the picture here shows. Such accoutrements could only be described as 'anti personnel devices' surely?

So, for most teenage boys, getting more closely associated with the female form meant keeping your eyes open for the shapely, and a good place for this was the seafront promenade in the summer. Here young geezers could be seen wandering along as close to the beach below as possible, simply in order to get just a glimpse or two of a well proportioned cleavage sunning itself on the sands below. Sometimes such attention to the task in hand led to young males walking right off the promenade when a turn in direction of the sea wall had escaped their notice or, more likely, collision with another hopeful group of yobbos coming the other way.

And then along came Mary Quant … or *'the blessed Mary'* as many a teenage lad had good reason to call her. The mini skirt and mini dress were a real eye-opener in more ways than one. Apart from being very revealing, they made something of a statement in that girls were now liberated, and whilst not exactly flaunting their sexuality, were perhaps at least acknowledging its existence. What's more, the female fashion trends emanating from the Kings Road and Carnaby Street further underlined the *ownership* of the youth culture; it seemed to be saying … *this is our thing, it only looks good on us and we're pleased that it will be seen as outrageous by many.* Combined with skinny rib jumpers and high heeled boots, girls certainly did look the part. The ensemble was not only revealing, it was also very smart, well designed, and artfully coordinated. In short, it was 1960's creativity at its best … and it also left many a spotty youth open mouthed in admiration… and a fair degree of lust as well, if truth be told.

'So, what about the fellas?' I hear you ask. Well, they weren't far behind. The London fashion elite realised pretty damn quick that there was also a big market to accommodate the desire to move away from the traditional jeans and leather jacket image, and as a result the new trendy 'mod' fashion for men was born. Like its female counterpart, this too was smart and well coordinated. Skin tight drainpipe jeans gave way to hipster trousers produced in ever more flamboyant patterns and colours. Complementing these were roll neck sweaters which as yet were unadorned with writing and advertising logos. Other notable additions might comprise a light tan coloured jumbo cord jacket in regency style, and a pair of smart leather Chelsea boots. These and other chisel-toed shoes rapidly replaced the uncomfortable winkle pickers of the late fifties, and the

Mod fashion – soooo non-greaser

[81]

previously coveted suede brothel creepers were no longer in sight.

Bear in mind also, that all of this came hand in hand with a deluge of advertising via the TV and magazines, new examples of which seemed to appear in their dozens. Secondary advertising in the form of the clothes worn by TV personalities and film stars also had a very marked effect: if it was good enough for Michael Caine in *The Ipcress File*, it was good enough for us. OK, for those of us who lived away from London, it took a bit of time to catch up. As a friend of mine from Devon says to this day: 'The sixties didn't even *arrive* in Plymouth until the seventies!'

Very true, but the evidence was there in the media, even if it took local shops an age to cotton on and cash in. As far as I was concerned, the sharp end of the market was to be found in the market stalls and associated 'fly-by-night' businesses that seemed to mushroom and then as quickly disappear. Never mind... the clothes purchased here may not have been of Carnaby Street quality, but at least they looked the part for a week or two, until your mum popped them in the spin drier and your skinny rib roll neck was skinny no more. Ah well, there was always next week's hard-earned to splash out on a smart shorty mac, or perhaps the down-payment on a Beatle Jacket. These curious garments had a sudden flurry of popularity when sported by the Fab Four at one of their publicity shoots. The garment's distinctive feature was its lack of a collar, and they were all the rage... for a short while. Those who did fork out the necessaries for a complete suit were alarmed to find out just how transitory fashion trends could be, for despite its association with the most iconic group of the sixties, the jacket faded out of sight with almost indecent haste.

And so it was that, as the pounds in our pockets slowly increased, we headed for the trendier tailors to get a 'decent set of threads' and for the first time this was to be made to measure. *John Colliers* was a national chain, and the TV ad constantly reminded us that it was '*the window to watch*'. Didn't cut much ice with me and my mate Steve though – we went to *Jackson the Tailor,* whereupon we ordered the same suit... in style, cloth and colour I mean - we didn't have to share it day and day about. And the cost? A princely £17 that's what. Seems ridiculous these days, but you may recall that as apprentices, we were all earning well under £300 a year. The average yearly wage for men was about £800, and women who were in full time work could expect significantly less than this. In the mid sixties, £1000 a year was an aspiration for most as it was a benchmark for those who were doing really well. To put such amounts into perspective, I remember being utterly scandalised at the cost of some of the pricier properties for sale on the leafy lower slopes of Portsdown Hill which commanded magnificent views across the city, the harbour and right away to the Isle of Wight beyond. But twelve thousand pounds?? *Twelve* thousand pounds?!! You've just got to be joking, surely?!

Never mind. We used our money as cannily as any other teenager in search of romance and success – i.e. without any real thought at all, and splashed out on anything that give the slightest appearance of making us as successful, popular and as downright trendy as Paul McCartney or Manfred Mann.

Truth is, there were so many things to buy, and so many enticements, nearly all of them delivered daily via the increasingly ever-present TV. Although basic by modern standards, the ads we were subject to at least left you in no doubt as to what you were buying. It seems that products nowadays frequently have names which bear little relation to what they might be used for - and titles such as *'Persuasion'* or *'Images'* might well leave the viewer baffled. Was the slinky lady wrapping her arms around the bloke with tattoos and a vest and deftly inserting her tongue in his ear thanking him for buying her a new dishwasher, a box of chocolates or an oven glove? I don't know. Not so in the sixties. Adverts were generally bluff, direct and left you in do doubt as to what you were being persuaded to buy:

Drink Red Barrel near or far, in pub or club or any bar
It's always good wherever you are'
Drink Watney's Draught Red Barrel!

And again:

'Only the crumbliest, flakiest chocolate'
Tasted like chocolate never tasted before...

Need I go on? I suspect you might well be able to add the closing words yourself, complete with tune and mental image of the young lady having her way with a Cadbury's Flake. Calm down now. Take a deep breath or two, and have a quick look over your shoulder to see if anyone's noticed you drooling. But at least you were in no doubt as to what you were buying.

One of the greatest- and affordable – temptations for teenagers was to take up smoking. The habit was endemic: just about *everyone* smoked, and advertising for tobacco products was perhaps the most common of all, and appeared just about everywhere: on bill boards, in newspapers, at the cinema, in magazines… you name it. And of course, it was at its most influential on the telly. TV jingles such as …

> **'You're never alone with a Strand'**

Or a jolly song (to the tune of *'Drunken Sailor'*):

> **'A man at sea will often hanker,**
> **For the flavour of an Anchor**
> **So much satisfaction!!'**

And again:

> **'Take a tip – take a Bristol:**
> **Today's cigarette is a Bristol,**
> **With a fine cool flavour you'll never forget-**
> **It's Bristol, today's cigarette!'**

… reminded us every hour of every TV day that smoking was sophisticated, it was cool, it was MANLY and it was sexy. *Got it?*

As a result, there were ashtrays everywhere – even on the backs of the seats in theatres and cinemas. We didn't think anything of it, and to be surrounded by a blue haze of smoke at the workplace, on the bus , on the train or the cinema was accepted as just part of life… indeed, it was more or less *expected.* Adults who did not smoke were in the minority. Fag ends were everywhere, and especially in the street; smoking outside was extremely common. Unless you had bronchitis, few of us gave much thought to the health consequences. Some manufacturers even tried to promote their cigarettes as a *healthy option*, believe it or not. The introduction of menthol into the tobacco mix provided smokers of such products with a curious minty, mouthwash-like taste, and we were told that menthol cigarettes were good for you. The best known brand

Consulate had the slogan –

'*Consulate cigarettes, cool as a mountain stream'*.

All homes – including those of non-smokers - were expected to have ash trays as part of their domestic provision, and the gift of an ash tray at Christmas or birthday was a common feature. Lighting up your fag in someone's home was just an everyday fact of life, and permission to do so was seldom sought.

So it's not really surprising that smoking was seen by many teenagers as a sure sign of adult sophistication. I am almost certain that my own mother didn't really like smoking, but she would have one or two when entertaining her friends, taking the odd puff on a *Du Maurier* king size - but never inhaling. It was so *de–rigueur* my dear - and with a name like *Du Maurier*, it must have something to do with fine writing and classy novels, surely? For those of us just starting with our first spluttering inhalations, purchases were inevitably directed towards the lower end of the market, and such interest was further accelerated by the arrival of the flip-top box. Strange to think that the packaging of a product could have such an effect, but it did. Prior to this innovation, fags were simply laid in rows in their packets, and if you wanted to offer one to a young lady, you fumbled open the top, pushed the silver paper to one side, tilted the packet towards her and shook. This would generally result in one of two outcomes – sometimes both. First, no cigarettes would appear at all, and despite frenzied shaking, not a single filter tip deigned to show its head above the packaging. Second, and rather more likely, all of the little sods would make a desperate dive for freedom and would shoot out of the packet and end up on the floor, or worse still, on a wet pavement. And as

Aptly named: all twenty were lined up ready for inspection in a cosy flip-top box.

scrabbling around trying to pick up your semi sodden *Players Weights* from the street left a lot to be desired in terms of the suave chat-up line, the dependability of the flip top was long overdue, and much appreciated. Now you could sidle up to the object of your desire and say *'Hi. Do you smoke? How about letting me press you to a Guard'* and with a deft flick of your thumbnail flip open the box to reveal a full packet of ciggies all lined up and apparently eager to be selected as the one to have its filter tip surrounded in a lipstick smear.

As you might expect, we raw recruits into the world of teenagerhood needed all the help we could get. Don't forget that we were also working hard and long hours were common, especially with the dreaded night school twice a week as well. As far as I was concerned, the weekends came as a blessed relief, and each Friday night I would pack away the old slide rule with no regret at all, and turn my attention to what delights the weekend might hold. And the conclusion? Well, by and large, life was pretty good. Some boys had bought scooters and were busy adorning them with a multiplicity of headlights, mirrors and just about anything else that was shiny. Many of us now had our own *Dansette* record player with automatic record change - and on a Friday night, our pockets might well be laden with a fair few bob as well. And I mean *laden*. The range of pre-decimal coinage in which we were paid our wages was large and heavy. Thus, you could well end up with a pocket full of change which might easily set up a momentum of its own when you were giving it all to Chubby Checker's *'Let's Twist Again'*. Bearing in mind many of us were wearing very low cut hipster trousers, it's really surprising that more didn't end up with these fashion must-haves in an crumpled heap around the ankles ...and its tricky trying to retrieve rolling coinage across a crowded dance floor with your trousers round your ankles, believe me - and certainly not a good image, when the age of fashion consciousness was well and truly with us.

Taking the broader view, the 1960's was probably the first time in history that there was a multiplicity of choice for the ordinary consumer - and the means by which to access it. Exciting? I should say so. With the *Liverpool Sound* and the *London Look*, UK teenagers were ruling the world, weren't we? The Yanks, all of a sudden, seemed a bit *fifties*, a bit old-fashioned. It might be something of an exaggeration, but as far as the young were concerned, confidence was soaring, and there was no upper limit – or so we thought. In a land which seemed to be spawning icons aplenty, one stood out head and shoulders above the rest in epitomising the new found spirit of the age: it was a little car – and everyone wanted one.

The 1960's Triumph Herald was an attractive and desirable car, especially as a convertible.

At the end of the fifties, there were some quite nice cars around, and the choice of colours and levels of trim were increasing rapidly. The Roots Group produced the sporty *Sunbeam Alpine* and the classy *Humber Sceptre*. The *Triumph Herald* made its debut in 1959, a well designed car that showed a strong Italian influence with its large windows and attractive layout.   Cars in general were now regularly providing those little extras which had been the preserve of the more expensive end of the market, like heaters and windscreen washers. But none of them had the pzazz – the absolute WOW factor of another car which made its first appearance in 1959, and became the darling of the sixties – **the Mini.**

For its size, the Mini certainly was spacious – but it is clear the ad men have got the 'little people' in again to ram home the point.

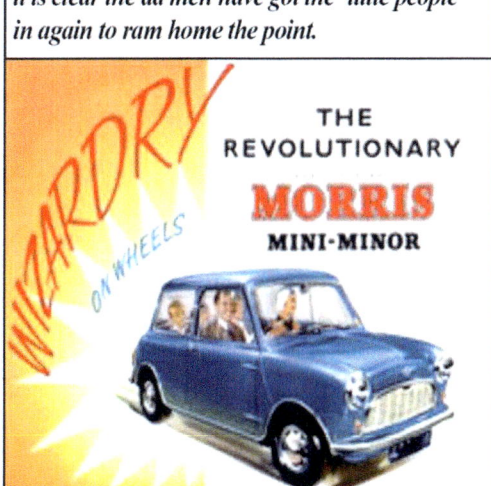

This deluxe model of the Austin Mini has an ever-so-slightly different radiator grill and chrome over riders on the bumpers. Cool eh?

It is not easy to overestimate the effect this little car had upon the decade: if you were asked to nominate just one icon of the age, surely this would be your choice. Its attraction lay in the fact that it was so utterly different, so absolutely *right* in every respect. The accepted view in the design world that *'if it looks right, it probably is right'* was absolutely the case with the Mini. More than that, its technology was like no other: fitting the engine transversely got rid of the need for a long bonnet, and providing the car with front wheel drive gave it an immediate road-grip feeling. Together with the fact that its wheels positioned in each corner were a lot smaller than was current practice and the centre of gravity was low, the car seemed to be on rails, and with little body roll, could be cornered at a speed hitherto considered immoderate, to say the least. It is interesting to note that the two most easily identifiable classics of the sixties should bear the same name – the *mini* skirt and the *mini* car. The name was not the only thing they had in common, for each attracted a huge dollop of lust, and I have to say that for many, the Mini car just eased its nose in front. Why? Because it was sexy, that's why. Clever marketing was one reason for this success, but the other was that, for the first time, your car could be *customised*.

The range of colours was, of course, just the starting point. The very fact that the manufacturer produced two versions of the car (the *Morris Mini Minor* and the *Austin Seven Mini*) meant that already there were aficionados of the two apparently competing makes. The fact that both were produced by the British Motor Corporation and differed only in the radiator grill and badging seemed to escape the notice of most. 'Brand solidarity' became a factor with all sorts of ridiculous comparisons:

'*Ahh*' you'd hear people say, '*The Austin Mini is built at Longbridge in Birmingham, the home of the mighty Austin Cambridge!*' To which the obvious retort was '*Yes, well of course the Morris Mini Minor is built at Cowley and comes from a long line of superb cars including the Morris Oxford and the* **original** *Morris Minor… and it was designed by the same bloke, so shut yer face!*'

In point of fact, the cars were exactly the same, both being powered by the same 850cc engine, and even had identical levels of sophistication in the two models each factory produced. The 'deluxe' version had additional instrumentation mounted in a central elliptical binnacle, and had more chrome work, particularly noticeable on the back and front bumpers.

But that was only part of the story. Apart from the revolutionary engineering incorporated into the little car with its space-saving innovations (sliding windows, deep door pockets, pull-string inner door handles to name but a few), what made the Mini so different was that it appealed to all sections of society. Though claimed by the young generation as the perfect example of how *distinct, together* and *different* we were, its appeal spread right across the age range like wild fire. It was the epitome of classlessness, and could equally be driven by a city gent as it could by a groovy hipster on his way to Carnaby Street. Men and women, boys and girls, each could adapt the little car to reflect his or her personality. A fine example of this was when the great comedian Peter Sellers added what can only be described as *wicker-work* to the body panels of his Mini – together with some very classy internal woodwork, and a whole mass of extra dials and gauges. It was very groovy – very desirable… very much the thrown gauntlet for everyone to start customising their own Mini in a bewildering array of alternatives, some of them quite bizarre.

That this obsession with personalising the original Mini went on right until it finally ceased production in 2000, (41 years and 5.3 million cars later) is quite extraordinary. ***But I digress!*** – for back in the 60's many thought it would be a good idea to make the little car a lot faster.

The final evolution of the original Mini, complete with electronic and power-assisted gizmos unknown in 1959.

And then along came John Cooper… who introduced engine modifications to the original quite modest power plant, and the up-rated Mini Cooper proved suddenly to be not only sexy but quite quick too. Next came Paddy Hopkirk who entered the little car in the 1964 Monte Carlo Rally, and won it outright – the first of three such victories. The car really *was* on rails, and he drove it at a blistering pace which left the rest more or less standing. The result of such performance-based interest resulted in the Mini Cooper S (for Sport) which, with an up-rated engine of 1275cc capacity was little short of downright dangerous in the wrong hands – especially as this was a while before the wearing of seat belts became compulsory.

The fact is, cars of the early sixties weren't even *fitted* with belts, and safety features such as collapsing steering columns were a thing of the future. As far as I was aware, no one had thought of rear screen wipers to enable you to see behind, and the technology of crumple zones was still way over the horizon. But nevertheless, by the mid sixties we had a car that was totally desirable and of universal appeal: it was classless, cheeky, colourful, adaptable, competitive, sporty, and as at home on the gravel drive of a stately manor house as it was street parked in front of a row of prefabs. I would also say that it was without doubt sexy.

See what I mean?

Thing is, most of us, boys and girls alike, aspired to own a Mini and like thousands of other aspirants to trendiness I decided that, much to the relief of the neighbours, my motor bike days were over. So, learning to drive was the next hurdle for many. In those days this nearly always meant having a go with your dad's car in the local streets, before polishing up with a few lessons from a driving school prior to the test. Perhaps this family based introduction to driving may account for the fact that so many dads of the preceding generation had that slightly haunted look and were just a little twitchy. I suppose continually screaming *'..no, the BRAKE, THE ONE IN THE MIDDLE YOU IDIOT!!'* had something of a lasting and indelible effect.

Regardless, most of us seemed to get through the test reasonably quickly, and after much scrimping and saving were able to fork out the necessaries for the deposit on a first car. The effect of this upon me was quite profound; for the first time ever, I had a little room all of my own. OK, it was mounted on four wheels, and had a big steering wheel, but it was mine… all mine. And what's more, I could keep stuff in it, and store my newly acquired string-backed driving gloves in the door pocket. To this day, I have no idea why **a)** you need gloves to drive a car and **b)** why on earth they should be made with a large proportion of string inherent in the design (the gloves that is, not the car). Now don't get me wrong, I like string; to be honest, I'm a big fan of the material, and see it as one of the foundations of the great British Empire, along with such things as custard and Oxo cubes. But a *string* glove? And for *driving*? I can only suppose that they were invented to enable your Auntie to buy you something for Christmas. Otherwise, they remain one life's great unanswered questions, and sit comfortably alongside such mysteries as how Neolithic people get those huge and heavy stones from Wales to Stonehenge, and the means by which the Egyptians managed to knock up so many pyramids without a JCB in sight.

'But enough of this philosophical fantasising' I hear you say. *'Where did you go in your new Mini? With which beautiful young lady did you share your new Smoke Grey plastic upholstery? What new horizons suddenly lit up your imagination and led inevitably to the great blossoming of wisdom and experience you so clearly needed?'*

Now come on! Far horizons? Exotic locations? Sorry. The first thing any new car owner had to do was to make sure he or she could get a little paraffin lamp to put out in the street each evening to stop the nasty policeman from fining us for having an unlit car on a public highway at night. If you've no idea what I'm talking about, let me advise you that at this time, **all** vehicles kept on a public highway had to be lit at night. No ordinary car battery then produced would stand the strain of the side lights being on all night for very long, and those who chose to do so would often be greeted with a noise similar to someone in the last stages of consumption when pressing the starter the following morning – a groan and then deadly silence. And when that sorry state of affairs did happen, the only recourse was to get the old crank handle out, thread it through the aperture in the front bumper, and then crank away like crazy. This was extremely hard work and indeed hazardous, in that engines which didn't wish to awaken from their slumber would quite often do a deliberate back-fire. Such a merry occurrence would result in the heavy steel starting handle suddenly rotating in the opposite direction, which always caught the cranker* unawares, and would often cause injuries which varied from hurt pride to a broken arm. And let me repeat, it was really hard and sweaty work and lasted until either the engine fired or you went to casualty to get your broken arm seen to… or you admitted defeat and crawled back indoors to call in sick.

So, we all had little night lights for our cars, OK? Now I don't want you getting over-excited and all of a lather, but I have something rather special to tell you, and it's this: being a trendy young chap, I was always on the lookout for something to show that I was a real sixties mover and groover, so obviously the old paraffin parking lamp, half painted with my mum's best nail varnish (to show red to the rear – we're not talking fettish here) was not really the image I wanted to project. So I invested in a state of the art *electric* parking light. Now, on the face of it, this might not have appeared to be a wise choice, for was not the new light powered by the car battery? And wouldn't it therefore cause this limited power source to discharge throughout the night? True enough, but it was only one small bulb, and therefore a lot less draining than all the side-lights on together, so for the more adventurous motorist, the risk was worth taking. Also, of course, it was provided with a handy bracket so that it could be hung from the top of the door:

* Please ...let's not descend to the vulgar

no more scrabbling around on the oil-soaked tarmac for me! I can almost sense your admiration at this bold move – and as if that was not enough, I have a treat for you, because *I still have that very parking light to this very day!* Yes, I know it's hard to believe, but well, some things are just worth keeping aren't they? And here it is:

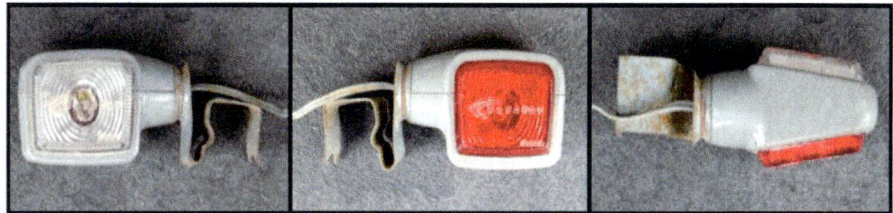

The view on the left is the one that an approaching constable would have seen from western end of our street, and the one next to it the rear view as he plodded past on his way to nick some other less well equipped and unlit parking criminal. The third view, included to ensure you get a complete picture if this trendy auto antique, is a view only obtained by either a very tall policeman, or a passing seagull. Shame that my original 1964 Mini is no longer there to complete the ensemble, but at least we've still got the window frame clip, so just let your imagination do the rest. I don't know; the things we did to be *with it*!

I suppose the risk of a flat battery was a bit worrying as the Mini had no starting handle; being built with a transverse engine, you'd have had to take the front wheel off to get the handle in, and that would surely have been a *losing the will to live* moment. Its saving grace, of course, was that the little car was quite light, and it was just about possible to bump-start it. For those of you too young to know what this entails let me enlighten you.

First, you need to push the car to get it rolling, then jump in and select second gear, then turn on the ignition, and finally let the clutch out. That's the theory. In practice you start by pleading with your mum to put down her toast, turn off *Housewives' Choice* and come outside and push your Mini up the road. That having failed, you put on your string-backed driving gloves, stand next to the open driver's door and push with all your might. When sod-all happens, you remember to release the handbrake before repeating this muscle wrenching procedure. Having got the car rolling, you then leap into the driver's seat, press in the clutch, select second gear, turn on the ignition and …. let the clutch out again. The trouble is, by now the car is barely moving, and thus you are lucky if the engine turns over at all. So the whole process has to be started again – especially as by now, your little car is stuck out in the middle of the road, and right in the way of other motorists who have had the foresight to have maintained a good level of charge in their batteries – or who have rather more cooperative mums willing to push.

So there you are; having an electric parking light was risky – but hey! We were Mini owners! Top of the tree, the grooviest geezers around! And boy, they seemed really nippy. The next step was to follow in Peter Sellers' footsteps and do our best to make our little cars different. The most obvious way was to put on straight-through exhaust, which gave the little 850 cc engine a pleasing roar even if it didn't enhance the performance much. And those blokes who had moved on to Mini ownership from covering their motor scooters with wing mirrors, now turned their talents to add as many dials to the dashboard as possible. And it really didn't matter much what the dials recorded, as long as there were plenty of them – rev counters, vacuum gauges, voltmeters, something to tell you what the time was in Bulgaria – as long as they looked good, and all lit up at the same time to resemble the inside of a fair sized airliner, it was just great.

And of course, as time went on, the Mini appeared in several different guises: in addition to the standard saloon, there was the ubiquitous Mini van, the Mini pick-up, the Mini Traveller, and the ever popular Mini Countryman. This last was a nod in the direction of the shooting-brake tradition of British car manufacturers, and followed in the footsteps of the highly popular Morris 1000 Traveller. The distinguishing feature of these useful estate-like vehicles was the wooden framing, which although entirely cosmetic, gave the air of solid country-living dependability… and all this on a vehicle whose wheelbase was only about ten feet. You half expected each of these vehicles to come from the showroom complete with a bale of hay and a couple of sheep in the back, with the sound-track of *'The Archers'* playing softly in the background. Also of note was the extension of the Mini range into the more sedate members of the BMC organisation. Whereas Morris and Austin were the main companies within that manufacturing conglomerate, there were also the Riley and Wolsely marques. These fine old companies had a considerable pedigree of not-quite-posh-but-not-far-off models to their names, and were, for example, used extensively by the police. Not to be outdone – and with a view to capturing the middle class market - both produced their own version of the Mini – the *Riley Elf* and the *Wolsely Hornet.* A glance will confirm that they were really little more than a Mini with a boot stuck on the back (where else?) and a bonnet modified to accommodate the traditional radiator grill and branding of each make. It made one smile: really both the *Elf* and the *Hornet* were produced to allow those who were being reluctantly drawn into the modern world the chance to participate, but very much at a 'toe in the water' level. Such things as walnut trim to the dashboard and thicker carpets were a given, and I dare say the rather posher glove boxes were indeed graced more frequently by tasteful kid and suede gloves than the string-backed variety. As noted before, the sportiest versions were the Mini Cooper and especially the Mini Cooper-S, but undoubtedly the sexiest by far and away was the *Mini Moke*. This crazy little jeep–like vehicle must

Members of the Mini family: on the left, the Countryman estate with its woodwork, and next to it the Riley Elf. If you can spot the difference to the Wolsely Hornet on the right, then a visit to your local ophthalmologist is entirely unnecessary. But the Mini Moke was, as they say 'something else'. A jeep? A beach buggy? A go anywhere anytime fun machine? Don't know, but for attracting young ladies it was 'sans pareil' as they say in France. Shame they only had the corrugated 2CV.

have been the product of inspirational 'let's *see where this takes us'* sort of thinking, and I believe it says a great deal about the confidence of an era which would allow such a bizarre vehicle to go in to production…. but if you wanted to pull the birds, the *Moke* had it in spades!

Well, I've banged on about Minis for quite long enough – but I seek only to under-line the major role this car made: it was really as much a 1960's life-style statement as it was a means of transport. It was the adopted darling and flag-bearer of the new pop culture. Odd, therefore, that most cars - the Mini included - *still* came without radios! Yes we now had heaters as pretty much standard equipment, and windscreen wipers for both sides (believe it or not, some cars of the fifties had only one wiper to clear the screen ahead; any front seat passenger therefore had to *ask* what was going on during a rain storm – not great, especially if the answer was just *'It's bloody raining!'*) and of course, every car was plentifully supplied with ash trays. So, a definite improvement on a decade before when those travelling by car might not be able to see outside, might be freezing cold and almost certainly couldn't listen to the radio, but at least everyone on board could carry on smoking themselves to death.

Many of us tried to get the new tranny to play in our Minis, but this was very hit and miss, usually because the reception was so poor, and wherever you stuck the radio and extended its little telescopic aerial, you could guarantee that it would fall with a crash to the floor at the next bend, or when you had to brake sharply in order to obey the traffic policeman who was wondering what you were fiddling with below the dashboard. So, listening to the radio in cars wasn't easy – and of course, despite it being the sixties, there was still so little pop music on the radio. That is, until along came salvation in the form of a fairly leaky boat moored off the coast of Suffolk. In 1964 we were rescued from pop starvation by the arrival of... the Pirates!

Of these, *Radio Caroline* was the first, and caused an immediate sensation. Whereas good old *Radio Luxembourg* had always been pretty hard to tune in to, *Caroline* seemed a lot easier – but more than that, it was in direct response to the needs of the young in the sixties. The BBC simply failed to tap into the market that was being created at an almost exponential rate: it really didn't get it. *Radio Caroline* did, and was probably the first employer of British DJ's who were to become household names – Tony Blackburn and Johnnie Walker for example, plus The Emperor Rosko, whose mid Atlantic drawl was especially appealing to an audience who still looked to the USA for much of its inspiration. Quite which empire the good Rosko ruled over was never made abundantly clear, but who cared? He and the others played the stuff that the people wanted to hear. That it was commercial radio added to its attraction – and the introduction of musical jingles such as:

'When you fancy a fruity treat – unzip a banana!!'

...was a first for British broadcasting and just added to the pzazz of the whole experience. For a population brought up with:

'This is the BBC Light Programme. We present 'Music to doze off by' the slickness and frequent humour of the new jingles were a complete revelation.

So pirate radio got off to a cracking startbin March 1964, and there followed a growing number of competing stations that were attracting new listeners in their tens of thousands. The odd thing is that the BBC's own audience numbers hardly moved at all… the significance of which eventually penetrated through the dusty recesses of the collective BBC brain to emerge with a long awaited - and screamingly obvious conclusion, which presumably went along the lines of:

'I say! There's an audience out there that we're not catering for. Does one think one ought to do something about it? Should one get one's finger out and tap into this new market? Shall one try and take on these pop pirate chappies? This needs further thought. Kindly pass me a Digestive biscuit'.

Fortunately the dear old Beeb did listen, and completely reorganised its radio output. Mind you, it took almost three and a half years, but in September 1967, Radios One, Two, Three and Four were born, and the old Light, Home and Third services were given a cup of cocoa and sent to a rest home somewhere near Bournemouth. Or something like that.

And Radio One was almost ALL pop. Yep … when Tony Blackburn put on the first disc – *'Flowers in the Rain'* by The Move, and used *jingles*, for heaven's sake, we knew that the future had arrived on the dependable old wireless at last.

Looking back, it's strange that BBC Radio took so long to take the plunge in to the pop era, because its counterpart - BBC TV - was far quicker off the mark. *Juke Box Jury* had been going since 1959, and in a sense flew the flag for BBC pop for a good few years on its own. OK, the programme was only *just about* all right: it always seemed to be a bit, well, *condescending,* in that it was still run by older people. Indeed, it seemed that the programme went out of its way to provide for as wide a clientele as it could get, and some of the guests could be described as rather more representative of the 'we know best' establishment, than of the groovy, hip, far–out kids that we all thought we were.

In retrospect, it was a clever ploy by the Beeb, as such presentation increased its viewing figures enormously and this broader appeal led to the programme being almost equally accessible to two generations of a family. As a result, it gave your Dad the right to say things like:

'Well, that's a definite 'Miss' if ever I heard one! **Doo Wah Diddy Diddy Dum Diddy bloody Dooo?** *What sort of language is that? What a load of rubbish... and they ought to get a good haircut... call themselves singers? Bring back Gracie Fields is all I can say!'* To which the usual teenage response would be a raised eyebrow and a withering look which said *'Yeah, but you're an old git, and this is our music, our generation so...............* I'll leave you to fill in the gap.

Nevertheless, JBJ continued to be a bit of a magnet throughout the early to mid sixties, and attracted viewing audiences of over ten million when groups such as the Beatles and the Rolling Stones were featured. But post 1963, it started to lose its teenage appeal and appeared fuddy-duddy compared with the new kids on the block: ITV's *'Ready, Steady Go'* in 1963 and the BBC's own *'Top of the Pops'* a year later.

RSG quickly built up a huge and dedicated following and introduced some innovative elements that left the old Juke Box gang in the dust. For a start, there was little in the way of glamorous studio scenery – in fact the sets were generally quite workmanlike, and TV cameras appearing in the mid-distance added to the feeling of immediacy, and a sense that the music was the all-important element, not the environment. All the chart-topping groups and individual singers were featured in the programmes, and the audience played a major role, dancing up close to the performers in such an energetic and creative way that most viewers were as much entranced by their gyrations as by the music. Indeed, it is said that programme producers had people scouring the London clubs in order to identify good dancers amongst the participants and to invite them to be in the audience at the next RSG programme.

Whether or not it was to counter the popularity of RSG, BBC TV launched its own pop flagship *Top of the Pops'* early in 1964. Its compilation contained similar elements to RSG, in that the DJ's mixed freely with the studio audience, and the dancing very much 'up close and personal' with the various acts. However, the whole presentation was more polished than its ITV counterpart: stage sets were artfully constructed to add glamour to the scene, and lighting and costume were also part and parcel of the overall production. The programme had an immediate appeal; compared to Juke Box Jury it had a much more intense pop feel to it, and was crammed with current music performed (and sometimes rather obviously mimed) by the groups of the day. As mentioned, the production was slick, and perhaps to some a little risqué: having youngsters, many of whom were mini-skirted young ladies actually dancing around the performer was a stroke of genius – especially as some of the cameras seemed to be set at a very low angle. As a result, some shots left many a teenage boy in a bit of a lather. Hell's teeth! Fab music, live groups in all the latest gear - and sexy girls doing their stuff… what more could anyone want?

The first show in January 1964 set the trend: groups featured included the Swinging Blue Jeans (*'The Hippy Hippy Shake'*), the Dave Clarke Five *('Glad All Over')* The Beatles *('I Want To Hold Your Hand')* and The Rolling Stones *('I Wanna Be Your Man')*. Interesting to note that the similarities in the titles of the last two set the tone for the Stone's more aggressive, demanding and uncompromising attitude, whereas the Beatles at that time were the good clean-living lovable lads from Liverpool. Not that we did much analysing you understand - we were all too busy pratting about on the dance floor at the *yoof* club or pretending to be our favourite singer in front of the bathroom mirror. So TOTP was an absolute must-see, and even though it would still be screened in glorious monochrome for nearly four more years, it didn't matter a jot; we were kids of the fifties, remember? Everything was grey in the fifties, and that included most of what we ate as well. Besides, tellies were still very small, and the 405 line presentation left a lot to be desired – but they were spread over just a fourteen inch screen, so it didn't matter much, and anyway, who cared? There was live pop on the TV, performed by the superstars of the day. And as far as the performers were concerned, it was all a matter of exposure: if you didn't get on TOTP ... then you didn't get on. As far as the adoring public was concerned, this was just about the *only* way you got to see what your heroes actually looked like!

That so much of the music created in the sixties still persists is testimony to the fact that much of it was really very good and as a result, many of the artists and groups that debuted there went on to become known, loved and followed worldwide over many years to come. The relatively modern phenomenon of tribute bands can only be attributed to such original popularity – plus of course, the fact that there are still loads of us feckless and now pretty ancient Baby Boomers still hanging around in the twenty-first century, generally getting in everyone's way and being a constant source of irritation to our children. But what we also do is turn up year after year at 1960's tribute band shows...and join in with every single word. Not that precise and exact knowledge of pop lyrics should come as much of a surprise: the purchase of records in the sixties became an almost mandatory requirement for many a young groover. Record shops were frequently besieged by avid teenage fans on the day of a disc's release, and the triumphant entry to the Youth Club clutching the latest disc from The Hollies or Manfred Mann was seen as a badge of some distinction

Bearing in mind that even the little 45rpm singles were relatively expensive – about 6s 8d (33p) in the mid sixties the massive sale of such records was something of a marketing miracle. Finding out how your favourite group was doing in comparison with all others each week became a matter of consuming importance, and as the decade proceeded, the term 'Hit Parade' was dropped in favour of 'The Charts'. The truly dedicated aficionado would fork out the cash to buy the *New Musical Express* or other contemporary music papers, but for most of us, it was just a matter of keeping up with the latest on TOTP, and trying hard to look exactly like Roger Daltry of *The Who* if you were a bloke, or Sandie Shaw if you were a dolly-bird. Come to think of it, there may have been a number of guys who wanted to look like Sandie Shaw as well, but at that stage, attitudes to sexual orientation were not up for debate. For the present at any rate, *'coming out'* simply meant emerging from your front door, usually with the newest 45 grasped in your hot little hand.

Now I suspect the thrill of seeing my all-electric parking light may have eased off a bit by now, so it's time to introduce yet more personal items. The 45's shown below are my wife's, and have been retrieved from our attic, where they have been stored in a grotty plastic bag for decades....but they are all genuine originals, and were purchased by her in the 1960's when she was a young and groovy teenager. Now, for those of you whose eyesight is not what it used to be, the discs thus

[101]

displayed comprise a pretty eclectic mix. The earliest trio are Jimmy Jones' *'Handy Man'* of 1960, 'Little *Town Flirt'* by Del Shannon and Kenny Lynch's *'Up On The Roof'* of 1962. Her 1963 purchases include *'It's My Party'* by Lesley Gore, (who is still quite possibly searching for her Johnnie) *'Don't Talk to Him'* by Cliff, *'Diamonds'* by Jet Harris and Tony Meehan, and the Beatles *'I saw Her Standing There'*.

It was 1964 that saw an upsurge in the group culture, and new names such as the Applejacks – *'Tell Me When'*, *'You're No Good'* by the Swinging Blue Jeans and *'Needles and Pins'* by the Searchers featured in her choice. Clearly, the Beatles were a favourite band, as the collection includes *'I Want to Hold Your Hand'*, *'I Feel Fine'*, *'Help'*, and *'Please Please Me'*.

Thereafter, devotion to the Fab Four moved on to LP's, which reflected not only intensity of interest in the group, but the ability to earn the money with which to buy such relatively expensive items. Others in the 45 collection reflect the growing breadth of the pop genre, and include several records by The Byrds: *'All I Really Want To Do'*; *'Tambourine Man'* and The Hollies: *'Look Through Any Window'*; *'I'm Alive'* and Manfred Mann: *'The One In The Middle'*. A few that caught my eye - and reflected how pop music was evolving and spreading its appeal - were *'True Love Ways'* by Peter and Gordon, Bob Dylan's *'Like A Rolling Stone'* and the innovative *'Good Vibrations'* by The Beach Boys. Also, there is a record which almost single-handedly epitomises the shift from the fairly simple boy-meets-girl scenario of the early to middle sixties, to something more reflective, more introspective... and in the case of this particular record, more puzzling. I refer of course, to *'A Whiter Shade of Pale'* by Procol Harum. Of this more in a minute, but the final members of the mini collection are also worthy of a mention: *'Kites'* by Simon Dupree and The Big Sound*, and *'Catch the Wind'* by Donovan. Released in 1967, both discs reflect

* *I was pleased to find this record among my wife's collection, as it is my one and only personal – and extremely tenuous- connection with the pop world. You see, Simon Dupree was the stage name for one of my mates at the old Southern Grammar School in Pompey. Derek Shulman and I were in the same year, and another friend, Eric Hine who plays keyboards on the record, was in the same class as 'Simon'. Blimey. Two SGS blokes who 'done good' as they say. I am tempted to make some reference to the Donovan song being in some way connected with another SGS friend, the flatulent Mick, but I think such a comment might be a bit OTT.*

a move towards the mystic and philosophical side of life, an opportunity for all of us Baby Boomers to pause for a moment in our headlong ambition to get a shiny set of fog lamps attached to the front bumper of the Mini, and to start dwelling on such themes as ***the meaning of life, man!***

1967 also saw a number of new BBC appointments to their DJ line up. Terry Wogan and Ed Stewart would in time become household names – and so would another newcomer, the amazing and totally irreverent Kenny Everett whose zany and creative broadcasting style was unlike any of his contemporaries. His continuity clips and the addition of imaginary contributors to his programme were exceptional, and a brand new experience for the listening public. Bearing in mind this was years before electronic mixing and multi-tracking techniques, the comedy effects he achieved were outstanding, and are an object lesson in great broadcasting to this day. So 1967 was something of a key year in *yoof* culture, and the introduction of Radio One and its pop-savvy DJ's played only a part – for the summer of that year was also....

The Summer Of Love.

It had been clear to those who knew about such things, that the pop scene was growing both in terms of output, breadth and focus. The earlier years had seen the great pop music breakout, where the absolute staple was the generally cheery optimism epitomised by Gerry and the Pacemaker's *'I Like It'*, and Herman's Hermit's melodic *'Woke Up This Morning Feeling Fine'*. Lyrics and focus were characterised as being broadly traditional, and consisted of the usual love trysts – or in the case of Roy Orbison, yet something else likely to make him burst into tears. However, the next big step was to move on from this, and such releases as Procol Harum's *'Whiter Shade of Pale'* set the mood.

Despite the fact that nobody really understood what the hell the lyrics meant, it didn't seem to matter that much and I genuinely believe that it was at this time that the term 'cool' came into popular parlance.

Suddenly things were *'far out man'*, they were *'cool'*, they were *'out of sight'*... and all of this was totally underwritten by what was going on in San Francisco.

In the spring of 1967, Scott Mackenzie had a seismic hit with the release of *'San Francisco (Be Sure To Wear Flowers in Your Hair)'* and suddenly everyone was talking about Haight Ashbury. For those of us whose gorm storage unit still had a fair degree of under-occupancy, the received comment *'Hey man, what about Haight Ashbury huh?'* was something of a challenge. As like as not, such an enquiry was embarrassingly misinterpreted to produce a slightly nervous response along the lines of:

'Well, certainly yes… Haight Ashbury? I never liked him - and Ashbury's a silly name anyhow'.

Once such gaffs had been overcome however, it was clear that the pop world had reached out to embrace the far-out, esoteric, psychedelic era… and as a result, the be-bop years were behind us. Bring on the fringes and bells man!

Haight Ashbury was, of course, the epicentre of this mini revolution, and for those who did indeed travel to what seemed an impossibly exotic location in the hills above San Francisco bay, it must have been a memorable experience – or *'mind-blowing, man'*. Certainly the release of such albums as the Beatles *'Sergeant Pepper's Lonely Hearts Club Band'* had a profound effect upon the huge popularity of *psychedelia* as it was called. The very fact that the BBC banned the playing of tracks such as *'A Day In The Life'* and *'Lucy In The Sky'* because of their apparent reference to drug-taking, made listening to them all the more attractive. And as if 1967 hadn't already done enough to put itself at the pinnacle of pop innovation, late November saw the Moody Blues release their ground-breaking album *'Days of Future Passed'*. For us hippy wannabes, the album's unique blend of pop and orchestral music finished off this fantastic year with a sublime flourish.

For teenagers still limited to the ordinary everyday round of work, Tech College, evening classes and slogging away with the old slide rule, it did seem all a bit distant, a bit out of reach. But fashions were changing, and the colourful mock eighteenth century dress uniforms worn by the Beatles were an inspiration, and had many a spotty hopeful wondering if sewing on a couple of gaudy epaulettes might in some way re-invigorate the discarded Beatle Jacket. Perhaps not.

Nevertheless, wearing fringed suede clothing, or for the less well off, ex-military topcoats became de-rigueur for the year.

But there was another aspect of Haight Ashbury which grabbed teenage attention: the fact that it was also advertised as a ***love in.*** This immediately summoned up images of a way of life which had the liberal application of *free love* at its centre. Wow! If scantily clad folk wearing not much more than a few daisies strung together over their erogenous zones was what we had to look forward to, then bring it on!

Mind you, practicality was always there just hovering in the background like an uninvited spoil-sport, and me and my fellow apprentices couldn't really imagine ourselves and the ladyfriend of our choice stumbling about on Southsea's heavily shingled beach wearing nothing more than a bunch of wilting gladioli, a nervous smile and a load of goose bumps - but there you are. San Francisco was a long way away. Still, we had Radio One, didn't we?

Despite the intrusions in to our free time demanded by the massive speculation such groovy events demanded, there were other matters to attend to as well. By 1967 most of us were nearing the completion of vocational training, and had BIG decisions to make about out futures. Being a keen advocate of sticking my head in the sand, I followed my natural instincts, and decided to go on holiday. Now all this talk of exotic locations may lead you to suspect that popular destinations for the average eighteen year old might include places such as the south of France, the Greek Islands – or at least Benedorm surely? Not a bit of it. Foreign travel was still very much the province of either the very well off, or the intrepid adventurer prepared to go it alone.

Most of us fell into neither category, and thus the vast majority of holidays were taken in the UK and usually not that far away. For someone living on the Hampshire coast, a visit to places such as Devon or Cornwall was the cause of a lot of excitement, and even something of a challenge. Although the railways were still – just about – offering a wide range of destinations, travel by train was slow and restricting. Therefore, the chance of going in or on your own wheels was intoxicating. Trouble was, the roads were crap. Bearing in mind that the first full length motorway in the country – the M1 – had not been opened until 1959 and that progress to provide more was inevitably quite slow, virtually all the routes we could take were on the old twisty, narrow two lane roads that criss-crossed the country in what appeared to be a fairly random pattern. Nevertheless, that's what we had, so they were used, and used heavily. The fact that many people now had paid leave *and* their own car, meant that holiday routes were frequently congested and often brought to a complete stop - a bit like the M25 really, but longer and thinner, and full of a mixture of shiny sixties cars surrounded by loads of old pre-war rust buckets.

Never mind; the thought of the sandy beaches of the West Country

Just like the M25, but thinner, and no service stations. The cars are typical of the time: although it was the mid sixties, most cars dated from the previous ten to twenty years. It looks like a motorcycle policeman is having a word with the lead car- perhaps telling the driver that the nearest public toilet is about twenty miles away.

kept us going. For those whose annual holiday consisted of little more than a pilgrimage to 'see the relations', it might have been that traffic congestion and delays represented a *welcome reduction* in the time spent with gran in Wakefield; in fact staring for hours on end at the back of the Morris 1000 Traveller in front was in some ways infinitely preferable to facing Auntie Margaret's suet pudding.

Anyway, on this occasion I had escaped family obligations, and with a couple of mates and a girlfriend squeezed into Geoff's tiny Vauxhall

Viva and headed off to Wales. And it's a hell of a long way to Wales, especially in those distant pre-motorway days. The only recollection I have of the journey was that, even with the delays and crowded roads it seemed even-tempered and fun; just getting out of the town was nice, and then to come across places with names you had not the remotest idea how to pronounce was a new and exciting experience. Besides, being away in west Wales seemed *so remote,* so totally different.

Being away from family was a novel experience too, although like the dutiful little souls we were, the first thing we did was to buy a fistful of picture postcards and send them home. With no access to the instant communication we have today, wherever you went, postcards home were an absolute must. Whether you were groovy young teenagers like me and my chums, or some old git who considered that wearing a knotted handkerchief for sun protection in addition to the grey socks and open-toed sandals completed a natty ensemble, it mattered not: you had to let the folks back home know you had at least arrived safely.

Mind you, care had to be exercised in ensuring you bought the right type of card for the intended recipient, as mixed together with such scenic shots as '*View of the Esplanade from the West Pier*' there were quite a few saucy seaside postcards, full of innuendo and accentuated body parts. That such open lewdness had become part of the established seaside tradition was something of a surprise, since sexual repression was still very much extant amongst the older generation. Perhaps such open suggestiveness reflected the momentary annual flicker of sexual liberation anticipated by parents (by which I mean Dads) who might endure the annual battle of getting everyone off on holiday all the more readily if they were consumed by the thought that perhaps…. just for once… with a nice view out of the window and plied with a stick of rock and a 'Kiss Me Quick' hat…well... you never know. I'm sure you get the picture.

Putting bawdiness aside for a moment, the actual *picture* post card was very popular because of course, most of us didn't have a camera at all, let alone one good enough to take in magnificent sweeping panoramas. The old Box Brownie didn't really cut it, and bearing in mind the fact that any phone contact with the folks at home was difficult, the postcard was about as good and quick as it gets. I suspect that snail-mail being the best option available might come as something of a revelation to the current generation who, it would seem, cannot walk thirty yards down the road without phoning/texting/e-mailing at least a dozen anxious friends with the vital message – *'Hey, it's me. You'll never guess what? I've just walked nearly all the way to Sainsbury's! I'll send you a picture of the offer on frozen langoustine on Facebook when I get there. Love you Babe!!!'*

So, being away was an adventure, and to holiday in places like the west coast of Wales was, for the likes of me and my friends, a real departure in more ways than one. But things were about to change.

In the middle of the sixties along came Freddie Laker, and he introduced overseas jet travel to the masses. Until then air travel was the preserve of the international businessman, or the well-to-do. Most air routes were covered by two British companies - the *British Overseas Airways Corporation* (BOAC) for long haul flights, and *British European Airways* (BEA) for short haul. Certainly, there were other UK airlines, but apart from *British United*, they tended to be somewhat peripheral as far as the public was concerned, and did not cater for the dormant mass markets which were waiting just around the corner.

But in 1966 Freddie Laker changed all that by introducing the country to cheap economy flights in jet aircraft which zoomed off to unbelievably exotic locations, principal amongst which were the long sandy beaches of the Costas in southern Spain. And these holidays were *cheap*: you could spend a whole week turning yourself so pink with unaccustomed sunshine that even a passing lobster might be moved to envy – and still have change from a sum well short of £100… and that includes all the sangria you can neck, all the lager you can swill, and all the paella you can wolf down. And you *still* had enough left over to purchase a stuffed straw donkey to bring home.

So, post sixty six, holidays that promoted sun, sand and sea (and of course, sex) had a meteoric rise in popularity. The only downside was that there were many stories of people arriving at their hotel only to find that it was still in a state of 'partial readiness' – i.e. only half built. Never mind. Leaping on board a Boeing 707 was now where it was at;

suddenly the traditional British seaside holiday looked fuddy-duddy with its endless traffic jams, draughty hotels and fearsome B&B landladies. In 1970, the incredible Jumbo Jet made its debut in the USA and its enormous carrying capacity secured the air holiday business for ever.

Not that everyone suddenly jetted off courtesy of the jovial Mr. Laker, but the writing was on the wall, and suddenly the general population became much more international. By that I mean that folk became aware of the fact that the continent *did actually exist*, and there were good times to be had over there. Up to that point, the other side of the channel was somewhere where you went to fight wars and generally put Johnnie Foreigner in his place. Not any more. Clearly, there was now a need to be dashing off to the sun, and if at the same time you could teach the Spanish to speak English by just shouting at them, then that was so much the better, wasn't it? And as for those swarthy, dark haired and be-muscled foreign torsos – my my! … and that was just the women! The mind boggled, as did various other parts, as I recall.

But it wasn't like that in north Wales. Mind you, we had a lovely time, and like most British holiday makers, made extravagant promises to new friends that we would keep in touch for the next century at least… only to forget almost instantly as the old home town crept into view as the faithful Vauxhall Viva struggled over the summit of Portsdown Hill. Home again. And a decision to make. A BIG decision.

You see, by this time I, like most others of the 1963 intake, had finished my apprenticeship, and was facing the future as a fully fledged GPO Engineer Technician 2A. Moreover, like most of my fellow trainees, I had achieved the giddy heights of 'Technical Officer in Training', and was destined to spend the foreseeable future in the business of Exchange Construction. Excited? Agog at the opportunities? Thrilled out of my tiny mind?

Well, no, not really. It was time at last to be honest with myself, and to acknowledge the little needling thoughts that would jingle in my mind every time I drove past the old SGS in the little green van with the ladder on top… *'Oughtn't you to be in there doing your A levels? Oughtn't you to be thinking about going to college full time? Oughtn't you to be paying attention to driving this van and stop wandering about all over the Eastern Road?'*

And quite simply, the answer to all of these was 'yes'. Problem was, as a technical sort of bloke, what could I do? I was beginning to feel that a lifetime of rearranging thousands upon thousands of little coloured wires into elaborate patterns was not really the right thing for me. Although I'm sure the myriad little conductors were very grateful to be so colourfully displayed before being set a-tingle with 50v of the finest DC current the GPO could provide, I felt I needed more!

Oddly, my quandary over whether or not it was time for a change of course work-wise had come to a head at Tech College, where even as part-timers, the powers that be had agreed that we were becoming *too* technical in our education. As a result, an obligatory session of *General Studies* was shoe-horned into the already packed timetable. On these occasions we were supposed to discuss matters of national importance like politics, the state of the world, current affairs, why there were so few girls on day-release in our class ... and other subjects of broad general interest. The problem for me was that I enjoyed this college session more than the techie ones. What's more, muttered conversations in the dinner queue led to a realisation that perhaps more trainees than I had suspected were having second thoughts about chosen careers.

So I decided I would be a teacher. Blimey. And the logic behind this decision? Well, I'd been surrounded by kids all my life, and had generally experienced no problem in getting along with most of them – indeed, I'd also been one myself. Also, at the suggestion of someone at the Tech, I got a book out of the library called *'An Experiment in Education'* by a lady called Sybil Marshal which proved to be a most powerful and engaging read, and that really did it for me. Added to this micro-acclimatisation of the practical pedagogy, came the assurance from another old SGS buddy who had just finished his first year at Teacher Training College, that it was an absolute blast! He was having SUCH a good time, and the place was heaving with young people, many of them of the female variety, and the lecturers were pretty cool (that word again) so what's to lose?

Well, only my whole career to date, that's all. So I agonised a lot, wrung my hands a lot, listened to records a lot, and wondered if the oil in my Mini needed changing a lot - and finally took the unprecedented step of resigning from the old GPO. Strewth! Perhaps at last, the level indicator on my internal tank labelled '*feck*' had crept up a shade from the EMPTY mark.

I have to say that the GPO was very good about it. Perhaps they were glad to see the back of me, but I don't think so. At my subsequent interview with the Executive Engineer – a really big cheese locally – he was gracious enough to tell me that he thought I had made a good choice. One of his children was a teacher. '*Oh, and by the way, Burden, if it all falls apart and you come back to me begging for your old job, you won't get it. You'll come in at least two grades down, OK?*'

Fair enough, I suppose. Four years of utter slog had been enough for me, but looking back, I didn't regret it… and I still don't. I had spent time in all branches of the Engineers, and met a very wide range of blokes representing a huge variety of skills. Some of them were very technical, and I could see a lot of evidence of the Tom Flowers side of the operation. Others were just the opposite, and superintending the work of the travelling contractors whose job it was to install new exchange equipment was a novel experience. These blokes were often pretty damn clever, but lived a curiously itinerant life, moving from one set of lodgings to another as the demands of an expanding electronics industry dictated. I well remember one such guy opening a tin of beans and then heating it up on the little gas ring in the exchange kitchen, with the tin lid still clinging on like a particularly lethal frisbee: no plate, no saucepan, no bowl – he simply explained that this was lunch, and would probably be better than what he'd get tonight at the his digs.

Other duties had taken me deep underground in order to repair or replace vast cables carrying literally thousands of wires – a pretty frightening experience if you're not happy with large moleskin-wiped solder joints heated to a terrifying degree with a pretty dangerous blow torch. It had also taken me up to the top of telegraph poles, where complete with safety belt, we were expected to do work on bare copper wires, porcelain insulators and bakelite distribution boxes – and not a reel of sellotape in sight! Of course, what all linesmen did to a new apprentice was to position themselves opposite the greenhorn at the top of the pole, and hold his nervous assistant's safety belt *just a little bit away* from the pole ... only to let it go moments later. Such action for the apprentice was about a hundred times more effective than a strong course of *Exlax*, and produced mighty guffaws from the merry japester who had caused you to lose at least three years off your life. It was the GPO's own version of the sky hooks and elbow grease initiation ceremony, I suppose. Still, *'never mind eh?'* as Charlie Drake would say.

So I applied to a College of Education in Bristol, and on the strength of the Maths I had done at Tech, and the amount of History and Current Affairs I was able to blag my way through, I was offered a place. And this was the Autumn or 1967... the Summer of Love! So, chucking everything that would move into the Mini, and donning my latest and grooviest hipsters, I set off to become a full time student.

Whilst acknowledging that learning about teaching might well be a central part of the three year course, I was of course keen to put first things first and make sure that I was a fully equipped with BIG hair, flared blue corduroy trousers, rope soled jumbo cord shoes, a string or two of beads and a fresh pair of Y Fronts. I decided to wait till I got to Bristol before buying some flowers for my hair as I didn't want to sweep into the college car park adorned with travel-worn and droopy freesias did I? After all, I was now a hip twenty something about to set the educational world alight wasn't I? And I had my Mini, complete with impressive wiper switch toggle extension and wing mirror, and that would surely be a big draw for the many young ladies who would need a lift into the city centre, surely?

Well, that was the plan. As it turned out, almost the first student vehicle I saw upon arrival was a *Mini* bloody *Moke* which was fully occupied by its trendy young owner-driver, and about seven or eight lovely females who were draped all around and over it...and him. Never were so many strings of beads, tiny silver bells, lengthy and luxuriant suede fringes, knee length boots and miniskirts so poorly deserved! Anyway, I was here to learn about education, so there.

Truth to tell, there were quite a number of students like me who had prior experience of the world of work before coming to college – some of them old enough to be married with families of their own. Perhaps it was that the education service was on a recruiting drive to provide for the upsurge in the birth rate – I don't know. All I was aware of was that college was a great place to be on the autumn of 1967, and I genuinely considered myself to be very fortunate. Although not particularly well prepared academically – there's not a lot of call for the technicalities of *Electrical Engineering B* in most primary and middle schools - they were prepared to let me have a go. Added to that, I had been given a full three year grant by the Local Education Authority! For the current generation of students, this latter must come as instant verification that the Baby Boomer generation had it easy. Well, yes, I suppose we did in some respects, and starting out a professional career without a large debt hanging around your neck was a massive boost. But that was the sixties for you: hard going in some respects, but still with the welfare state firing on enough cylinders to support the likes of me – and countless thousands of others – in the quest to achieve our ambitions.

One thing I will add, though, is that nationally, the aspirations of many young people were not high enough; too many school leavers were channeled into work that others thought would be good for them… and that was not necessarily what they could have excelled at had they been given half a chance.

But in the autumn of 1967, I and my new found college chums were having a great time – how could you not? Diana Ross and the Supremes were belting out *'Reflections'* on the student union disco machine, hugely flared trousers were flapping around legs which varied from spindly to muscular, the college bar was selling cheap beer and the Summer of Love looked set to hang around right into the autumn, winter, spring and beyond. Talk about sex, drugs and rock and roll! ....which reminds me: drugs - the other third. I haven't mentioned them much yet have I? Well here's the reason.

Let me remind you of my comments in the Introduction to this worthy tome concerning the current popular convention that:

'If you can remember the sixties, then you weren't there'
As explained earlier, the implication is that **'hey man… you were too**

spaced out... you were out of sight baby, you were away on the dream machine... you were cutting some grass with no lawn mower in sight...' to which I say an emphatic: '**Nope !**'

Admittedly, there was certainly a lot of TALK about drugs, and the number of trendy young blokes recounting their (largely imaginary) experiences of the particularly vibrant and *'beautiful colours, man'* parties they had attended over the past week was more than a few. Invariably, such discourse would have been along the lines of:

'Well, you should have seen Joe – he fell over the coffee table, grabbed hold of Celia's beads and they both ended up sprawled out in an absolute heap behind the sofa... completely spaced out of course! We were all tripping out man!'

No you weren't! The only *tripping* you did was the stumbling pinball like process you weaved through the furniture and various recumbent party-goers to answer a pressing need to get to the loo, you posing git!

In reality, for the vast majority of youngsters there were very few drugs around at that time. The little that did make its way to student parties was mainly *'hash'* or *'weed'* - cannabis which rightly or wrongly was considered to be at the less serious end of the scale. Although registered by only a few at the time, perhaps trendy students would have done well to have reflected upon the fact that the only other time when the word *'weed'* had attained a media profile was when it had been used repeatedly back in the fifties on children's TV. Remember BBC's **'Bill and Ben the Flowerpot Men'**?

Their jerky marionette perambulations in their monochrome TV garden were frequently interrupted by the sudden arrival of a wobbly little plant with a cherubic flower face. This character always elevated itself from a horizontal position - (which in retrospect might be described as *'spaced out, man!'*) to a more erect stance, at which point its only contribution to the dialogue, always delivered in the same squeaky voice was:

'Little Weeeeed!'

That the second word of this greeting was extended, seemed at the time no more than a personal signature, an amusing dialectic aberration introduced by the goodly plant for comic effect. Now, like all kids in the fifties I had taken such brief and frankly uninspiring dialogue as no more than the character introducing herself to her flowerpot chums. It did not occur to us innocents that her only contribution to the sparkling conversation might have been punctuated with question mark after it, and that she was therefore actually **offering her garden mates an opportunity to engage in some illegal practices.** Certainly, their inordinately lively reaction to her – hopping up and down and yelling: *'Flub-a-lub-a-lub–a-lub!!'* might have been an indication that they were pretty high already, and were therefore extremely chuffed at the thought of scoring some more of *the right stuff, baby!!*

Or not… so let's skip forward again to the decade in question, where the sort of hallucinogens we heard that various figures in the pop world were experimenting with were virtually non-existent as far as the students at my college were concerned. The same can, I think, be said of the wider student population of the city, with whom we had frequent contact – but that didn't mean to say that they wouldn't have been tried had they been available. As far as most of us could see, the drug experience of most of our contemporaries was *talked up* a lot… but actually *experienced* only a little. Its position in the folk-lore of the mid to late sixties was therefore much overrated. Talking about it? Yes. Actively participating in it? For a small minority, yes I suppose so, but for the vast majority - no, not at all.

Besides, there was so much else to do, man! As well as our student studies – and there was a lot of that, believe me - the world was moving on apace, and some of it was definitely not for the better. The Yanks were getting really tied up in what was becoming an increasingly disastrous and horrible war in Vietnam, and the Civil Rights movement was rightly incensed at the callous and brutal assassination of Martin Luther King. Gruesome stuff of course, and brought nearer to home when his killer James Earl Ray was arrested in London. No doubt we were relieved to have our minds taken off such horrors by the arrival of *'Joseph and his Amazing Technicolor Dreamcoat'.*

Apart from all this serious stuff, student life was jam-packed with activities, clubs, societies, sports - and keeping a wary eye out for marauding Welsh students who seemed to enjoy nothing more than coming across the Severn bridge to test that all our college fire extinguishers were in full working order. And, of course there were endless parties, and the need to make your flat as groovy as possible. This was the age of the poster, and although some were stuck on walls to cover cracks, blemishes, holes and various stains of doubtful origin, they were generally a very welcome addition... and the one that stands out quite literally head and shoulders above them all? Well, Che Guevara, of course.

To be honest, one of these trendy black and white jobs was just about mandatory in any student flat: as a heart-melter for girls it had no equal, and it gave opportunity for even the weediest of males to boost their ego just a smidgen by identifying themselves as *'just a bit of a revolutionary myself!'* All too frequently, and depending upon how much cheap *Don Cortez* wine had been consumed, such a statement might be followed with a load of pseudo-revolutionary bunkum, more often than not adding in an impressive desire to '*travel to Cuba, man, so that I can help the revolutionaries there throw off the yoke of capitalist oppression*'. What might have been more truthfully added was: '*...that is, just as soon as I've finished this essay on the Ladybird Keywords Reading Scheme, and done an in-depth analysis of 'One thousand things to do with an abacus*'.

But I mustn't be too harsh. The sixties as a whole was something as near as dammit to a second renaissance: that it should have been surrounded by so many iconic images and impressions is therefore hardly surprising. Che, of course was high on the list, as was the wonderful Mini. But so too was the fabulous E-Type Jag. And I'm going to include it here simply because I can't bear not to. OK?

As an example of the **wow factor** in design and engineering, it is still breathtaking today. You can imagine therefore the effect it had in the sixties when it was unleashed on a population still getting to grips with the

Just drool!

Vauxhall Victor – a car so prone to corrosion that even if you just sneezed in its vicinity all that would be left was a large brown pile of rust, four tyres and the odd windscreen wiper. The E-type was simply gob-smackingly beautiful, and with a top speed of 150 mph it was also pretty damn quick – so just like its cheeky companion the Mini, it was very close to the top of 1960's Hall of Fame.

Now I know we've dealt a lot of icons in this chapter but hey! – this was the sixties man! This was an age when *everything* changed, so you'll forgive me if I mention just one more?

Evidently, one member of the audience in a 1965 *Ready Steady Go* production was a young lady by the name of Lesley Hornby. Like many others, she had been noted by one of the TV show's operatives whose job it was to scour clubs and dance halls for trendy young folk who

[117]

would then be invited to participate as one of the groovy ensemble circulating around the various singers and groups strutting their stuff in the studio. Lesley's striking good looks and dress sense made her a natural choice ... and as a result, her career as perhaps the world's first ever super-model took off. If you are unfamiliar with the name *Lesley Hornby*, then try that by which she became a great sixties celebrity:

Twiggy.

That this young lady took the fashion world by storm was something of an understatement. She was only sixteen when she was named by the Daily Express as *'The face of 1966'* and voted *'British Woman of the Year'*. Strewth! If ever there was confirmation that the Baby Boomer generation had arrived big time and had established itself at the centre of society, then surely this was it.

Twiggy in the mid sixties (The date I mean)

I recently came across one episode of a TV programme on BBC 4 entitled *'The People's' History of Pop'* and was particularly pleased to note that it was narrated by none other than Twiggy herself. It was a lovely programme, and without ever going over the top, gave a thoughtful, engaging and joyous tour of that wonderful time – a time when the pop culture suddenly came of age. Most of all, I was struck by something Twiggy said right at the end of the programme:

'I was just a typical teenager, lucky enough to be born into a generation who were experiencing something that their parents never had: pop.... the music, the clothes and the clubs – all of it giving us a new way of expressing ourselves, and a new way of saying who we were'.

I couldn't have put it better myself.

5 Vertical Hold

Rather like the radiograms and wireless sets of the 1950's, the first TVs were as much pieces of furniture as they were items of new technology. Their relative rarity and considerable expense made them features to be proudly displayed, and during the fifties in particular, having people round to *'watch the telly'* was common; it was a source of pride for many a family to extend this technological largesse to those still aspiring to such dizzy heights of ownership. By the sixties however, TV ownership, if not universal, was getting pretty damn close but that still didn't stop many house-proud owners from treating the set almost as a family member of some note. Indeed, its every need had to be attended to in terms of regular polishing and shading from such vulgarities as bright sunlight and excessive dust or marked temperature changes - or someone sneezing within a radius of about half a mile, or so it seemed. And that's because early TV's were temperamental ... and unreliable ... and heavy, and let's be honest, sometimes just downright sulky. They were just about as far removed from our modern flat screen, paper thin, superbly reliable and beautifully engineered Smart TVs as you can imagine.

For a start, the fundamental piece of hardware lurking within the

BBC TV's first logo

Although distinctly 50's looking, there were still loads of these around in the early sixties.

glossy wooden cabinet was a cathode ray tube. Now, not only was this essential bit of kit large and pretty heavy, it was also a bit unreliable, and would frequently start doing odd things, the most common of which was to start rolling the picture in the vertical plain. Thus, the top of the picture was lost, but by way of compensation, it re-appeared at the bottom of the screen. As you may imagine, watching such an odd combination of split pictures required a certain re-calibration of your brain, and didn't add to the pleasure or indeed the accuracy of interpretation. Say, for example you happened to be trying to follow the particularly delicate and dramatic procedures encountered by the heroine when going through childbirth on *'Emergency Ward Ten'*. Such instability with your TV's vertical hold could make following baby's delivery a bit tricky for the viewer, especially when the infant, in the process of being coaxed from between the shrieking woman's legs was displayed at the *top* of the screen, whilst Mum's head was putting in an entirely weird appearance at the *bottom* – well below where all the obstetric action was taking place. If you try to substitute this particular scenario into the split-screen interference shown on the picture above, you will get the idea of the sort of complications such electronic problems caused the dedicated viewer. It was not a happy combination - and what's more, once your TV had got it in mind to completely mess up your programme enjoyment, it would quite spitefully increase its intervention to include a *continuous* roll so that the lady's head would appear to push her nether regions out of the top of the screen, only to have them reappear and steadily climb up the screen from the bottom, if you see what I mean. Once this had reached a sufficiently robust rate of vertical roll, you were lucky indeed if your brain could make any sense at all of the rapidly rotating images – perhaps just the odd waving hand or slightly

Ready to roll... a TV picture in the early stages of climbing up the screen, and cleverly reappearing at the bottom.

bewildered looking new born baby flashing by as it zoomed towards the top of the screen.

Quite obviously, something needed to be done, and this is where it starts to get technical. If you think that the dusty recesses of the internal organs of valve radio sets were something to wonder at, then the TV was so much more. For a start, the back of the set was where the delicate arse end of the cathode ray tube lived, and it was surrounded by a cat's cradle of important looking wires and other gizmos, all of them filled with very high voltage sparky stuff just dying to tempt the unwary to poke their fingers through the little ventilation holes. As such an exploration could lead to a real life visit to a real life A&E department, it was not to be recommended. And yet, it was only by fiddling around at the back of the TV that you could calm the poor soul who was attempting to help her baby enjoy its first feed at her breast whilst rotating at increasing speed around your 14" TV screen.

Very close to all the life-threatening bits at the rear of your telly was a tiny panel which contained some very small knobs labelled: *Brightness; Contrast; Height; Width; Horizontal Hold...* and last but most importantly *Vertical Hold.* The trouble was, these controls were at the *back* of a large and weighty piece of equipment, and so you had to do the necessary adjustment by touch alone, as you needed to watch the screen *at the front* for the anticipated improvement. It doesn't require lot of imagination to predict that the  accuracy of groping your way around this inaccessible control panel resulted in a large number of wrong buttons being twiddled, the visual outcome of which was frequently rather more haphazard than was required. Still, it sometimes produced some nice knitting patterns.

And that's not all; getting your 405 line 14" black and white picture in the first place was down to having a good aerial and this, of course, was a perennial problem. Whilst the fifties and early sixties saw a massive proliferation in the number of roof top TV aerials, picture reception was still pretty unreliable, and rightly or wrongly led to a lot of shouting at pigeons and seagulls who had the nerve to land - and probably crap - on your otherwise pristine antenna. The arrival of the first portable sets with their trendy V shaped telescopic aerials brought yet more tuning challenges, and it was somewhat dispiriting to find that the best picture on your new Pye portable was to be had with the aerial about two feet below ceiling level in the airing cupboard.

There were, of course, no remotes in those days, and so watching TV was a lot more calorie consuming than it is today, what with taking it in turns to hold the portable aerial just below the curtain rail, or of it being your turn to rush into the street in order to shout at the birds roosting on the chimney pot version. Added to that was the regular need to leap out of your seat to change channels (always with a big hunky switch on the side of the set which made a satisfying *ker-chunk* noise when turning to another station), to alter the volume or indeed to delve into the dusty recesses of the back of the set to adjust the dreaded *vertical hold*.

'And what of the programmes?' I hear you ask. Good question. As might be predicted, there was something of a change in TV output in the sixties. No longer was the medium considered to be the special and extraordinary preserve of the affluent minority. Mass viewing was at hand, and TV was rapidly becoming the common social currency of the age. The changes were subtle but present across the entire TV genre. Take for example, a popular TV comedy of the late fifties called *'The Army Game'*. As its title suggests, this was very much a product of the post-war period, and the comedy largely centred around the confrontation between an army regular (Sgt. Major Snudge played by Bill Frazer) and a bunch of National Servicemen who were out to do as little work as possible, the chief character being Private *'excused boots'* Montague played by Alfie Bass. As National Service itself finished in 1960, the programme was date vulnerable, and although its *cheeky chappy* type humour was well written and delivered with skill, it was all of a sudden a bit old-fashioned, and the programme was withdrawn in 1961 after a four year run. Replacing such offerings in the BBC schedule came some comedies which moved away from the traditional simple end-of-the-pier style to something much chancier and for its

time quite experimental. A perfect example was *'Steptoe and Son'* which hit the screens in 1962 and in a way set the scene for a whole new direction for TV comedy, which artfully combined current social tensions with comic situations.

Another innovation was the introduction of much more experimental comedy. It could be argued that what the Goon Show did for radio comedy, Michael Bentine's *'It's a Square World'* did for TV. His madcap humour which used a considerable amount of technical wizardry paved the way for programmes such as *'The Goodies'* in the 1970's and especially, *'Monty Python's Flying Circus',* first broadcast in 1969.

That's not to say that the break was complete – *'The Army Game',* for example, metamorphosed into *'Bootsie and Snudge'*, where Alfie Bass and Bill Frazer continued their comedic sparring in Civvy Street, and comedies such as *'The Dickie Henderson Show'* continued to be successful with the more traditional variety show format.

Children's TV also took a big step forward, and whereas the slapstick and homely comfort of *'The Sooty Show'* was still quite popular and the participative attraction of *'Crackerjack'* with its must-have coloured propelling pencils still drew huge audiences, the *'Blue Peter'* genre of active engagement for all viewers was gaining ground. Participating in naming various canine chums, funding lifeboats, supporting guide-dog training and the like - enabled viewers to be part of the programme. Indeed, to be made to feel that they were active contributors opened up a whole new context for children's TV. Whilst Richard Hearn's *'Mr. Pastry'* was still popular, Jimmy Edwards' *'Whack-O'* depicted a lifestyle that was becoming increasingly unrecognisable by the new generation of school children, and it was no surprise therefore that Gerald Campion, the star of *'Billy Bunter of Greyfriars School'* shrieked his last *'Yaroo!! You beasts, you absolute beasts!'* in 1961. Later in the decade, John Alderton's brilliant portrayal of a harassed secondary modern school teacher in *'Please Sir!'* was a perfect example of TV edging towards reality broadcasting – in this case a move along the education/comedy spectrum which would eventually culminate in *'Grange Hill'* of the late seventies.

The transition to a more active audience participation style was underwritten by another ground-breaking programme called '*Vision On*' which was first broadcast in 1964. This innovative programme was designed with the needs of deaf children in mind, but it quickly became a draw for a much wider audience – quite a proportion of it adult. The imaginative ways in which visual stimulation and entertainment could be provided was a complete revelation for many of us, and played a significant – and at the time largely unrecognised – part in the reassessment of how the general public viewed disability.

Even the programme logo was stimulating. Clever stuff.

The brilliant and kindly Tony Hart was central to children's growing realisation that they too could produce some really creative art work and the *'Gallery'* part of the programme, where viewers' own creations were displayed was proof positive that there was a massive wealth of juvenile talent just waiting for the chance to blossom forth. If you can't remember the tune that always accompanied the *Gallery* part of the programme – and I'm certain most of you can – take a moment to use your internet skills and listen to **'*Left Bank 2*'** *by* a band called the Noveltones. If there was ever an iconic piece of music to encapsulate children's TV of the 60's, then this must surely be a strong contender.

And other big changes? Well, one that crept in almost unnoticed was the fact that the schedules were really filling up. In the fifties programming started late and finished early, and there were sometimes odd gaps which had to be accommodated. These were called *Interludes,* and a short piece of film was shown to plug the gap. The most memorable of these was *The Potter's Wheel* which, as its name implies showed the hands of a potter throwing a new creation on his wheel. As far as I can recall, you never got to see the potter himself, or indeed the finished pot, but I suspect that I am joined by many thousands of Baby Boomers in that I can still hear in my mind the piece of light orchestral music which accompanied this brief in-fill.

By the mid sixties programming was a lot tighter, and *Interludes* had all but disappeared. Nevertheless, TV broadcasting was still far from being the twenty four hour coverage we have today, and apart from schools' programmes, morning TV for the wider population didn't really exist. What we did have, however, was the test card. This was screened prior to the commencement of broadcasting each day, and its purpose was to enable you to tune your TV set to its most precise and accurate setting. In other words, it was recognition that most TV sets needed time to overcome their initial grumpiness at being woken up, and required you to spend at least a quarter of an hour or so putting your life at risk of electrocution by delving around in the musty depths of the fine tuning controls

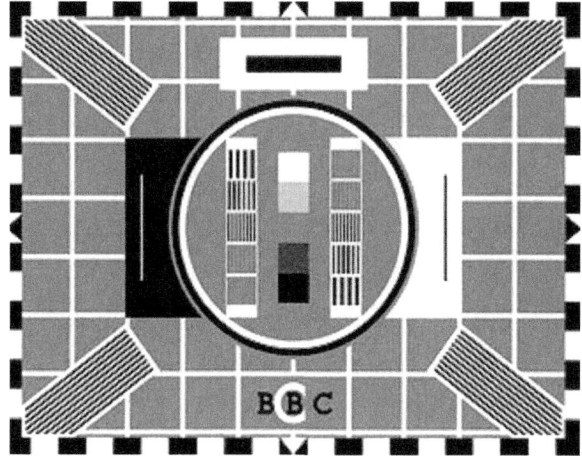

mentioned earlier. The card itself provided a whole range of lines and shapes which, we were informed, had to be precisely recreated on your own set to ensure that *Yogi Bear* didn't appear more pear shaped than required, and that all the shades of glorious grey were accurately represented and properly displayed on your 405 lines of venetian blind.

And while you were at it, it was worthwhile changing channel: just because things were OK on BBC, it didn't mean that ITV was equally well catered for, and may therefore require a whole re-distribution of seagulls and pigeons on the chimney pot aerial to get anything approaching a decent picture at all. In some respects, I suppose it was a blessing that at the beginning of the decade there were only two channels to choose from, and that channel changing via the clunky switch on the side of the old Fergusson was just a matter of one clunk either way.

That is until 1964, when the dear old Beeb introduced another channel – which it imaginatively called BBC 2. Wow! A *third TV* channel? Has the world gone mad? And what's more, the number of lines was increased from 405 to a dizzying 625! Although counting them became a lot harder than with the old 405, there were still people grumbling that they were sure that *'the damned seagulls on the roof mean we only get about 610 on our set... last Thursday fortnight we were down to 390 on the BBC - I'm getting on to the Council....'*

Hey ho... technology for some was always a challenge. What was more to the point, however, was that the original BBC channel had to change its name, and thus with what was fast becoming an almost legendary lack of corporate imagination, we were totally unsurprised that the station now bore the title 'BBC 1'. Hooray.

Which brings me to the **white spot**. *'Another programme?'* I hear you ask. Well, no, not really. That's not to say that most of us at some time or other didn't witness hour upon hour of the white spot's transmission, but that was only because we'd fallen asleep when broadcasting had closed down for the night, usually between 11pm and midnight. At the schedule close each day, the station announcer would say something like:

'The BBC is now closing down. We wish you all a very good night, sweet dreams, don't forget to lock the back door – you know what that bloke at number thirty seven is like - mind the bogey man doesn't get you, put the cat out, and for heaven's sake remember to clean your teeth.'

OK, perhaps not quite as detailed as that, but there was still something of the 'Auntie' in the BBC. Following this announcement, the National Anthem was played together with pictures of Buckingham Palace and suchlike. The implication was that the Queen had drawn her curtains and was at that moment busily winding up her alarm clock and Philip was just sluicing out the Horlicks mugs, and so IT WAS TIME TO GO TO BED…OK?!!

Once the National Anthem was finished, the picture disappeared and was reduced to a white spot right in the centre of the screen. This was accompanied by a fairly high pitched whistling noise which really got on your nerves – as it was designed to do, for it was the audio warning that *'You've left the telly on, you useless git – turn it off before the little white spot bores a hole through the end of your cruddy old black and white TV between lines 202 and 203 on BBC 1 and 312 and 313 for you posher people (who should know better) on BBC 2'.*

So the gradual development of TV entertainment started to gather pace in terms of programme appeal, content, and technology. As far as the latter was concerned, the next big thing of course, was COLOUR. Strewth! Rumour had it that the Yanks had been enjoying colour TV for several years already, but then they had everything didn't they? And anyway, lots of people said that their system was rubbish and their programmes were crap, and they didn't even have *Sooty*, so there!

Nevertheless, once the Beeb announced that it would start colour broadcasting on BBC2 towards the end of 1967, there was something of a collective sigh of relief: the UK was keeping up at last! The fact that initially it would only be for a few hours each day didn't spoil the sense of national achievement, and anyway, our colour was going to be much better than the Americans... much less brash... much more tasteful, refined and well ... British. Anyway, the results would be a damn sight better than those crummy little adverts in the classified Ads which had declared quite brazenly in the early sixties '...*You can have colour TV TODAY for just £3/10/6d*!!' And so you could. What you got was a screen-sized rectangle of thick lilac coloured cellophane set in a plastic frame which attached to the front of your monochrome TV set ... and voila!! There you have it... colour TV! And provided you didn't mind absolutely everything being a shade of violet, you were well pleased. I kid you not. These things actually were advertised and bought by gormless folk in the belief that the *Acme Colour Screen TV Company* of Neasden had stumbled upon an economical way to enliven your broadcasting pleasure without the need to develop complex technology. And some people fell for it. Anyway, *my* screen lasted quite well, and was only discarded when it was put to more effective use as a 14" lilac tea tray, and subsequently fell prey to the over enthusiastic application of very hot *Brook Bond PG Tips*. Never mind.

Anyway, who cared? Real colour TV was on its way – not that the vast majority of us had much chance of seeing it for a while, as the sets were very expensive indeed. Although they were quite a lot larger - and a popular size to which many aspired was 26", - the cost was in the region of £350. Bearing in mind you could buy a quite reasonable second hand car for that in 1967, it put such sets beyond the means of many for the time being. As a result, TV rental firms did good business, and it was not long before everyone was looking at the old monochrome sets and wondering if they could be off-loaded on to someone who had never heard of the new technology.

Bizarrely, one of the very first TV shows to be broadcast in full colour was *'The Black and White Minstrel Show'*. One can only assume that the irony of such a choice was lost upon the BBC executives who commissioned it, and I suppose their defence would have been that the show had already been running for six or seven years in glorious monochrome, the costumes were very colourful, so why not?

Another seismic shift caused by the birth of colour TV was the effect it had upon the movie industry. It could be said that *'Glorious Technicolor'* had been its last defence against the creeping menace of the small screen, and now this too, had been swept away with the introduction of colour TV. Suddenly, the local cinema, once a focus for a great night out was looking down-at-heel and just plain old-fashioned. Even the noisy and colourful adverts put on by Messrs. Pearl and Dean seemed to be less relevant than their TV counterparts, and being urged to knock back a few Martinis *'Any Time, Any Place, Anywhere'* by some flashy geezer driving his Alfa Romeo Sports along the seafront at Cannes seemed suddenly irrelevant. *'Babycham? I'd Love a Babycham!'* Oh really? Well *you* might love, but the rest of the world's learning a lot more about the benefits of bubbly dish-washing, because, as we were all being told at least ten times every night:

'Now hands that do dishes can feel soft as your face, with mild green Fairy Liquid'*

So, did the film industry take it lying down? Did it just curl up and die? Well, to a considerable extent, yes it did. The mid to late sixties saw the

*Come on, admit it... if you're over 65, you've got the advert music in your head right now. And what's more, you can probably remember the obnoxious little kid who introduced the ad by asking her mother why her hands were so soft and smooth in a voice so babyish it seemed to be coming out of her nose. Also, I'm sure you'll remember with startling clarity that the final word of the jingle was always pronounced 'lick-weeeeed'... to make it sound posher.

closure of thousands of cinemas across the country. In my own locality, the Gaiety cinema which had formed an essential and seemingly irreplaceable element to the backdrop of my life went out of business… and was converted into the first supermarket in the area, called *Fine-Fare*. And that was just the start. Although some cinemas tried to up their game by sub-dividing the often cavernous interiors in order to provide two or more programmes, this was a costly investment, and only really came into its own a decade or so later.

The only other way was for cinemas to provide entertainment which relied heavily on sheer scale – something with which the small screened TV would find it difficult to compete. It was no doubt with this in mind that some genius came up with the idea of *Cinerama*, a trade name for a means of providing an almost 3D experience by screening three linked images together over a massively wide and sumptuously curved screen. Impressive and hugely effective though this was, it could not be projected on a normal cinema screen. The other problem was that the Cinerama films themselves were visually fantastic, but otherwise quite boring: some were really little more than simple travelogues - but on a huge scale, and I guess that after a while, even the mighty Niagara Falls or the thundering migration of a million wildebeest over the central African plain might get a bit tedious. What was needed was something that was visually difficult to replicate on the small screen, but also immensely compelling in terms of plot and screenplay, and, to put the cherry on the cake, *would be better viewed en masse.* And there was. By the end of 1965, a film was launched which really did show the way in which cinema could fight back against its small but powerful living room competitor. It was **'*The Sound Of Music'*.**

The film's opening sequence throws down the gauntlet: in drawing back from the image of a young woman apparently doing aeroplane impressions, the camera reveals that the grassy knoll upon which she gambols is actually the top of a gorgeous alpine mountain, and that the novice nun in question might be well advised from getting too near the edge lest she be swept away to the valley bottom about a zillion feet below. But the point was made: such panoramic scenes simply could not be replicated on the small screen. What's more, the screenplay, and especially the captivating music made the whole presentation one you wanted to enjoy *with lots of other people...* and see again, and again....and again. One woman in Portsmouth hit the headlines in the local paper by claiming that she'd seen the film on every single day for a over a year. Now that's what I call dedication... or obsession perhaps? OK, the film was very entertaining, based on a true story and included those whacky funsters the Nazis, so there was plenty of intrigue... but *every day for over a year?!* Despite the cuddly and adorable children, the wise Mother Superior and of course, the incredibly wholesome and well-spoken leading lady whose matchless enunciation and pitch-perfect voice were things of wonder, I think such daily devotion might have been a tad too far.

And in any case, I have a bone to pick with the lyrics of one of the film's most popular songs. To be honest, I feel we were all a bit short-changed in that memorable ditty *'Doh a deer'*. You see, any reference to the tonic sol-fa immediately takes me back to my early days at Highland Road Juniors, when the fragrant Miss Grant would wield her little cork-on-the-end-of-a-stick up and down her musical tonic sol-fa staircase. Now in those days, when men were men (and so were quite a few of the women, or so it seemed) we never had trendy and thoughtful mnemonics to help us master the tonic sol-fa ... it was just:

Doh, re, me, fah, soh, la, te, doh.

But in the 1965 film, according to the lovely Maria Von Trapp,

'When you know the notes to sing
You can sing most any-thing'

Well, I beg to differ. All of us scruffy little eight year olds dutifully learnt the old T-S, but at the end still could sing bugger-all. Nevertheless, the song's lyrics imply that learning this sequence makes a successful career in music a virtual certainty. Oh yeah?

To be fair, it's all OK until you get near the top of the old T-S staircase: you've started well with '***Doh**, a deer a female deer'* and then '***re**, a drop of golden sun'*, moved swiftly on to '***me**, a name I call myself* ', next '***fah**, a long long way to run'*, and all seems to be going swimmingly well as we ascend to '***soh**, a needle pulling thread'*. At this point we are eagerly anticipating getting close to the very summit of the musical escalator when it comes to a juddering halt with:

'La - <u>a note to follow soh'</u>.

A note to follow soh?! What kind of a memory aid is that? If that's all you can think of, why not make ordinal references in all the other parts of the song, e.g.

'soh a note that comes after fah, and next but one before te, but still quite a long way off doh..*(the second one that is)*'?

I don't suppose that I was alone amongst film aficionados in feeling somewhat short-changed by the kindly Maria. To be honest, with mnemonics like that, I'd have made a right mess of **'High on a Hill Stood A Lonely Goatherd'** by probably missing out every *'la'* note encountered in the score. And it would have been so easy for the film's scriptwriters to put in something more creative, so much more memorable for the note, such as:

'La - half of an award-winning magic land'... or even:

'La – the incorrect phonic interpretation of a large city in California'. Surely one of those would have done?

But despite this single misgiving the more attentive filmgoer might have had about *'The Sound of Music'* it certainly showed that the cinema was far from dead and buried – in fact, by concentrating on scale and diversity, the film demonstrated that it could compete effectively against the seemingly unstoppable tidal wave of TV programmes. And of course, it did just that.

It would, for example, have been impossible to have screened a new Bond movie on the TV. Even with the new 26" coloured screen, it would just not have been right to see James Bond sitting in your front room. Bond was a creation of the cinema, and that was the place we all flooded to when the next in the series was presented. Although my personal favourite will always be 1964's *'Goldfinger',* the eager anticipation with which we went as a group to the flicks to see what our favourite secret agent was up to next, knew no bounds. And of course, 007's sexual exploits – when he and his faithful Y Fronts soon parted company - were a huge attraction for teenagers, and really represented the most explicit on-screen sexuality most of us had ever encountered. For that reason alone, watching James Bond in your front room with your Mum and Dad spluttering in outrage over their cocoa ensured that the cinema would continue to have a large and appreciative audience. Although ITV was showing *'The Saint'* and *'The Avengers'*, neither really hit the cutting edge that the big screen Bond films represented.

Having said all that, the little screen did produce a lot of memorable stuff, and one area which went almost unnoticed – because it was so much a part of everyday life - was the cartoon. ITV could claim to be at the forefront of this, and the Popeye cartoons were hugely popular with younger audiences, and set the scene in the early years of the sixties.

Quite why Olive Oyle never quite seemed to grasp that any association with the unshaven lout Bluto was bound to end in trouble remains a mystery to this day – and is only matched by Bluto's continual misreading of the situation regarding his opponent's predilection for tins of spinach, and the massive effect that the consumption of the product always had. *Why*, we asked ourselves, *didn't Bluto knock back a couple of cans for himself?* He must have noticed that once the sailor-man had got his hands on the formidable vegetable, his own lascivious advances on the lovely Olive were doomed. As it was, each cartoon had a goodly outcome in that Popeye - a rather unprepossessing one-eyed sailor with arms bearing a good resemblance to inverted frying pans, always got the girl. Oh, and by the way, he was a regular smoker with a pipe grasped permanently between his teeth. Despite the obvious detrimental effect this would have on his ability to defend Miss Oyle - and the inherent worries about asthma and associated respiratory complaints - this still didn't prevent our spinach-filled hero from giving the villainous Bluto his weekly pasting. Am I going in too deep here? Is micro-analysis of Popeye's medical needs a shade too far? In my own defence, I took *Huckleberry Hound*, *Top Cat* and the wonderful *Flintstones* at face value.

In what appeared to be a spin off from cartoons, the sixties also saw a big increase in the number of animations. Of course, *'Thunderbirds'* was perhaps the best known and most influential: it was loved by all ages, and many of us raised an eyebrow or two when our mums expressed considerable admiration for Lady Penelope and her chauffeur, the imperturbable Parker. I mean, who wouldn't want to own a pink Roller? And even though Parker seemed to have a permanent head cold, his manners were impeccable.

The genre continued with *'Fireball XL5'* and *'Captain Scarlet'*, but the one that really captured the nation's imagination from October 1965 was *'The Magic Roundabout'*. Created by Serge Danot in France, it was commissioned by the BBC when the brilliant Eric Thompson dubbed in an entirely new soundtrack to the original French production. The characters included a rather matronly cow, a stroppy but inquisitive dog, a polite little girl, an old bloke who turned the roundabout, an intellectual snail, a spaced-out and really rather groovy rabbit and a bloke with a big moustache, a rather scrawny body whose legs were replaced by a large spring apparently shoved up his bum. No wonder he never looked entirely chuffed.

Eric Thompson's sublime script was so popular with adult audiences that it was screened on a daily basis in the prime spot just before the six o' clock early evening news. In the days before video recorders it was many an adult who rushed home to make sure he or she was ready for Florence, Dougal and co by 5.55 each evening.

The Magic Roundabout – a national favourite. When the BBC moved its time slot there was a huge outcry from adults who couldn't get home in time to see it. The Beeb quickly back-tracked...and everyone was happy again.

In similar vein, the BBC's '*Camberwick Green*' with the endearing Windy Miller was a huge favourite with its intended audience – and again, more than a few adults as well. Following on from this was the wonderful '*Trumpton*'. I challenge you now to ask any Baby Boomer dinner party to complete the roll call which you start with: '*Pugh, Pugh, Barney McGrew*', and you'll be hit with an avalanche of people roaring '*Cuthbert, Dibble and Grubb!*' So much for adults turning their noses up at kids' TV.

A couple of years later, the equally engaging '*Clangers*' hit the screen. For the few of you who have no idea who or what I am talking about, I demand that you pick up the old *I Pad* (other tablet and smart phone appliances are available) and type it in this minute. I mean, what more do you need? Little pink animals with long noses that live on a neighbouring planet and are dependent upon the largesse of a *soup dragon* for their continued sustenance and well-being – can't be easy, can it? Oh, and when you realise that they only communicate with just whistles… how good can a programme get, for heaven's sake?

The early seventies saw something of a return to cartoons – or to be more precise, *wobbly* cartoons. '*Crystal Tipps and Alistair*' had a gentle and slightly spaced-out appeal, whereas '*Roobarb and Custard*' were in every way the real deal with the brightest of bright colours, grinning main characters and blaring music. Subtle it was not – loved it was.

But back to the sixties. Another area where the TV found it hard to compete was in the area of pop films, and chief amongst these were '*Hard Day's Night*' and '*Help*' from the Beatles. It simply wouldn't have been right to see either of these films in the privacy of your own home. Beatlemania was a *collective* phenomenon; you have only to look at the mass of footage of teenagers screaming their heads off at concerts to absorb the fact that doing this sort of thing individually in your own sitting room in front of the old 14" black and white would have been something of a non-starter. So, bearing in mind that most of us didn't get to see the group live, the next best thing was to go to the flicks with as large a group of appreciative mates as you could gather, and do the collective appreciation bit there. An added advantage was that you could all exit the cinema yelling…

'I…… should have known better with a girl like you,
That I would love everything that you do'

…complete with your best effort at harmonica accompaniment but without the harmonica. Better still was a group rendition of…

'HELP! I need somebody,
Help, not just anybody;
Help, you know I need someone,

ending with the crescendo   …..'*HEEEEELP!!*'

Group therapy at the Odeon was still a lot better than watching pop films on the TV.

Occasionally, famous groups such as the Beatles would be scheduled to sing live on the telly, and this was a cause for great excitement. In the sixties, every TV programme was introduced by a continuity announcer and each station had a small staff of such people. Their job was to appear between programmes and to inform viewers of immediate and forthcoming programme details. Bearing in mind there were no on-screen programme guides in those days and no way of recording programmes, they performed a useful role. Often, an announcer would become a celebrity in his or her own right, and probably made a bob or two opening local supermarkets and so on. Telly people were still held in awe, and when they got to remind their own audiences about programmes of such massive interest as the Beatles appearing live, they often seemed beside themselves with excitement. Shortly after the Fab Four had released their 1963 hit single *'She Loves You'*, I can remember our dinner-suited continuity bloke beaming with almost unrestrained excitement and saying to the camera something like:

'And don't forget later this evening it's 'Yeah, Yeah, Yeah …Yeah!!!'
All a bit embarrassing really - on two counts: for him as it was painfully apparent that he had little experience of pop music and might well have been more at home reading the Shipping Forecast, and secondly for me… because if you have no recollection of the Beatles' song lyrics, you will have no idea what the hell I'm banging on about. Oh well.

Something else that populated a good deal of TV time in the sixties was what is now called a game show. Amongst the earliest of these was a programme that was really little more than a televised panel game, called *'What's My Line?'* It was hosted by the ever cheerful Eamonn Andrews, and the celebrity panellists had to deduce from the actions and question responses elicited from a stranger what was the nature of his or her profession. OK, it was not really that gripping, but it drew a reasonable TV audience in the early sixties, and was a comfy programme in that viewers liked the familiarity of the show's elements and the low key jocularity that accompanied them. As to actual quiz shows, ITV seemed to take an early lead – perhaps because the independent companies could be more generous in terms of prizes. An early example was called *'Dotto'* which required contestants to recognise the face from a picture of a well known person. The trick was that the picture was sub-divided into many dots, rather like newspaper images of the time. Contestants were allowed to see an increasing number of dots which built up into the full image – but the fewer dots used meant the higher the prize money for a correct identification. Exciting? ... I'll say! It was £5 for each unused dot, for heaven's sake!

Mind you, with the sort of dodgy reception and persistent interference most of us got on the old 14" back in 1960, home based identification could be a bit wide of the mark, and especially if the vertical hold was playing up at the same time. Trying to identify a dotty face whose chin appeared above its eyebrows was always going to be tricky, especially as the picture was rolling up the screen with increasing velocity at the same time – so variations in interpretation as wide as King Kong and Doris Day were sometimes equally plausible.

The first real game show was presented by Michael Miles and bore the title *'Take Your Pick'*. This popular show clocked up thirteen years, and drew big audiences right up until its withdrawal in 1968. The prizes offered were way beyond anything the BBC could muster, and the fact that ordinary participants could win prizes as spectacular as a new car ensured a regular following. One particular part of the programme – *'The Yes/No Interlude'* was as excruciating as it was compelling. The contestant was asked a series of quick fire questions to which he or she had to answer without using the words 'yes' or 'no'. Since all the questions would normally require just that response e.g. *'Did you enjoy your summer holiday?'* or *'Do you like mustard on your sausages?* it was hard for the contestants to remain focussed enough not to use the proscribed response. Added to that, there was someone else standing at the contestant's elbow with a gong, and whose job it was to hit the instrument if 'yes' or 'no' were used by the poor

The great Michael Miles

contestant. Now, you may be familiar with the J. Arthur Rank geezer whose job it was to introduce blockbuster films by flexing his muscular and well oiled arms and giving a vast screen gong a mighty thump ... well this little bloke on the telly was about as far removed from that image as you can imagine. He was short, wore a blazer and grey trousers and specs. Now, nothing against the visually impaired I hasten to say, but the overall effect was somewhat *weasely*, and he did seem to take enormous pleasure in catching someone out. Nevertheless, the programme was a great hit and apart from the numbing tension of the *'Yes-No Interlude'*, had viewers on the edge of their seats when audience members were invited to urge contestants later in the programme to either:

'TAKE THE MONEY!!' or *'OPEN THE BOX!!'*

You'll appreciate that at the time TV audiences at home did not have the technology to participate in this choice; there was no:

'If you think Daisy should OPEN THE BOX then dial 071234 001, but if you think she should TAKE THE MONEY then dial 071234 002. Remember, calls from your local phone box may be completely messed up by some old git in front of you who can't find four pennies to put in the slot and even if he could, pushing button A would probably give him a seizure. Alternatively, you might consider sending a carrier pigeon'.

So, in the sixties, home reaction to TV programmes which elicited a response, such as the monumental questions regarding *opening the box* or its alternative, were reduced to simply shouting at the TV... and then basking in reflected glory - and perhaps awarding yourself a chocolate digestive - if your choice happened to be proved correct.

Another great favourite was *'Double Your Money'* hosted by the affable Hughie Green. Again, as an ITV production, it was able to introduce big cash prizes – to a maximum of £1000. For many in the mid sixties, this sort of sum was seen as a goal for the yearly salary to which they aspired, so offering it as a prize was no small beer. Even though Mr. Green's oft repeated sincerity (*'and I really mean that, friends, I really do'*) could be a little overpowering at times, he was pretty good at his job, and the show attracted huge audiences for much of the decade. That Hughie knew his job well was undoubted, and despite the repetitive form of the show, he always managed to seem interested in the contestants, and to extract a fair amount of humour from such a well trodden formula. The programme became something of an institution, a familiar part of the everyday lives of telly viewing people – i.e. most of the country. Again, such a simple question and answer format allowed all viewers to participate by shouting out their own answers at the screen, and to take family adulation from the amount they would have won had they been there. The boast of *'winning the thousand last night'* was therefore not uncommon.

Because of its charter to *'inform, educate and entertain',* the BBC was in no position to compete with such shows, and could only really persuade people that its own quiz programmes were ever so slightly high brow in comparison – tacitly implying that it would not lower itself to the vulgarity of offering money. Well, perhaps that's a bit strong, but when you compare a shiny new car as the star prize on *'Take Your Pick'* to a propelling pencil on *'Blue Peter'*, you get the idea. Nevertheless, the BBC did pretty well with its strictly non-commercial approach, and built on it quite successfully, even attracting younger audiences through the highly competitive *'Top of the Form'*. Originally a radio programme, it transferred successfully on to TV in 1962. At this important juncture, the BBC used its immense resources of wit, wisdom and creativity to come up with the outrageously new and funky title *'Television Top of the Form'*. With billing like that, how could it fail to attract the eager masses of youngsters keen to pit their wits against St. Margaret's Grammar School for Girls, Hythe? And it didn't.

The plucky kids of Great Britain queued up to get in the contest, and for many a year the closing *'Three cheers for the boys of St. Bruin's Episcopalian School Ashby-de-la-Zouche'* rang in the ears of the tens of thousands of viewers. It was noticeable, however, that although seen by quite a large audience of adults as well as the kids for whom it was intended, the verbal confidence with which such older viewers responded to the questions was a great deal more muted. It was pretty much OK to get a question wrong with Hughie Green, and to offer timely advice to Michael Miles as to whether or not the bleedin' box should be opened, but to get kids' questions wrong? That was something else!

Clearly however, the BBC recognised the mileage in creating quizzes with a wide age-range appeal, and thus introduced a programme called *'Ask the Family'* in 1967. This cross-generation game invited parents and children to submit themselves to humiliation or glory in front of a huge TV audience, so a certain amount of bravery was required, especially as the quiz master on this occasion was the ever-so-slightly abrasive Robert Robinson. Although always absolutely polite, one frequently had the feeling that after the show, he would be perfectly happy give out a detention or two, or perhaps a hundred lines to any family members who had let themselves down.

This rather schoolmasterly approach was further underwritten when Mr. Robinson went on to play a central part in another semi-intellectual 1960's panel game entitled *'Call My Bluff'*. On this occasion however, light-heartedness was ensured by the inclusion of Frank Muir as one of the team captains. That Frank was a great comedy script writer meant that the show could never be all that serious, and so it became a watchword for clever word play and devious interpretations. Frank Muir's own career in comedy always shone through, and not surprisingly as he and the great Denis Norden co-wrote the BBC's famous *'Take It From Here'* radio show, and transferred to the TV with *'Whack-O'*. On the big screen, Denis was also responsible for the famous line from *'Carry On Cleo'* when Kenneth Williams, playing Julius Caesar, finds himself the unwilling recipient of a number of rather sharp knives and cries:

'Infamy! Infamy! They've all got it in for me!!'

Surprisingly, however, the intellectual high ground of quiz shows was not held in the sixties by the BBC at all. Despite its charter to *Inform, educate and entertain'*, ITV snatched the accolade as far back as 1962 by introducing one of TV's most enduring programmes - *'University Challenge'*. Now a stalwart of the BBC, the original series was put out by Granada, and had as its host the memorable Bamber Gascoigne, whose smooth and friendly style set the tone for a decade and more. Given the fact that many folk in the sixties still regarded university education as something which was held in awe, it is not surprising that a goodly proportion of the weekly audience – me included - didn't even understand what *sort* of answer the urbane Bamber was looking for. Was it a number? An article of clothing? A scientific formula? Your inside leg measurement? And this was *before* making a desperate stab at an answer.

Mind you, just occasionally you'd strike it lucky when out of the blue a question might drop into your lap, and then there was a good degree of kudos to be gained from your success. But such happy coincidences were few and far between, and I lived in hope that more accessible and practical questions such as '*In the 1950's, what was the number of the Portsmouth Corporation trolley bus which served South Parade Pier and Cosham Railway Station?*' might become the norm. Despite this, the show was remarkably popular, and there was a certain cachet in letting the odd intellectual fact gleaned from the previous night's programme drop casually into a subsequent conversation. For example, in responding to an adverse comment quoted from the Football Mail concerning the inability of your local team to get anywhere near the goal mouth, it might be possible to hit back with:

'Well yes, the Mail may be right, and perhaps Smithy shouldn't have fallen over his boot laces and burst into tears right in front of the posts ...but wasn't it the great Roman orator Cicero who in 56 BC said 'It is the peculiar quality of a fool to perceive the faults of others and to forget his own?'

You see? Just a little snippet of info from Bamber's boys (and girls) and you were away. It's a good job the long running TV show is still available today: provided you can ignore the likely response you might get from Jeremy Paxman were your ridiculous answers to be made known to him when you shout at the TV, there's still a chance to make a suitably good impression down the pub later.

It was not until 1972 when '*Mastermind*' made its debut that a sort of happy medium was reached, whereby pretty hard-ish questions were asked of pretty ordinary people, many of whom rose to the occasion and gave a good account of themselves. It seemed to be a bit like University Challenge for ordinary people, and was immediately popular… and remains so today.

'*So, enough about the intellectual challenge of TV quiz shows!*' I hear you chorus, *'What about drama, crime, current affairs and variety?'*

Well, there were lots of them, that's for sure. The schedules were filling up, and pressure on the empty slots in both morning and afternoon Test Card time was growing. Imports from the USA were very popular, and none more so in the early sixties than the classic western. Having been brought up in the previous decade with a combination of early TV and Saturday morning pictures providing graphic insights to the world of famous gunslingers such as *'The Lone Ranger'* (*'who was that man wearing the tiny black mask that only just covered his eyes and did no more to protect his identity than a pair of fairly small sunglasses? Blowed if I know. Why not ask Tonto?'*), *'The Cisco Kid'* (*'Hey Pancho, you want guacamole on your tortillas or what?'*) and *'Hopalong Cassidy'* (***Oi!! Why can't I have a proper super hero name too?!'***) it was but a small and welcome step to the sexier, more sophisticated world of *'Wagon Train'*, *'Rawhide'* and *'Bonanza'* on TV.

OK, *'Champion the Wonder Horse'* was pretty damn exciting, but Clint Eastwood's entry as Rowdy Yates was the one to set many a teenage girls' hearts a-flutter. These programmes were so popular that combined with the less sophisticated 'Cowboys n' Indians' diet with which we had been bombarded at Saturday morning pictures the decade before, the wild west for many of our generation was as homely and familiar as a digestive biscuit and a cup of tea. In some ways, a present day visit to the western states of the USA is a bit like coming home and in moments of idle gazing upon a western scene, you suddenly realise that it all seems oddly familiar… and you find yourself wondering if the great spread on that lonely hillside over there must be the Ponderosa Ranch surely? And isn't that the sound of Hoss coming galloping over the plain with Little Joe hot on his heels? Westerns were ingrained deep in our collective subconscious.

With the advent 007 on the big screen, a level of sophistication – not to mention the sex and violence – was reached that was hard for the small screen to emulate. The monochrome goings on in dear old *'Dixon of Dock Green'*, in the comforting presence of Jack Warner suddenly seemed a bit old hat, and even the popular *'Z Cars'* came over as just a little bit pale in comparison. Nevertheless, Patrick McGoohan's *'Danger Man'* and *'The Prisoner'* were welcome additions to the TV diet, and the perceptive Chief Detective Superintendent Tom Lockhart kept things on a pretty even keel each week in the long running ITV series *'No Hiding Place'*. So, although the small screen couldn't match the pzazz of its larger brother, it managed to keep us pretty near to the edge of our seats more often than not, and with a certain homely feeling that *right would always prevail*. As far as I can recall, there was virtually no mention of drugs or terrorism - or the serial killers that seem to stalk our TV screens in the 21st century. These were good old-fashioned villains of the *'it's a fair cop guvnor... you got me bang to rights'* variety, so at least we all knew where we were.

Not that we were entirely devoid of the criminal realities of life. The Great Train Robbery of 1963 genuinely shocked and upset the nation, and the thought that criminals could steal such a vast sum of money (£2.6 million) was almost inconceivable. Outside broadcasting brought us location shots of the crime scene, and programmes such as *'Panorama'* and *'This Week'* kept us well informed of current events and issues. At a lighter level, a popular post 6 o' clock News broadcast was one of the first TV magazine programmes. Called *'Tonight'* it was hosted by the popular Cliff Michelmore and his co-presenter Derek Hart. Together they built up a little team of contributors, notable amongst whom was a craggy Scot called Fyfe Roberson, whose gentle Highland lilt added to the charm of his investigative reports. That some of Fyfe's efforts to discover the solution to a particular matter ended inconclusively didn't seem to matter all that much, and his concluding phrase *"... and as to the truth of the matter, well we don't know... we just don't know..."* became one to watch out for.

A knowing look The craggy Fyfe Robertson was very popular on BBC TV's 'Tonight'.

It was on the *'Tonight'* programme too, that another great TV name made his debut: Alan Whicker cut his teeth doing travelogue pieces for the programme, and his distinctive style and informal approach made him a great favourite. Such pieces were the pre-cursor to his massive contribution in making us all aware of the vast horizons offered by the planet earth through his subsequent *'Whicker's World'* programmes.

Back in the *'Tonight'* studio, the pattern of magazine programmes was set when Robin Hall and Jimmie MacGregor introduced a guitar based musical interlude, and were joined by another contributor, Cy Grant, whose West Indian calypsos – often of a topical nature - were both amusing and very popular.

And all-round entertainment of the period? Well, it's hard to know where to start. Many of the programmes we have today saw their incubation and birth in the sixties. A good example would be when William Hartnel hit the screen as the very first *'Doctor Who'* in 1963. It should not be forgotten that at that time, the blue police phone box which was the exterior of the Tardis, was still a familiar sight in the towns and cities of our great land and perhaps the programme had greater immediate impact as a consequence.

'Emergency Ward 10' completed a decade of gripping hospital dramas in 1967, but could easily be seen as the forerunner of programmes such as *'Holby City'* and *'Casualty'* today. *'Coronation Street'* was in its tenth year by the end of the decade, and shows no sign today of waning any time soon – indeed it is as popular now as it ever was, and the vivid personalities of the show's many memorable participants are as sharp and perceptive now as they ever were. Whether or not the redoubtable Ena Sharples remains the programme's most acerbic character is, I am sure, a matter of debate. In the sixties, she was certainly thought to be the real harridan viewers loved to hate – especially when she was lauding it over her two timorous cohorts, Martha Longhurst and Minnie Caldwell as they sipped on a glass of milk stout in the Rover's Return. Hark at me! I didn't even watch the programme on a regular basis, and yet such a powerful production has etched these indelible images into my mind – and many of yours, I bet. Such is the power of television.

Of course, Corrie is not the only sixties show that is still with us, and some are even more popular today than they were then. The example that springs immediately to mind is, of course *'Gardener's World'*…… *no it isn't* - just teasing! It's just got to be *'Come Dancing'* hasn't it? The programme actually started in 1950, for heaven's sake! In those days the voluminous dresses worn by the ladies were almost too big to be squashed into the old 14" screen, but such was the draw of the show that such indelicacies were quite immaterial. Now, of course, the word *'Strictly'* precedes the original title but the content, although much more glamorous and *very* much more revealing, is virtually identical: young people dressed to the nines and zooming around the dance floor in a dazzling shower of sequins, sparkly bits and overlong eyelashes… and that's just the blokes. Nevertheless, it remains a vastly popular production, and for those of us less than transfixed by such extravagant goings on, seems to last for months. Am I letting my personal views cloud the issue? Do I have a problem with the odd hundredweight of sequins? Well, perhaps so… but the show remains a master class.

So too, were many of the variety shows. Whereas *'The Good Old Days'* inevitably stepped well into the past, the one that kept us abreast of current thinking was impresario Val Parnel's *'Sunday Night at the London Palladium'*. Introduced by a resident compere – and amongst the first of these was the incomparable Bruce *('I'm in charge!')* Forsyth – the show was variety at its best. The format of the Sunday night get-together was a comfortable amalgam of singers, dancers, special guests and some audience participation. The latter came in the form of a mini game show called *'Beat the Clock',* where contestants had to re-arrange a seemingly random selection of words into a well known phrase or saying. And all of this within thirty seconds in front of about nine million viewers…. all of whom were shouting at their TV sets…

'No you idiot!!! It's WHERE THERE'S A WILL THERE'S A bleedin' WAY!!! … not WHERE A WAY WILL THERE… are you blind or something??!'

Such raised blood pressure had the next few minutes of commercial break to resume its normal status, and the second part of the show was when the BIG stars were on. It was common for the latest pop groups and singers to appear to tumultuous applause at this point. Comedians

Bruce 'in charge' at the London Palladium.

also got star status, as well as more specialist acts like ventriloquists. Ray Alan's *Lord Charles* was popular, mainly because he was risqué enough to say 's*illy ass'* in such a way that made it sound like *'silly arse'* - how daring! Amongst guest magicians, Tommy Cooper was an obvious favourite, but so too were speciality acts like the little Italian mouse *Topo Gigio,* which was a marionette operated by 'invisible' puppeteers clad in black.

That the show became something of an institution is undeniable, and its family-friendly appeal was largely down to the all-encompassing jolliness exuded by the host compere. Quite apart from anything else, it certainly brought the nation up to speed with the fact that *The Tiller Girls* had very long legs, and could dance linked together in quite enormous chains of comely limbs, flashing smiles and glittering costumes *like anything*. And the finale to each show was *sooooo* orchestrated to make you aware of what a good time you had had. You see, the performing area included a very, very large rotating stage, and at the conclusion of each show, all the participants would stand behind huge illuminated letters spelling out the name of the theatre. The stage would then rotate and all of the performers got about 120 degrees worth of waving and smiling exposure as the giant rotating motor eased them round and round at a less than giddy pace. It was all jolly good. Really.

Doing a turn: Brucie and the entire show's cast take a leisurely spin at the end of another successful 'Sunday Night at the London Palladium'.

So, variety was pretty well covered… but you couldn't honestly say the same of sport. Outside broadcast technology was nowhere near as sophisticated – or even portable – in the sixties as it is today. Whereas the main sports were covered, the amount of scheduled time was small by comparison. Against this however, you have to be mindful of what coverage was like just a decade or so before: simply listening to sports coverage was always going to be a much more 'arm's length' experience, and even the most gifted commentator would be hard pressed to engender the sense of immediate excitement that actually seeing the event would provide. Thus most televised sport was greeted with a high degree of enthusiasm just because the experience was so much more immediate. Obviously, there were real highlights: watching annual events such as the Boat Race was new to many, and provided the joyous speculation that eight of the most educated folk in the kingdom might again end up floundering about in the muddy waters of the Thames as their streamlined pencil of a boat suddenly gave up the unequal task of remaining buoyant under such a muscular load.

Another sporting event which achieved unexpected popularity during the period was, believe it or not, *wrestling*. Now I don't really remember wrestling being a sport at all when we were kids at school. Sure, there was a lot of wrestling going on in the playground, but this was of the more unseemly *'kick your shins and pull your jumper over your head'* type, and usually ended up with a hefty slap from the incomparable Miss Grant, who on such occasions seemed to be a little less fragrantly appealing than normal. So when the mid-Atlantic TV commentary of Kent Walton introduced such hairy gorillas as 'Big Daddy' and 'The Crusher' to us on a Saturday afternoon, we were not quite sure whether to class it as sport, operatic drama, or a minor declaration of war. I suppose this was one instance where the lack of colour TV might have been just as well.

Football? Yes of course, but with nothing like the coverage today. The most famous match was without doubt the World Cup Final of 1966, and BBC commentator Kenneth Wolstenholm's final sentence: **'They think it's all over… it is now!!'** has quite rightly taken its place in the 1960's TV hall of fame.

One could go on and on giving examples of pioneering TV throughout the decade – and I suspect you might be at the point where a spot of gardening/car-washing/staring at the wall…or just about any damn thing might come as a merciful relief. But bear with me just a little longer, because what I haven't mentioned yet is perhaps the most momentous TV programming of the whole decade.

I believe that the occasion that really defines our age was the fantastic coverage given to the Apollo Space Programme. If ever it needed to be brought home to humanity just what an important part the new medium of TV had to play in our lives, this was it. Imagine if you can, how different the momentous, historic and ground-breaking events of 1969 would have been without experiencing live the coverage of man's first steps into space via our little television screens.

For me, there were two occasions when the true wonder of what man could achieve was really brought home in a most breathtaking and dynamic way. The most obvious of these was, of course, Neil Armstrong's wonderful *'One small step for man, one giant leap for mankind'* moment when we witnessed a fellow human being stepping on to the surface of another planet for the first time – July 20th 1969. Wow! But there was another - and sometimes forgotten - event which, at the time drew the highest ever number of TV viewers worldwide, and that was something stupendous at the close of the previous year.

In December 1968, Apollo 8 was the first manned space mission to leave Earth orbit and to travel to the moon. Its purpose was skim the lunar surface, to measure the effects of such a long journey and to test out lunar navigation and return in the run up to the moon landing scheduled for 1969. Apollo 8 orbited the moon ten times, and thus revealed for the first time its the hidden 'dark' side. That it turned out to be just about the same as the side of the moon which we see on a daily basis was hardly a surprise, though I suspect it disappointed conspiracy theorists of the near barking-mad variety who anticipated the place to be choc-a-bloc with little green blokes, cheese factories, and a number of soup mines. But for the majority of the world's population the abiding image was that of the planet earth taken from way out in space. For the first time we were shown a live picture of the beautiful celestial spaceship that is our home – and what a thing of wonder it is.

The breathtaking beauty of the Earth photographed from Apollo 8 on Christmas Eve 1968

OK, we knew it was round, we knew it would be blue-ish, and that a lot of it would be covered in cloud… but to see it in all its splendour, set against the impenetrable darkness of outer space was a heart-stopping moment. It was only with a supreme conscious effort that I refrained from dashing off a poem right there and then. The following day, the other photograph of the age 'Earthrise' - showing our home planet emerging above the moon's rocky horizon – was beamed to the earth, and immediately became a much deserved sensation… but I suspect that I am not the only one to feel that the previous day's portrait of our mother planet floating serenely in the vast emptiness of space was the one to cherish.

And so we leap forward to July 1969 and this most memorable and astounding decade is almost at a close. With or without a supreme sense of irony, Creedence Clearwater has a hit with *'Bad Moon Rising'*, the Stones seem to have a bee in their bonnet concerning certain *'Honky Tonk Women'*, and Johnny Cash is stressing his masculinity with *'A Boy Named Sue'*.

On the domestic front, the UK is very much at the cutting edge of state of the art inter-planetary exploration with the introduction of a large bouncy rubber ball with handles attached and called the *'Space Hopper'*. Am I over-stretching credibility in claiming that this juvenile *must-have* introduced many a child to the experiences of free-fall, and thus could be seen as excellent training for their future role in expeditions throughout the solar system?

The Space Hopper -very popular with kids and budding astronauts. You can still get them now.

On a rather more practical level, the maiden flight of

Concorde, the world's first super-sonic jet airliner took place, and the amazing jump jet, the Hawker Harrier entered service with the RAF, proving that although regarding space exploration the UK might only bounce along just a few inches above the ground on a rubber ball, we were still better than anyone at producing superb aircraft.

Also in April 1969, the voting age was suddenly reduced from twenty-one to just eighteen, and thus the old custom of acknowledging your 'majority' on your twenty-first birthday suddenly became a thing of the past – which was a bit of a shame for those who were over eighteen but not yet twenty-one on that day, and who had been looking forward to the traditional big party on their twenty-first. All of a sudden, their future was behind them, so to speak, and Baby Boomers born at the end of the forties must have been feeling somewhat short-changed, to put it mildly. Good job we were well-hard, say I; kids brought up with marbles in the gutter, ice on the inside of bedroom windows and tapioca pudding were made of tougher stuff. That we managed to overcome each indignity with a cheery smile and sturdy resolution should come as no surprise to those of you who bravely slogged your way through the first book of this series*.

And yet, even with such heroic 1960's stoicism, some knocks were hard to endure: take for example, August 1st 1969. For those of us brought up with ye olde imperial system of weights and measures, another blow was struck on this date when the old ha'penny was withdrawn. As if losing the farthing wasn't bad enough, here was another nail in the coffin of all our work with the lovely Miss Grant… and by the way, how on earth were we now going to be able to buy a couple of Fruit Salads with the necessary coinage removed? I dunno! Sometimes you could murder for a Fruit Salad… but had we done so in the later months of 1969, *not to worry* – for the Death Penalty was finally repealed just in time for Christmas – so that's all right then.

But of course, for all mankind, the defining image of the decade – indeed of the twentieth century - must be that of the moon landing on 20th July 1969, when at 4.18pm mission control - and the rest of the watching world - heard those immortal words:

*'The Time of Our Lives' published on Amazon in 2021. It's a great read. Honest!

'Houston, Tranquility Base here. The Eagle has landed.'

I suppose there could have been no better way with which to end a decade that was full of the most amazing and astonishing events. Even given the optimism with which the sixties were approached, I suggest that no one could have foreseen the scope, diversity and sheer brilliance of the developments that took place within such a brief span. The world in general, and the UK in particular took a great leap forward, and society changed forever. The arrival of global TV played a pivotal role in widening our perception, in allowing everyone to participate in all that was going on with an immediacy that had been inconceivable even a decade before. More than that, the teenage revolution that was hinted at in the fifties had developed into a tidal wave of what seemed at the time an unstoppable roller coaster of creativity: suddenly the world was a young, vibrant and exciting place, and its infinite possibilities were there at our finger tips.

Is this all a bit strong? Am I over-egging it? Possibly. Perhaps me and my Baby Boomer chums were just lucky to plant our feet firmly on each stepping stone of opportunity as it arose. But I would say that the decade offered an extraordinarily large number of stepping stones, and despite receiving what in retrospect could be seen as a sometimes quite brutal education, the experience seemed to fit us well for taking advantage of the opportunities offered. All I can say is:

The 1960's? I'm glad I was there.

6 Shell Suits, Vertical Artex & Other Mistakes

You have to feel a bit sorry for the seventies. I mean, the sixties were so identifiable, so different, so confident. There has probably never been a decade which was so self-aware of the new path it was cutting through society, a period that was so alive with ideas, creativity and the joyful appreciation of all that was happening.

So when the next decade came along – where could it go? There was no chance that it could replicate the immense leap forward that had happened ten years before - the great changes brought about by universal TV ownership and consequent access to the wider world, the music scene, the educational and employment opportunities coupled with teenage empowerment and emancipation - these had already been made. So it seemed the best the following decade could aspire to, was simply to build upon this inheritance. Thus the seventies, and perhaps the early eighties too were really characterised by *'more of the same'*.

But not necessarily better. Let's takes a simple example. At the very end of the sixties, there was a move to personalise footwear by making the soles of shoes a bit thicker. In the 70's this developed into the full blown fashion item that was the platform shoe. If mine were anything to go by, comfortable they were not, but that's not really the point. They were not designed as practical footwear, they were a fashion accessory. Oddly, they came at the same time as bell-bottom trousers – now called

Cuban heels had been around for ages, but were mainly worn by cowboys and, well, Cubans I suppose. The seventies, however, took this footwear design feature to new heights – quite literally – by raising not only the heels of shoes, but the soles as well. Clumping around in such lofty footwear was a skill to be acquired

flares - extended their southern-most circumference to almost pillow case proportion, the result being that provided your flares were of the right length – i.e. scraping the ground - your newly acquired platforms disappeared beneath the bell-tent like enclosure of the trouser leg. The only way to show off your expensive platforms therefore, was either to sit down with one leg crossed over the other at a crotch-wrenchingly horizontal angle, or to wear your flares so short that they finished an inch or so above your shoes, a bit like an up-turned trombone hovering six inches above the ground - not a good look. So there you have the 1970's in a nutshell: muddled thinking brought about by the panic when everyone suddenly realised it wasn't the 1960's anymore.

Worse still, at the beginning of the new decade, that absolute pop icon the Beatles split up, the Labour Party was all over the place … and the country was about to abandon the imperial system Yes! No more rods, poles or perches! Goodbye to the ten bob note, and as for your threepenny bits, well they were things of the past. Mind you, decimalisation itself was a bit of a good old British compromise in that it really only involved the currency. Despite there being every intention of adopting all sorts of foreign stuff like kilogrammes and metres, there seemed to be a lack of detail as to when and how. Let's just say that the ownership of such un-British units remained an aspiration… we still had the hundredweight and the ounce to worry about, for heaven's sake.

Also, of course, we cunningly managed to hang on to quite a few coins which managed to sneak through the barbed wire barrier that was decimalisation. Thus the good old shilling became the 5p piece, the florin the new 10p coin, and most bizarrely of all, the trusty tanner - the *sixpence* - that a decade before would buy you three gob stoppers, a sherbet fountain and a copy of the Beano, was still there, and was worth a very un-decimal like **2½p**. So you'll be glad to know that our brand new **decimal** system gladly incorporated **fractions**. How pleased Miss Grant would have been that even well over a decade later, all those arithmetic lessons at Highland Road Juniors were still proving their worth. There was even a new **half pence** coin – a little bronze coloured jobby that managed to squirm its way down to the bottom of your pocket, or purse and jam itself into any handy crevice in such a tenacious way that it simply refused to come out. And we still had pints, and yards and acres and fathoms, so all was not lost – but you get my point that the seventies was a bit of a mish-mash right from the start?

What was difficult to get your head around was the *equivalence* of the new coinage. Despite being given lots of handy little conversion charts, most people spent months going around muttering to themselves such things as:

'... now if 75p is the new fifteen bob, and a florin is now 10p, have I been overcharged at Timothy Whites for a new broom handle, a tin of Brasso Magic Wadding and a small packet of Aspro which came to one pound fifty three and a half pence?'

It was all very confusing, and people were all pretty sure they were being ripped off – the main argument being that the smallest value coin, the new half pence, was now worth *more* than one whole, complete, utterly-as-nature-intended old penny. How could that be? How could things possibly be cheaper - or even the same - on February 15th 1971, when the smallest coin in the realm was now worth *twenty percent more than the smallest coin the day before?* For such grumblers, the fact that by 1971 the number of things you could buy for a single penny could almost be counted on the fingers of one finger - let alone one hand – was largely ignored by those who saw the move to decimal coinage as part of a sinister plot to make us all ***foreign.*** No wonder some looked back to the previous decade with ever greater nostalgia when comments such as: *'I can remember the good old days when you could buy an LP for eighteen and threepence three farthings, and half a crown would buy you twenty Woodbines, a tin of Ajax scouring powder and still leave you with tuppence ha'penny change'...* were frequently accompanied with a stifled sob and the need to dash a tear from many a manly eye. And that wasn't the only thing that set knees a-trembling.

In 1973 the government decided to have another go at joining the Common Market – this despite the fact that in 1967 the president of France, the monumentally ungrateful Charles de Gaulle, had for the second time in four years vetoed our application for membership with his famous reaction which boiled down to just one word: '**Non**!'

Well, back in the confident sixties, you can imagine that society's reaction to such repeated rejection could be summarised as:

'Well, up yours Froggy, we don't give a toss…. Oh and by the way, don't expect your onion sales to increase anytime soon!'

OK, perhaps not the government's formal position, but probably a pretty accurate summary nonetheless. So perhaps decimalisation of 1971 was a way of showing our continental chums that we really were serious about becoming more European – blimey, we even had a few centimetres knocking about the place for goodness sake – how much more convincing did they need? Mind you, the fact that the pint remained firmly entrenched in the nation's pubs was a source of great comfort in these changing times. But by 1973, I suppose we were starting to get a bit used to all this new stuff, and just as well, for on 1st January Edward *'The Grocer'* Heath, our portly Prime Minister signed us up for the EEC. In case you're wondering, that's the **European Economic Community** – the forerunner of today's EU. So after a decade or so of trying to get in and being rebuffed by De bleeding Gaulle, we were in! The Common Market, as it was more colloquially known, now had us as its newest member. Were we excited? Were we enthralled? Did we all dash out and buy a French onion and a Volkswagen to celebrate?

Well, no, not really. Lots of folk regarded such a move with suspicion, and the prospect of getting much benefit from what the politicians regarded as a seminal moment was lost on many. I suspect most people just gave such reports a glance and then turned to the sports pages to see how the footie was going. We were British after all… no need to get over-excited at the prospect of Johnnie Foreigner turning up on your doorstep with multi-coloured peppers and a sack full of aubergines anytime soon, surely?

More to the point, our new membership would boost our chances at the forthcoming *Eurovision* bash in Luxembourg, wouldn't it? Hopes were high… surely GB would sweep the board - after all, we'd joined their damned club, and after last year's win by someone called Vicky Leandros with a song no-one could pronounce (*'Après Toi'* for heaven's sake) then Cliff's rendition of *'Power to All Our Friends'* was a done deal surely? I mean, come on! Even the title alluded to the fact that we were now willing to be friends with all sorts of foreign people, so voting would be little more than a formality wouldn't it?

Well, you can imagine the disappointment when Cliff's excellent delivery only accumulated enough points to come in a plucky third…

and even worse, the winner was Luxembourg! Again! Two bleeding years running! And with yet another totally unpronounceable title: *'Tut Te Reconnaitras'!* The only compensation was that Germany came eighth and France came second to bottom, so at least that was OK.

So, attention turned to more immediate, more local issues. There were things to be getting on with, and many a Baby Boomer with a very tentative foothold on the bottom rung of the property ladder found that there was a good deal more to occupy free time than worrying about what went wrong with the most recent failure in our Eurovision bid. Home ownership then as now, was a big deal, and getting somewhere nice to live played a major part in most people's aspirations. In some cities – and mine was a case in point - the early sixties had seen the final so called 'slum clearance' programmes which had provided space for high rise blocks of flats. I can remember gazing with awe as prefabricated sections of these massive tower blocks were hoisted into place – complete with external pebble-dashing, glazed windows, and all plumbing and cabling ready installed. The only thing missing seemed to be a window box full of geraniums.

At the time, these impressive structures seemed to be the answer to the housing need created by the loss of so many tiny back-to-back houses. But a decade later, serious questions were beginning to emerge about such high rise blocks. Rather than being the light and airy solution to the pokey and primitive houses they replaced, a considerable proportion of them seemed to be developing unthought of problems of their own: people felt isolated; connecting walkways and corridors were sometimes long and intimidating; there were few recreational areas where people could meet - and the lifts didn't always work. So by the mid seventies, it was not surprising that those with the wherewithal to do so were looking to other housing solutions.

As a result, their eyes turned to that other icon of the age - the vast new housing estates that were springing up all over the place. Bit by bit, the serried ranks of large-windowed but very boxy little two and three bedroomed houses came to adorn many a field and hillside around the edges of towns and cities. It is perhaps surprising for the current home-seeker generation to note that these new homes in the 1970's were much more sought after than older Georgian and Victorian houses. Seems unbelievable? Incredible to think that these often tiny and hastily constructed units should have an appeal greater than their solid and well constructed predecessors?

Well, again, it's a matter of context. The Baby Boomer generation was coming of age, but was immersed in its own tidal wave of modernism that had been generated in the sixties. The unspoken mantra seemed to be *'all that was modern must be good'*. And in some ways such a view was right. For a start, all new homes were dry, and they had the built-in sophistication of fitted bathrooms and internal toilets. Generally speaking too, they were relatively draught free and warm – some even having central heating - a very new concept for the majority of the population. Another attraction was that estates were constructed with an eye to being a self-contained community, with an infrastructure of shops, library, church, doctor's surgery and a school and so became very appealing to a generation keen to start family life.

Yes, we were aware of the concerns about uniformity… had not the satirist Pete Seeger got himself a hit in the sixties with his song *'Little Boxes'* - houses *'made of ticky-tacky and they all looked just the same'*? Well, that was true, but to be honest, to a generation increasingly keen to use its Mothercare gift vouchers, living in a dry, warm and comfortable house with its own parking bay and space for a pram in the hall was the absolute priority. The fact that a proportion

were shoddily constructed was not always given the attention it merited - but at the time it was really much more a matter of saying goodbye to damp and unpleasant flats, and getting your own roof over your head.

In addition, it should be borne in mind that the majority of affordable Victorian and Edwardian homes that were on the market at that time were un-modernised. To say that re-roofing, re-wiring and installing modern plumbing in these otherwise substantial properties was beyond the skill and affordability of most aspirant home owners, is to put it mildly. For many the choice between old and new was simple: had the term *'no brainer'* been around then, it would have been in frequent use.

That is not to say that the choice of a modern home didn't have unforeseen consequences for some. Rather conspicuous amongst these was the fact that some recently purchased modern houses seemed to be sagging a bit. The summer of 1976 saw a protracted and very hot dry spell which rapidly declined into a proper drought. Whilst many were attracted to the local authority's advice to save water by *'taking a bath with a friend'* (I kid you not) others were more concerned that a number of ominous looking cracks had suddenly appeared in the walls of their new semi. The problem was that quite a goodly number of new homes had been constructed on land which was susceptible to shrinkage in times of drought, and thus the inevitable movement in the foundations was causing a lot of structural problems. As a result, many young home owners found themselves heading for the nearest hardware shop to invest in a packet or two of Polyfilla. To be honest, even our staunchest friend, the ubiquitous roll of sellotape, was not really up to the job of holding the house together, and it was therefore perhaps fortunate that 1976 was just about the start of the DIY craze.

Sure, there had been many a keen home handyman before this time, and the famous *'Practical Householder'* magazine had been popular since the 1950's. However, to the new generation of home-owners, it seemed perhaps just a little bit old fashioned. Also, the self-build suggestions within its pages were daunting for the average young home owner: it was not everyone who could turn their hand to creating a whole new dining suite from just three wooden orange crates, two eight foot lengths of four by two timber and a roll of Fablon sticky-back. What was needed for the aspirant 1970's home-owner was a warehouse that was full of stuff which you could purchase and sling up on the wall to hide any nasty cracks… and the newly popular DIY stores were just the job. Here you could, for the first time, peruse what was on offer to convert your little two up, two down terraced house into a fine example of contemporary living complete with built-in furniture, multi-shelved room divider and trendy table lamp made from an outsized Cointreau bottle. Groovy or what?

And another advantage was that you could amble around the DIY store without fear of making yourself vulnerable to the sort of advice that owners of smaller handyman shops were so keen to offer, and which so often revealed your embarrassing lack of experience to undertake the proposed work. Local experts always seemed too ready to offer advice which was normally preceded by a raised eyebrow and a long and audible intake of breath followed by the like of:

'Well, if you take my advice, you need at least half a dozen galvanised double hanger brackets each attached by threaded two inch Whitworths, and even then I wouldn't put any weight on it; to be honest, Evostick is all right for mending a flip-flop, but for building in your twin tub and over counter draining board... well, rather you than me son!'

Nevertheless, DIY was immensely popular in the seventies. To be sure, it was largely out of necessity as such improvements were a lot cheaper, and if you wanted to turn your little pied-a-terre into a trendy must-have residence, filling up the trolley with the necessaries and digging out the old paint brush was the way to do it. And didn't the seventies offer some decorative choices?! If you ever wanted confirmation that the decade was seeking desperately to give itself a separate identity, then you need look no further than the area of what was considered to be *chic* in the contemporary home decoration market. This can most easily be summarised as **LOUD** and **COLOURFUL**.. I blame Dulux.

At this time a whole new range of paints became available - a riot of different colours in matt, eggshell and gloss finishes could be purchased at modest prices and in large amounts. As well as that, woodchip paper suddenly appeared, and this was the perfect answer to the home which had recently acquired a number of interesting cracks in its internal plasterwork. Woodchip paper was, as its name suggests, a heavy and lengthy roll of coarse paper impregnated with a mass of splinter sized bits of wood. I suggest it had probably been invented by someone who had just completed pasting a piece of wallpaper when a thoughtless spouse opened the window on to a garden where the next door neighbour was getting seriously out of control with a chainsaw. A gust of wind - and hey presto! ... the perfect amalgam for rough wall covering, just right for literally papering over the cracks. What's more, it hid all imperfections by making **everything** look imperfect! All you needed now was to slap on a load of paint, and there you were.

Unfortunately, such heady enthusiasm seemed to promote a national condition which can best be described as *'extreme lack of taste'*. Thus, the 1970's homeowner could frequently be seen purchasing large tins of violently coloured paint, in the misguided belief that strong colours would cheer the place up, and make the sixties look old-fashioned. Oh dear. Just how many thousands of homes witnessed bright orange woodchip covered walls we shall never know. Worse still, a deep rich brown gloss became unbelievably popular, as did luminescent yellow and a rather frightening shade of green. Subtle it was not. In addition, wallpaper manufacturers realising that the world had suddenly gone completely bonkers, started churning out the most garishly printed stuff ever seen. Chief amongst these were massive orange, purple or magenta flowers. I can still remember the comment of a friend of mine who came round to our house after we had finished papering our front room with wallpaper of this type. He entered the room, and turned to us and said *'You're very brave!'*

Well, you can imagine our chagrin; we'd spent over three quid on two rolls of famous Vymura wallpaper, nearly seventy pence on paste, plus the cost of two pairs of sunglasses so that we could look at the result without exposing our eyeballs to too much brilliant visual stimulation, totally necessary after a hard night on the Don Cortez cheapo wine. Not only that, our florid chimney breast was central to the whole chic lounge /diner ambience, for heaven's sake; we'd even gone so far as to buy a few bricks and a couple of planks to make a bijou and semi rustic shelving unit for our flash new music centre, of which we and Currys were proud part-owners. So what's not to like?

Well, just about everything, really. The one saving grace of the Vymura wallpaper range was that it was really a sort of paper-backed thin plastic sheet, and taking if off again was therefore a doddle. All you needed to do was to prize up a tiny corner of the plastic, and then you could tear away the whole piece, leaving the paper lining behind. To be honest, it became such a rewarding experience – especially compared with the traditional method of soaking wallpaper with water, then scratching away with a rusty old scraper only to get about a quarter of a square inch off at a time – that I swear some people bought it just for the pleasure of ripping it all off again.

Yep... this is it: our front room. Bear in mind too that the photo has faded over the fifty plus years since it was taken. Aspirin anyone?

But woodchip paper was something else, especially if it had been painted with brown gloss. Such a combination was impervious to any form of attack short of a flame thrower or pneumatic drill: the only way of overcoming your decorative indiscretion was to cover it up with another layer of paper, and hope to hell that the brown didn't seep through. But woodchip paper was thick and knobbly - so what could you cover it up with? Why, *more* woodchip paper, of course.

So in this way, many a DIY Baby Boomer, after applying several layers of this dubious material found that there were serious shortcomings to the process: for a start, as the layers went on, rooms were getting correspondingly smaller, and windows and doors which once opened easily enough were now much more reluctant to do so. Furthermore, there were several folk who, after the most recent application of yet another woodchip layer, found themselves thinking - *'you know, I'm sure there was a serving hatch between this room and the kitchen, but where the hell is it?'*

Regrettably, such decorative madness didn't stop at wall cladding alone. Oh no. You have to bear in mind that for many, this was a first foray into the world of home ownership, where the luxuries of having your own kitchen, bathroom and toilet were a given – not something all of our parents' generation could depend upon, certainly. That such provision came at the same time as the seventies decade was desperately searching for its own identity and decided to go for the ***totally flamboyant and completely over-the-top look,*** was just an unhappy coincidence.

Thus, many a standard white ceramic bathroom suite was ripped out to be replaced by something more plastic, and certainly more colourful. Perhaps a tasteful butter-cream shade? An understated hint of primrose? The merest misting of a subtle rose pink perhaps? Nope. Not a bit of it! What we went for were deep maroons, a yellow that would have outshone the double *'No Parking'* lines in the high street, and best of all, a morose and angry green *avocado* – the sort of colour that made early lino seem almost cheerful.

Given today's predilection for light, neutral shades, you cannot really imagine the visual assault such decoration had upon the senses. For a start, there was the completely bonkers idea that painting bright colours on the walls would make your house brighter and livelier too. Of course, it had the reverse effect and made returning after a heavy day to your little maroon and avocado nest something of a challenge to even the hardiest adherent of such extremes. I'd like to say it ended there – but it didn't. Someone suddenly realised that there were other means of covering up cracks, and another new material was pressed into service to not only cover up the blemishes, but to add warmth as well… and thus *polystyrene tiles* made their debut.

Now on the face of it, these thin, light, easily fixed little tiles seemed just the job: they were simply stuck to walls or ceilings where they looked nice and white, or, of course, you could paint them. With a bit of extra paste, they could even be persuaded to stick to woodchip paper, for heaven's sake. Added to this, was the fact that they were good thermal insulators, so you got all sorts of benefits with just one easy application. What's more they could be cut with a pair of scissors if you didn't want to fork out for a nifty little battery powered device that heated up a wire and allowed you to cut all sorts of intricate shapes by melting the stuff. Sure, it released a fairly noxious odour when doing so, but hey! - your new cosy ceiling cladding was only a few dozen tiles away! And so it was. Some tiles even had a cracked ice pattern cunningly etched into the surface. That no one at the time seemed to notice the irony of using a deliberately cracked look to cover an already cracked ceiling defies explanation; perhaps it was the nineteen seventies version of *'hiding in plain sight'*.

The problem was, polystyrene tiles had a habit of detaching themselves from time to time, and for no apparent reason. Although their fall posed no immediate threat to those beneath, it could be embarrassing if a gust of wind slammed the door, and a number of tiles came floating down to adorn your new shag pile at the very moment the neighbours had popped in to listen to your Barry Manilow LP on the new music centre. Also, it might have been helpful if someone could have done some pretty basic tests on polystyrene, as although it was an efficient thermal insulator, it was also a fire risk in the sense that once ignited, it gave off noxious fumes… so all in all, not a particularly suitable material with which to clad your walls and ceilings?

At the risk of going on endlessly, let me just take a moment more of your time, which I hope will bring this sorry decorator's tale to an end. The one other material which people turned to in droves in the seventies was **Artex**. Now this was something which could not easily be applied by the enthusiastic amateur. It was, after all, a plaster based treatment, and needed a bit of skill to apply successfully. The process involved coating ceilings with a thin layer of plaster, and then stippling it all over to produce what amounted to an inverted mountain landscape… thousands upon thousands of little jagged stalactites, all brilliant and shiny white, their deeply etched peaks and troughs covering up all sorts of ceiling blemishes with an efficiency neither paint nor paper could hope to emulate. And it was so durable! You could slam your doors to your heart's content and relax in the knowledge that such drama would never be accompanied by an unwanted shower of little pointy bits of plaster. Some people liked it so much, that they also had it applied as a durable and trendy *wall covering*. And that's probably where certain doubts may have started to creep in. You see, even with a coat of paint, the little pointy bits remained just that – pointy… in fact, really quite sharp. Thus tripping over a rug and putting out your hand to arrest your fall could in itself be pretty hazardous: in short, Artex covered walls could be painful.

Now if, like me, you would prefer to have your house decorated with stuff that doesn't actually attack you, then having a wall covering that was a close cousin to a particularly well endowed cheese grater doesn't seem a great idea. What's more, once on it was almost impossible to get it off again – not without completely destroying the original plasterwork upon which it was laid. Many a DIY fanatic would attack an unwanted patch with little more than a wall paper scraper, a piece of sand paper and a look of grim determination. If the very opposite of Vymura wallpaper stripping gives you a picture of the impossibility of this operation, you will not be surprised to learn that most people in this predicament either just knocked off the mountain peaks and convinced themselves the resulting lumpy bumpy mess was really quite attractive, and didn't at all look like someone had *'smeared the wall with porridge'* as the yob next door had suggested, or they discovered that the only other realistic solution was to move house.

If the seventies lacked the distinctive and unique charisma of its predecessor, then one of the ways it did make its own mark was in the world of small screen entertainment. The notion of the nation-wide audience really took off in the decade, and there were some really ground-breaking programmes which achieved audience numbers previously unheard of. For the young generation (and Baby Boomers still considered themselves young ... or at any rate young-ish) *'Monty Python's Flying Circus'* was a major hit, and did for seventies' TV what *'The Goon Show'* had done for fifties' radio. That it was misunderstood by many of the older generation who preferred the predictable security of *'Terry and June'* gave the programme even more allure, and the latest episode frequently became the topic of conversation at work the following day. Thus at any one time in any coffee bar, sandwich shop or works' canteen, there would be thousands of people doing their best to imitate John Cleese's *Ministry of Funny Walks* routine, and probably coming a cropper at the all important 'about face, direction change' moment.

At the other end of the scale, was BBC's *'It's A Knock-Out!'* which had the added frisson of competition between towns... and later between countries. Although the series started in the late sixties, it really took off in the seventies, and became a must-watch for thousands of families grouped around their TV – many of which were now colour sets. And a good job too, for the colours in 'Knockout' were anything but subtle – but then, neither was the programme. Come on now... what could be better than seeing someone dressed up as a massive orange and purple squirrel booting another similarly encumbered rodent into a pool of bright green slime? And if the victim happened to be a bloke called Fritz from Dusseldorf, then surely, it had to be the best thing ever, didn't it?

1973 saw the first broadcast of another TV show which drew an enormous audience, and had an added bonus in that it promoted a huge amount of unexpected audience participation. The show was *'Some Mothers Do 'Ave 'Em'* starring the brilliant Michael Crawford as the unique Frank Spencer. Endearing and exasperating in equal proportions, the character of Frank was like nothing we'd seen before: to say he was 'accident prone' would be like saying Niagara Falls are a bit damp. Not only were the stunts carried out by Michael an absolute sensation (in fact, as soon as you put this book down, I demand that you go and look at the roller-skating episode on YouTube) but they were like nothing seen before in a British sitcom.

And the audience participation? Well, not everyone was keen to roller skate while holding tight to the passenger rail of a bus, not to mention zooming between the wheels of a speeding juggernaut – but what just about every bloke who ever watched the programme *did* do, was to adopt a shocked expression, put his knees together and raise his fist to his mouth and say '***Oooooooooooh Betty!!!***' - a catch phrase which probably had the biggest following of any in the decade. Doesn't sound much? Well, that short phrase alone led millions of blokes into believing that they were great impersonators, as well as providing the stimulus for an animated discussion of the '*and did you see it when he dropped through the roof?!*' type.

So this was the telly-glue which went a long way towards holding families together at a time when many younger members were drifting off to far flung places with strange sounding names... well to Weston-Super-Mare at any rate. And that's not all. There was a whole range of new TV programmes which lit up our lives, and which have remained favourites ever since: *'Dad's Army', 'Yes Minister', 'Porridge', 'Fawlty Towers'* and *'The Good Life'* to name but a few. In 1973, the popular *'Tonight'* early evening magazine programme was replaced by the appropriately named *Nationwide* which was screened every weekday after the news. It was a major player in introducing the notion of local TV by programming in regional slots within the overall programme – a

If ever a title was self- explanatory, this was it. BBC1's Nationwide meant that we all knew what everyone else was up to wherever they lived.

At a time when home brewing was popular, wasn't being further self-sufficient like Tom and Barbara Good simply the next logical step?

new departure for the time, but one which went a long way towards knitting the nation together, and helping people to feel less isolated.

Of course, there were the more serious programmes like *'Panorama'* and ITV's *'This Week'* to keep you up to date with the grim realities of life. Because the seventies turned out to be an uncomfortable time politically, there were all too many of these, and of General Elections there seemed to be an over-sufficiency. Also, there was a great deal of industrial unrest with the trades unions frequently at loggerheads with management. Pictures from picket lines throughout the country were commonplace, and as the eighties commenced, industrial relations appeared to be at an all time low. Such negativity seemed to diminish the country's ability to make good decisions regarding what it should manufacture to satisfy consumer appetite, and nowhere was this more clearly demonstrated than in the British motor industry.

From 1973 until the early eighties, British Leyland (an amalgam of several old and famous companies including Austin and Morris) tried desperately to convince its customers that the *Austin Allegro,* introduced that year, was the answer to all their motoring dreams and aspirations. It wasn't. It was really pretty awful. For a start it had a **square** steering wheel. Now I don't know about you, but to me the most dependable – indeed *essential* - characteristic one might ascribe to any wheel is that it should be ROUND. The Allegro's wasn't. Heaven alone knows why, but it may be that the designers thought it would be a bit *edgy*, a bit of a *groovy design statement...* something indeed, of which no other car could boast. Well, they might as well have agreed to make the road wheels square as well, or put the headlights inside the boot for all the difference it made. That the anticipated sales never really materialised is hardly surprising. Mind you, square steering wheel aside - and the fact that most mechanics quickly

Quite attractive for the time, but the Austin Allegro developed an unenviable reputation.

[168]

came to refer to the car as the '*Austin All Agro*' as it was a bit of a beast to work on – its one saving grace was that it did in fact look quite nice. So if you wanted a British car to just sit in the drive looking quite inoffensive, then the Allegro may have been just up your street. In fact probably the *only one* up your street, as the relatively small number that were sold spent quite a lot of time down at the local workshop having bits replaced.

Lest I seem to be victimising poor old British Leyland, let me remind you that other home-based car manufacturers didn't exactly cover themselves in glory either. Although there were some very popular designs, such as the ubiquitous Ford Escort and the Vauxhall Viva, the biggest problem was not with the design, it was with durability. Let me give you a personal example. In 1980 we bought an eight year old Morris Marina – another of BMC's less than glamorous products. Nevertheless, it was OK, reasonably comfortable, and big enough to accommodate on the back seat the carry cot of a very small person who had just recently joined our family. Before you jump up and down in rage and reach for the phone to call the appropriate authority to report a forty year old case of child negligence, let me remind you that in those days, Health and Safety didn't really exist. Children could sit on the back seat totally unrestrained. Although there were seat belts, their use both in the back and front of cars was not rigorously enforced. However, let me help you to smooth your troubled brow by informing you that we were not so careless of our new-born that we didn't strap the carry cot in. That this precaution was far less robust than the full body armour into which children are inserted these days is simply an indication that car safety – along with just about every other area of personal well-being and survival - was 'a work in progress' at that time.

So let's get back to the old Marina. Unfortunately, like almost all other cars of the period, it was plagued with what might be called 'body shell durability' problems. In other words, cars of the period were very, very prone to rust. Ours was a case in point; despite being less than ten years old, there was ominous movement beneath the shiny bright orange paintwork, and soon little brown speckles started to appear around door sills, wheel arches and… well, just about every other area really. Slowly but surely, the surface area of the car was taking on the appearance, relief and texture of wood chip paper. That the car was largely held together by the unreliable envelope of its bright orange paintwork was fairly apparent, the proof being that when we came to sell it, a potential purchaser rested his hand on the nearside wing, and putting just a little pressure on the area was somewhat surprised when that very hand disappeared in a shower of rust, and ended up on the top of the front wheel. My explanation that … *'Yes, there is a little surface corrosion, and anyway, the newly revealed aperture gives the lucky new owner an improved means of checking on how tyre wear and upper suspension brackets are progressing'* didn't really cut the mustard.

But our dear old Marina was not alone. Rust was a really bad problem, and seemed to affect British cars more than the new arrivals from the Far East: the Datsuns and Nissans of the period seemed to be much better in almost every respect. Poor old British Leyland. Even with its new lineup featuring the Mini Metro did little to halt its eventual slide into oblivion. In 1980, the Morris Ital was introduced as an updated version of the Marina. It was supposed to be *New! Exciting! Having all the flare and passion of its Italian parentage!* Shame really. It was so obviously just a Marina with a few bits added to make it look a bit trendy, but was no more convincing than if, say, a city gent wearing a pin striped three piece and a bowler hat, had stuck a false moustache on his upper lip and said: *'Look! I'm French!'* And the name? What's an **Ital**, for heaven's sake? Another home goal, that's what, because like the All Agro, more than a few nicknamed the car the **'It'll'** on the grounds that **'It'll** *spend most of its life in the garage'* … ho ho.

So if motoring was pretty poor at home, where better to turn than to our transatlantic pals to see if their automotive industry was doing any better. And there was indeed something to admire, because the mid seventies suddenly had an injection of something big, powerful and noisy – the American fast-back sports coupe. Head and shoulders above the rest was the car driven by the new TV heroes Starsky and Hutch. Not only was it a fast and aggressive looking car – it also had a novel and awe-inspiring paint job: a white stripe that extended from one front wheel arch to the other via the huge doors and rear of the roof. Wow! How good was that?!! Well, pretty good by all accounts, for all of a sudden such extravagant paint jobs began to

A cool dude: Starsky & Hutch's wheels

appear on customized British cars as well. Mind you, the white stripe applied to a humble Austin Metro somehow failed to hit the spot and made it look... well, completely ridiculous really. It seemed to have escaped the notice of those motivated to plaster their motor with such iconic paintwork, that it was the *performance* and *rough handling* qualities of the car that were of much more important than the white stripe. So if your third-hand Ford Anglia on its spindly little wheels struggled to get from 0 to 60 mph in a shade under a quarter of an hour, you were somehow missing the point a bit, weren't you?

And as if to rub it in, shortly afterwards came another American TV series with a robust car: '*The Dukes of Hazzard*' with the mighty Dodge Charger nicknamed General Lee fulfilling the required motoring role. Rather than a trendy white stripe across the roof, this car featured a large **01** plastered across its bright orange door. And guess what? There were more than a few (thousand) British car owners who decided to emulate such a butch go-anywhere-anytime vehicle with the said numbers. Laugh? Well no, not really.

Although it would be quite wrong to say that there were no good British cars in that period, the industry as a whole could be seen as just a symptom of the sad overall malaise which seemed to have settled over the country. Regrettably, the late seventies and a lot of the eighties were difficult times for British industry. Industrial relations reached an all time low with the miners' strike, and the confrontation between police and pickets at Orgreave Colliery in 1984 was perhaps the ugliest example of how the unwillingness of both sides to listen to the other can quickly lead to chaos. Not a happy time.

But it was not all four day working weeks, power cuts, strikes and confrontation! With our nation's inherent ability to find cheerful and happy things in the midst of all sorts of bad news and grim reality, we did just that. For as well as watching *'It's a Knockout'* with its ever present gleeful prospect of seeing some foreigner plastered from head to toe in pink blancmange, there was a new hobby that quite literally helped us to forget the day to day problems of the world by producing a sometimes quite startling level of inebriation: **home-brew.**

It's perhaps a little hard to imagine that just forty years ago, the availability of booze was still very restricted. For a start, closing times in pubs were strictly adhered to, and the traditional call of *'Time, Gentlemen Please'* at 10.30pm was still very much in use. Pubs opening all day long was virtually unheard of and added to that, buying anything alcoholic to take home was still quite a performance. Supermarkets were only slowly gearing up to the revolution in booze supply that was just around the corner, and the trip to the off-licence was still the main source of alcohol in the home. That is until some bright little spark started hit on what appeared to be a fantastic solution: why not take the nation's affection for DIY one stage further by re-directing the enthusiasm for building *room divider and matching nuclear fall-out bunker* to **Do–It–Yourself booze?**

What a great idea! Thus was born the craze for homebrew. Now, that is not to say that wine or beer had never been produced in the home before. Clearly, there was a long tradition, especially in rural areas for the production of country wines such as *Dandelion and Burdock*, or *Rosehip and Birch*. What was different now however, was that the practice and process of producing both wine and beer at home was actively promoted as a pleasurable, rewarding and deeply satisfying use of your spare time. All of a sudden, your local parade of shops would be joined by an establishment proudly displaying all the equipment you would need to keep yourself, your family and friends happily smashed out of their brains for the foreseeable future - and all for next to nothing!!!

Well, that was the theory – indeed it was the vision that many a young chap had as he strode manfully into the homebrew shop, and was immediately confronted with something akin to a medieval alchemist's laboratory: row upon row of shiny glass demijohns, a few miles of plastic piping, rubber bungs by the thousand, little plastic jobbies that stirred old memories of the chemistry lab back at school, and which were stuck into the tops of your brewing equipment to make continual glurping noises for the next six months... and so on. And there was always some very keen bloke in corduroy trousers and short-sleeved argyle jumper bursting to tell you about how he had just finished brewing sixty five gallons of *'Old Rot Gut'* milk stout as well as three dozen bottles of *Stinging Nettle and Marrow Peeling* wine that *'tasted just like champagne, but better'*. Oh yeah?

Mind you, the sales patter must have been pretty good, because I was only one amongst thousands of gullible idiots who raced home with a considerable yardage of plastic piping, a dozen demijohns (just to get me started, you'll understand) and many a packet of odd-smelling stuff which would convert itself into foaming pints of beer and glistening flutes of the finest wine in the merest twinkling of an eye.

And so began the national pastime of trying to impress upon friends and neighbours that the booze you had produced was in any way worth drinking. All too frequently, the results of home brewing became a matter of hoping that your ghastly, over-sweetened mess - whose main feature was an overwhelming flavour of sodium metabisulphate sterilising fluid - would be passed off as *'interesting'*. Honesty forces me to confess however, that the response to such a scenario was a depressingly consistent **'Strewth... What the hell is that?!!'** Often this was quickly followed by the ungrateful recipient hopping around the living room with a hanky rammed in his mouth before heading to the nearest loo to part company with the fruit of your labours.

Mind you, we should have known. The liberties that many a Baby Boozer took with the home-brew process were huge. For example, just about anything organic was included in the recipe, a good example being the 'banana skin aperitif' produced by one of my friends. It was great if you wanted a tonsillectomy, or to rid yourself of unwanted woodchip wallpaper, but as a sophisticated pre-dinner tipple it lacked that certain something: fitness for human consumption, for a start.

The trouble was, you had to be prepared to take *time and trouble* if you wanted to get anything near a reasonable outcome. That's not to say the results weren't alcoholic – they most certainly were. The fact that this was the case was probably the reason why most people kept up the hobby for such a long time: if you could neck the stuff down fast enough, you could very quickly get to the stage where you were immune to the vile taste ... in fact you were probably immune to just about everything that was going on all around you. Suddenly, from your horizontal position behind the sofa, with your right leg beguilingly lodged in the waste paper basket, the world was a beautiful place... and the people in it were also beautiful ... and perhaps that *peapod and cauliflower root* booze wasn't so bad after all, provided you sieved out the green lumpy bits with your teeth before you swallowed. Hey ho.

Despite the fact that some folk persevered and really did produce some good wines, I would say that for the majority of Baby Boomers, the experiment could well go down in history as a gallant failure, and I wouldn't mind betting that there are still thousands of attics around the country which right at this moment are the final resting place for many a demijohn - and have been so for many years.

With the coming of easily accessible, reasonably cheap and even better - DRINKABLE booze - many home brewers turned to the easier option, just keeping a few remaining bottles of home-brew for extra Christmas presents for someone you *really* didn't like. There were even those who had the temerity to take such offerings to a bring-a-bottle party, in the hope that they could slip it on to the table when no one was looking, and then proceed to drink everyone else's store-bought wine. Disgraceful behaviour? You bet! And in case you think it was me... well, shame on you! I didn't. I used mine in the garden to clean the slimy mildew off the fence - and very effective it was too.

And so to other aspects of the domestic scene. It won't have escaped your notice that the narrative so far has alluded a few times to the next generation gradually coming onto the scene. Yes, for many a Baby Boomer the late seventies/early eighties was a time to put aside childish things such as free time and getting up when you felt like it at the weekend: this was the time to forsake your weekly visit to *Burtons the*

Tailors … and get on down to *Mothercare*! The time had come when babygrows and terry towelling nappies were suddenly getting in the way on the washing line, and the tiny space many a bloke had allotted to him in the bathroom cabinet had suddenly been totally taken over by tins of baby powder and bottles of tasty gripe water. The early eighties in particular found many of us spending the wee small hours endlessly pushing a pram up and down the front room in a desperate attempt to get the howling off-spring to sleep whilst muttering: **'give it a rest and go to sleep for gawd's sake! I've got to go to work on three hours' time, and I think the battery's flat on the Allegro!'**

Regrettably, such reasoned logic seldom had the desired effect, and fatigue was a constant companion, making the affixing of a fresh nappy each morning an even more hazardous operation. You see, in those days there were relatively few disposable nappies; babies' messy bits were swathed in a great square piece of towelling, and this had to be folded in a particular way to fit even the least bit comfortably – and then kept in place with a gigantic safety pin whose enormous spiky bit was, quite frankly, a threat to life, limb and fingers of parent and baby alike. So, given the fact that both Mum and Dad had probably endured a sleepless night, the bottle steriliser had developed a crack and leaked all over the kitchen floor, the pram had big scratches all down the side where you'd collided with the Artex wall during your night time attempts to pacify the grumpy little git, it was really quite remarkable that survival levels amongst our nearest and dearest were so high.

Now don't get me wrong – we weren't in any way reluctant or careless parents. On the contrary there seemed to be stacks of advice about how to do *this*, how to do *that*, how to ensure your child grows up to be a happy and fulfilled adult – and by and large we followed it all to the letter. And it all felt terribly *modern*, so *new age*, such an *advance* upon what we had been subjected to when we were kids, surely? But of course, it was nothing of the sort. Devotion to an infant has always been – and will always be – an instinctive reaction, and we were no better than any other generation.

Mind you, in comparison with our own babyhood, we did have a lot more kids' TV to provide welcome entertainment for our tinies. BBC

TV's *'Playschool'* and the like were great for junior – and provided a welcome distraction for many a hard-pressed adult fretting over the apparently out of control rate of inflation, the state of the nation's economy and where the hell had you put the last two books of Green Shield Stamps you had spent at least eighteen months collecting?

In fact, the adult world at that time was heavily populated with concerns about money. Unrealistic wage demands, the industrial strikes they provoked and other unrest in the work place were depressingly common, and there was a bit of a feeling of 'just try to keep your head down and carry on'. …and increase the volume on the music centre.

If you are unfamiliar with the latter, it was a machine which combined a record player, radio and tape deck all in one lavishly dialled wood-veneered box – and the more smoky grey plastic covers and cute little dials and knobs, the better. Also, they often had separate speakers which could then be sited at various locations around your lounge,

Lots of buttons, lights and smoked glass: the perfect recipe for a trendy music centre.

providing perhaps for the first time a magnificent opportunity to go arse over head when you tripped on the wire whilst carrying a tray full of home-brew for your friends. Despite these hazards, such equipment was popular, even though each part of the ensemble seldom did as good a job as those bought individually. Never mind! They looked nice on the brick-and-plank shelf unit, and despite the tendency of cassettes to inexplicably wrap about a furlong of thin audio tape tightly around just about every spool and pinion within a six foot radius of the machine, the music centre was a source of considerable pride.

And there was some exceptionally good stuff to play on it too - for all of a sudden, the period's music seemed to find a confidence that hitherto had been dwarfed by the pre-eminence of the sixties. Although at one end of the market there was still such memorable stuff as the ever subtle *'Leap Up and Down, Wave Your Knickers in the Air'*, the same period encompassed such wonderful numbers as Simon and Garfunkle's *'Bridge Over Troubled Waters'*, and Kate Bush's ethereal *'Wuthering Heights'*. And, of course, this was also the age of Queen. When Freddie Mercury produced *'Bohemian Rhapsody'* in 1975, it caused a sensation, especially when combined with the ground-breaking TV promotional footage which was pumped out full blast on *Top of the Pops*. There were a lot of others doing good stuff too – Abba, The Police, David Bowie and Michael Jackson to name but a few.

TV too seemed to step up yet another gear; I don't know if it was the influence of the huge bright foam rubber costumes so popular in *'Jeux Sans Frontieres'* (nee *'It's A Knockout'*) that did it, but two other programmes appeared to take such technology a stage further. The first of these was Jim Henson's *'The Muppet Show'* whose soon-to-be famous list of characters included Kermit the Frog, Miss Piggy and Gonzo the Great. The music hall setting featuring both front of stage acts and behind the scene dramas was a stroke of genius, and added a whole new level of comedy.

Not far behind was *'Spitting Image'* which moved political satire into a brand new realm. Again, foam rubber was the principal material used by Peter Fluck and Roger Law to create the instantly recognisable characters. If there was ever a decade in which it was necessary to take the piss out of our political masters, this was it... and it was done so well. I suppose you could say that the brilliantly depicted caricatures were really a 'live' version of the political cartoon – indeed, they were often very hard-hitting, and sometimes verged on cruel. Nevertheless, the programme had a huge following and was really quite influential. When the Social Democratic Party under David Owen and the Liberals under David Steel got together to form a political alliance which lasted for most of the eighties (and morphed into the Lib-Dems in 1989), Spitting Image always presented David Steel as a tiny little fellow totally overshadowed by the tall, dark and sinister David Owen. The former later said that such imagery was a constant source of aggravation, and that such lampooning had had an effect upon his political career. Well, that may have been the case, but suffice it to say, the programme certainly brought politics to the fore, and gave everyone a weekly opportunity to laugh at their political masters.

The two Davids on Spitting Image. I'll leave it to you to work out which is which.

So there you go. The mid-seventies to the mid-eighties was a period when we Baby Boomers realised that we were not quite the young and trendy groovers we had been just a few years before, and found us surrounded by other depressingly grown-up responsibilities. Chief amongst these was earning the wherewithal to feed an extra mouth or two, and even getting all serious about school choices for the kids. Set this against the other pressing needs of the age – such as finding out just where you could get a good deal on Farley's Rusks, and urgent issues like wondering just how much longer you could put up with the gross excesses of the floral wallpaper - and you can see that it was not all plain sailing. Confidence, as ever, was the key – and to plaster your Ford Anglia with Starsky and Hutch stripes took a hell of a lot of that. But hey! ... this was the age of diversity, when anoraks with go-faster stripes down the sleeves were everywhere ... and for blokes, a really weird snorkel jacket was king.

This curious garment was a development from the parka anorak worn by the Mods in the sixties – except that it was now made out of a brightly coloured quilted synthetic fabric whose crowning glory was a strip of what looked suspiciously like rat's fur around the end of its capacious hood. I say *hood*, but when the whole ensemble was zipped up to its full extent, this normally benign part of the design took on a life of its own by converting itself into the shape of a horizontal tube projecting a good six or eight inches out from your face – hence the 'snorkel' description of the garment. The theory was that when you wore it completely done up you felt utterly insulated from anything the weather could throw at you. The problem was, you were also completely insulated from *seeing* anything around you as your field of vision was now similar to that of one of those early deep sea divers with

Someone who thought an anorak with red go-faster stripes was a good idea. Yes, it's me.

the big metal helmets... and they had side windows! The snorkel did not. The result was that blokes would go blundering about holding conversations with people who had taken their leave several streets ago, totally oblivious of just about everything. To find out where you were, you had to do a complete three-sixty, and even then you couldn't see your feet. But at least you were warm... lost, but warm.

And there's no need for you ladies to smirk at how foolish the blokes looked – for not long after came the introduction of the SHELL SUIT. If you think that green rayon snorkels were the most bizarre thing ever, then think again. I can only surmise that some designer somewhere had noted that there was simply no more room anywhere to sew on yet another set of trendy stripes to a track suit, and decided something radical was needed – and preferably something that would highlight the vast array of garish colours that were now available in the new synthetic materials. Thus the dreaded shell suit was born... and worn by thousands and thousands of dear souls – from tiny toddlers to the quite elderly, who should have known better. Accompanied by the compulsory white simulated leather trainers, each with its own starkly vivid array of *GF* stripes, the look was immensely popular. And the name? Well, I can only suggest that the term 'shell' was chosen because the shiny colours of the material possessed iridescence not unlike that of the mother-of-pearl interior of many a sea-shell. The difference was that the natural array of colours was subtle, delicate and refined: shell suit hues were anything but.

As an act of kindness, I've deliberately kept these shell suit images quite small.

[180]

I suppose the one saving grace of the snorkel was that at least it restricted much of the reflective glare you had to tolerate when in the vicinity of a shell-suited devotee, but I cannot in all honesty say that this descent into the awful was restricted to the female of the species. They were popular with blokes as well – especially if you came from Liverpool and had a mop of thick black hair to contrast with the eye-catching colours. Ouch!

'So what', I hear you ask, *'has happened to good taste and self-restraint? Did such desirable and discriminating qualities simply desert the seventies and eighties?'* Well, no... but as you might guess, there was an awful lot of competition. Modern art was popular, and the provision of large framed pictures featuring lots of colourful blobs in apparently random application fetched many an admiring glance. Such works of art also had the benefit of providing anyone who wanted to impress fellow viewers with the opportunity to say such things as:

'Ah yes, well you can see what the artist is getting at, can't you? The quintessential apotheosis of the work strikes at the very heart of neo-collectivism, and betrays a wider and deeper appreciation of the psyche, don't you think? By the way, is there any more of that peapod 'n' stinging nettle homebrew around?'

But it wasn't all self-opinionated twaddle. Oddly, another artistic craze swept the nation, and there could have been few homes in the early eighties which didn't have an example of a curve stitched sailing boat or windmill quietly collecting dust in the corner. The nice thing about it was that all you needed was a cork tile, a few dozen panel pins and a length of string and you were away.

And as if that wasn't enough to keep your idle hands purposefully occupied every minute of the day, the

Curve stitching was easy to do, good to look at and fantastic for accumulating dust.

period also can claim credit for introducing an entirely new pastime to the country, and one that remains popular and time-consuming up to the present day. It was: ***Find the Tupperware lid!'***

Hard to imagine now, but there was once a time when there were no Tupperware containers, and thus the need to perpetually mismatch container and lid simply did not exist. Now that the inevitability of never ever being able to find the correct lid for the container of left-over beef stew you desperately want to put in the fridge (so that you can throw it away next Thursday week) is a daily occurrence, we tend to ignore the humble beginnings this occupation had. Funny to think that people would fall over themselves to go to *Tupperware Parties*, where apparently sane adults would spend an evening salivating over the many choices of plastic container that might be purchased and carried triumphantly home. Once this was done, you could rest assured that your once-used container and its matching lid would thereafter be destined to live a life apart… indeed, despite increasingly frantic searching, it seems likely that they would not even be in the same room together ever again. Searching for the matching lid thus became the 1980's version of locating the Holy Grail, and despite such a forlorn hope, the process became something of national preoccupation.

So, there you are: the middle Baby Boomer years were certainly pretty chaotic, but the good and bad elements mixed up into an experience that was at least memorable. That it was also the period when we came of age – became truly grown up, I suppose – it will always be associated with the fundamentals of putting down family roots, and making your way in the world.

Not so very different from the present day and age? Perhaps not… but I have to point out that it's not every generation that has to put up with homebrew, vertical Artex, woodchip wallpaper and shell suits all within a decade is it?

Again, the BB's *well-hardness* proved itself to be a continuing asset.

[182]

7   Acid Drops

I hope that readers will agree that the essence of this book and its predecessor *'The Time of Our Lives'* can be summarised as an **affectionate commentary on the life and times of the Baby Boomers.**

Now that we're well into the 2020's, the fact is that although a proportion of those born in the decade after the Second World War are no longer with us, there are still loads of BB's who are. Thankfully, the old NHS has kept us going, and we're still here bumbling about, moaning about the weather, looking for our glasses, wandering around looking slightly bewildered in shopping malls and generally getting in everyone's way. You must have noticed us, surely?

Inevitably the ladies will be fumbling in their handbags looking for their bus pass, spare hearing aid battery or a receipt from Marks and Spencer for that girdle which looked such good value at the time, but unbelievably seems to have shrunk on the way home. The blokes, on the other hand are generally just standing about with their hands in their pockets, uttering the occasional long-suffering sigh and wondering for the millionth time why it takes the wife such a long time to go to the loo in Sainsbury's… and why on earth he has been tasked with going to find out exactly what the shop is offering by way of a special promotion on sets of teaspoons.

Exasperating indeed, especially as the shopping trip got off to a bad start because of the argument with the bus driver of the 9.25 am, occasioned by the fact that his arrival was seven minutes late. So technically speaking, it was two minutes *after* the 9.30 am threshold for pensioners' bus passes, '*…so let us on! it's not our fault you're late!* Getting the picture?

In contrast, for the oldies who can remember where the polling station is, a whole lot of Baby Boomers are now in a position to flex their muscles as the influential 'grey vote' and, it could be argued, are probably more politically aware than preceding generations. Furthermore, it has to be acknowledged that when the post-war largesse of the welfare state is seen in tandem with the opportunities provided by almost full employment in the sixties, it has led to many of this fortunate generation being surprisingly well provided for in terms of finance. Clearly, such a happy state of affairs is not universal, but in comparison with those who reached retirement age in the mid twentieth century, many post-war kids are doing pretty well.

And you don't have to take my word for it: just casting a brief look at the age range of those sloshing on the sun tan lotion in the Maldives, or leaning over the upper sundeck rail of just about any cruise ship bobbing around the Caribbean will testify. For these folk I suppose Harold MacMillan's famous phrase *'you've never had it so good'* would be even more appropriate now than it was when he coined it in 1957. The Baby Boomers have indeed been incredibly fortunate – but the downside of this is that such generous bounty bestowed by fate is seen by more than a few of the succeeding generation as a strong indication that the Boomers are little more than a load of smug and self-satisfied old people who are oblivious to the wants, needs and sometimes thwarted ambitions of those who follow.

The suggestion that such folk are squandering the nation's wealth and prosperity in an orgy of self indulgence is one which is cropping up increasingly as we get further into the new century. Although such a view is understandable, it frequently appears to ignore both *detail* and – especially – **context**.

Certainly, the Boomer generation has had what at first glance seems to have been a charmed life, but perhaps we ought to reflect that its origins were based firmly in a period of the greatest violence man has ever known - the Second World War. The reason for its very existence as a recognisable group is down to just one simple fact: *its parents survived that awful conflict*...and the corollary to this truism is that many children who one *might* have anticipated being born in the late forties were not, because one or both of the prospective parents didn't make it. Sobering thought, isn't it?

It was our mums' and dads' generation which suffered the war's appalling privations, sadness and loss… and as a result of their sacrifice, those who survived were able to have a clear view as to where, in 1945, the nation went next ... and it certainly wasn't *more of the same.* The General Election of that year swept Clement Atlee's Labour government in to power, and our parents were at last able to provide those fundamental elements of life which had been at best patchy – and in some cases almost non-existent – in their own formative years. In this brave new post-war world there was to be no more scraping by, no more access to the basic rights of health, homes and education depending upon how much you could pay: from now on, these would be free and for *everyone*. Wow!

Thus, the Baby Boomers were the first to benefit massively from the exuberant and altruistic social reforms of the post-war years when the opportunity for everyone to enjoy clean, secure and hygienic housing went hand in hand with vastly improved diet and access to full time education. And, of course, underwriting all this good fortune was the fact that we were guaranteed free and unconditional provision for our health and well-being via the wonderful and brand new National Health Service. From 5th July 1948, the Welfare State was up and running.

Through the efforts of their immediate predecessors, and rather like travellers crossing a river in full torrent on precarious stepping stones, the Baby Boomers were able to plant their feet firmly on each. They were borne along on their journey by the confidence of youth which was able to flourish in the welcoming and commodious setting that the fifties and sixties provided. And that's not all. Complementary to free and universal education were really quite generous grants to enable those willing and capable to aspire to qualifications and positions hitherto considered unattainable. The early sixties featured a host of job opportunities at the very time Boomers launched into the world of work – and at the same time, whilst progressing along this charmed journey, we were accompanied by the brilliant innovations brought about by the timely revolution in domestic technology. The post-war kids were the first TV generation - and this at a time when creativity and its attendant levels of opportunity were going through the roof.

So it's not at all surprising that the label of smug self-satisfaction is appended by some. Considered against twenty-first century opportunity, such criticism should not be lightly dismissed, especially when current economic and social pressures appear to be narrowing people's choices.

So, is a critical view of the BB generation accurate and justified?

First, I have to say that in my experience, people of the BB generation are very ready to acknowledge their good fortune, and it takes but a few moments of lively debate to reassure oneself that this appreciation is both perceptive… and genuine. Boomers are also keen – and perhaps a little defensive – to explain that our early experiences were not *all* plain sailing. To put them into perspective, you need to examine post-war realities a little more closely before comparing them with what is seen as 'normal' for the twenty-first century. Whilst acknowledging there is a tendency to drift towards the extremes so beautifully portrayed in Monty Python's famous 'Four Yorkshiremen' sketch (*'We used to dream of living in a corridor'…*) some illumination is required.

For example, living conditions in the fifties in particular, were still really quite spartan, and of the creature comforts commonly expected and enjoyed in modern Britain, there was a dearth. Children's clothing for most working-class kids was still pretty basic, and often a much-altered hand-me-down. On getting my first pair of long trousers at the age of ten, I'm sure I was not alone in being told that:

'You'll have turn-ups at the bottom and braces at the top just like your dad and Uncle Norman. I don't care what Bill Hayley's wearing… and stop grizzling!'

Tough times… and don't forget, you 21st century softies, sweets were on ration until 1953… EIGHT sherbet lemon-less years after the end of the war!

Central heating in ordinary homes was unheard of, and although *'scraping the ice off the inside of the bedroom window'* is in danger of being relegated to an apocryphal tale to recount at dinner parties, it was in fact absolutely true for a very large number of kids. In addition, plumbing was still very basic with many otherwise quite well-appointed homes still having an outside loo. It is hardly surprising therefore, that bedrooms in a large number of homes were always equipped with chamber pots which were usually placed under each bed. Faced with the alternative of getting up in the icy stillness of the night and making your way out of doors to the loo, or taking a quick pee in the pot… well what would you have chosen?

Although fitted bathrooms and kitchens were on many a wish list, for the majority they remained something of an aspiration rather than expectation until well into the sixties and in the meantime we made do with the leaky old geezer* in the bathroom, and the Ascot over the kitchen sink. If there is truth in the saying that *cleanliness is next to godliness,* then it is little wonder so many of us got sent to Sunday School to redress the balance.

For ordinary kids the daily round of chores about the home was probably a lot more onerous than those faced today – the never ending instructions to '*just pop down to the corner shop and get me a couple of carrots and a bag of sugar*' or the need to '*clear the grate, help get the coal up and re-lay the fire*' being just a couple. And need I remind you that in the early post-war years we were still *PRE-SELLOTAPE*?

As you may recall, our schooling both at primary and secondary level was pretty basic and certainly lacked a coherent wrap-around curriculum, or such elements as the pre-school experiences and after-school provision so common today. And to be honest, secondary education was at times really quite rough and ready, with an emphasis - for boys especially – on the former. There is little doubt that were teachers today to indulge in such acts of random and unrestrained corporal punishment administered as they were then, they would be in deep trouble with the law in no time at all. That we still have such affection for our old schools in spite of such treatment does beg a question or two, doesn't it?

You have also to bear in mind at in those days there was perilously little Health and Safety. '*Bloody good job too!*' I hear you say. But wait a moment… over-bearing, unnecessarily complex and stifling it may appear today, but in all honesty, would anyone *really* want to go back to the days when corporate neglect and failure to ensure sensible working conditions and practices led to so many preventable and often life-threatening accidents? Don't think so. Just remember, seat belts in cars were not even *fitted* in the fifties, and neither was it compulsory for a

*Leaky geezer – no, not our granddads suffering from urinary problems, but the name for unreliable gas powered water heaters installed over the bath. They frequently leaked water, and sometimes gas as well when a gust of wind via the bathroom window blew the little flames out.

motor-cyclist to wear a crash helmet, so the chances of you having all your electrical sockets checked every year or your fire alarms regularly tested and maintained were pretty much approaching zilch. And don't get me started on domestic smoke detectors; to be honest, so many people smoked in those days, then even if such devices had been available, they would have been going off all the time. Carbon monoxide? *'Never heard of it, mate'*. Good thing homes were so draughty.

Mind you, if you did manage to survive all these avoidable physical hazards, there were still a whole range of other challenges, many of them financial. Chief amongst these was when many BB's tried to scramble on to the first rung of the housing ladder: it's now hard to believe it was even more difficult in the seventies than it is today. Despite recent interest rate rises to low single figures, it may come as a surprise to the younger generation that about fifty years ago, when many Boomers were still desperately trying to get a foot on the first rung, annual interest rates rose to an all time high of *fifteen* per cent. Yes, I did say *fif*-bleeding-*teen!* What's more, to have any hope at all of getting a mortgage, you had to have been a regular investor with a Building Society for at least a couple of years, and to have demonstrated your ability to repay the yearned for mortgage through crediting your account with a considerable proportion of your earnings on a monthly basis. Even then, you were by no means guaranteed a loan, and if the Society's quota for a particular month was gone – then hard luck – try again next month... by which time the price of the accommodation you wanted to buy would have risen by a lot. Rampant inflation in the property market is not a new thing, believe me.

Another point made by many Baby Boomers in defensive mode, is that we had very much lower expectations in terms of what are now considered the essentials of life. In short, we were much more willing to make do with whatever we could get in terms of personal property in general, and household provision in particular. Of high value items such as TVs and tape recorders, not many owned their own, and remember, mobile phones and home computers had not even been invented. I'll just say that again: *In the 1970's there were no PC's, no mobile phones, no apps, no internet, no games consoles, no SKYPE and no credit cards to buy anything with.* Plastic had been invented, but credit cards hadn't and if you wanted to buy anything, you went to the shop with cash or a cheque. In fact, as far as a comparison with the life of a modern consumer goes, there was *a whole lot of nothing.*

Yes, most people owned their own tranny, and you might be lucky enough to have part share with a flat mate of a twin-tub washing machine and a beaten up three piece suite from your student days, but that was about it. In order to scrape together enough cash to get on the housing market, many an old car was sold, and the ancient Raleigh *Jack of Clubs* push bike heaved out of your dad's garden shed for a second life. Spending large sums of money on expensive cups of coffee and the latest in sun glasses design was nowhere close to being on the priority list, and Blue Ray speakers and universal WiFi access, even if they had been invented, would probably not have been seen as a must-have.

If you were lucky enough to get a mortgage, your first house or flat would be furnished with all sorts of hand-me-downs from parents and friends. Things that are considered essentials today – central heating, fridge-freezers, double glazing and built-in dish washers, would not have even been considered as pre-requisites for the start of your home-owning experience. OK, some of today's essentials had not yet been invented: the only *surround sound* experience you were likely to get was the noisy exuberance of the water pipes as they gurgled their happy way around your sparsely furnished abode. Wardrobe fridges, microwave cookers and en-suite bathrooms were yet to come, and it is interesting to note that even in the seventies, most people still did not have a shower.

By that I do not mean that we were unhygienic and went about the place reeking of an excess of accumulated unmentionables – it was just that the shiny bathroom fitments that we know so well today, simply did not exist. Showers were things associated with sports changing rooms, swimming pools and the like. Once the idea that having *a shower at home*, rather than trying to clean yourself in two or three inches of lukewarm bath water started to catch on, the gradual move to taking a regular shower in the privacy of your own bathroom became a practical possibility. Unfortunately, the best most people could aspire to was one of those crappy rubber stethoscope type attachments you shoved on to the bath taps. More often than not you were either scalded or frozen, or both, and ended up wrapped in a plastic shower curtain whose clammy constraint seemed deliberately to entwine itself about your shrivelling torso.

So there you are – not necessarily quite the easy ride so many of the younger generation assume it to have been. Nevertheless, showers and other modern attributes notwithstanding, just about everyone agrees that our generation *was* extremely fortunate; undoubtedly, we were in the right place at the right time... which leads one to the inevitable question:

With all these advantages, did we get it right?

Well, of course we didn't. We made some terrible mistakes – but we're human, OK? And that's what humans do.

I stumbled across a TV programme a couple of years ago called *'It was All Right in the Seventies'*. Evidently the format of this particular episode followed the same pattern as others in the series, the essence of each being to examine a particular aspect of life through the historical lens provided by what we watched on TV during the decade in question. Thus, each programme comprised a number of snippets from the TV programmes of the era, and to new viewer like me, the episode had therefore little to distinguish it from many similar compilations of light entertainment. Bearing in mind that the focus of this particular programme was on comedy, it looked as if it was going to be nothing more than an amusing trip down memory lane. For me, it wasn't.

What made this programme different was the fact that modern day entertainers - most of them well known in the world of comedy – were invited to take an active part in the programme by viewing the snippets themselves, and having their immediate reactions televised live. Thus, during the course of each 1970 comedy clip, the programme producer would cut away to record the immediate reaction of the celebrity guest, and at the end of each section, allow him or her to speak at some length about their reaction to the piece shown.

Almost to a man /woman the response to the provided clips was one of incredulity, shock or horror – and quite often all three. Now this may lead you to deduce that the clips themselves were from programmes whose content was most likely to elicit a negative response – but they were not at all. On the contrary, they were from standard comedy and light entertainment programmes of the era – the sort of programme designed to appeal to popular taste, and to keep well within the bounds of current sensibilities. You may remember some of them:

- *'Are You Being Served?'*
- *'It Aint Half Hot Mum!'*
- *'The Two Ronnies'*
- *'Till Death Us Do Part'*
- *'The Goodies'*....and so on.

What it boiled down to was an analysis of the attitudes and tastes of seventies' society in respect of some pretty fundamental aspects of life - the most evident being racial attitudes, gender stereotyping, misogyny, prejudice, equality, toleration and sexual orientation.

Well, it was perfectly clear from the responses shown during the programme that those who enjoyed these programmes forty odd years ago had a great deal to answer for. Clearly, just about every one of the viewing celebrities was aghast at the things they saw - and by implication therefore, their responses reflected badly upon those of us who found such entertainment innocently amusing at the time.

And just why are the seventies so important to Baby Boomers? Why do we feel so … sort of *responsible?* The reason is, I believe, that the decade was our 'coming of age': we could no longer pretend to be trendy teenagers; suddenly life was real and life was earnest. The Baby Boomer generation grew into full adulthood in the seventies – and by that I mean becoming the new core of society, buying homes, having our families, integrating into the world of work, contributing to the economy, paying taxes… and using political clout through the ballot box. But we were also passively responsible for what was popular and what was not, what was considered acceptable and what wasn't. If the sixties had taught us anything it was that people power had the ability to exert massive influence on popular culture. Thus, the things we looked at, the things we supported and enjoyed on TV and at the cinema were acceptable to, and therefore reflective of, the way in which we lived our lives.

So, were we as a generation racist, misogynistic, intolerant and prejudiced? Well, if the reaction of the modern day contributors to the *'It Was All Right in the Seventies'* programme was anything to go by, then we were guilty as charged, without a doubt. So let's take a closer look at these sensitive issues.

As regards racism, *'The Black and White Minstrel Show'* was probably as good an indicator as you are likely to get, but by the late sixties there was a growing sense of unease amongst many, and the show was eventually dropped. Racial stereotyping was also an essential ingredient of *'Till Death Us Do Part'*, and the use of terminology by the outrageous Alf Garnet would quite rightly be considered highly offensive today*. The show was cut in 1975.

Nevertheless, apparently narrow racial attitudes continued to be well represented in a number of programmes, the most obvious being *'It Aint Half Hot Mum'*. Michael Crawford's portrayal of bearer Rangi Ram was brilliantly acted – but the fact that he was a white Englishman and therefore had to black up for the part says a lot. In addition, the other parts representing Indians were at least played by actors native to that country, but the script meant that they were generally addressed in a manner totally identifiable as that belonging to the Victorian days of the Raj. If you are the proud owner of Book 1 of my series (*'The Time of Our Lives'*), then referring back to the first *Camp Coffee* advert in the chapter 'Cupboard Love' will give you a good idea of what I mean.

Even variety shows containing well known stars such as Stanley Baxter, might well have clips where it was necessary to black up to make the joke. And it didn't stop with caricatures that needed a lot of

---

* *Interestingly, a recent BBC programme 'Sitcoms: Laughing at Ourselves for 60 Years' provided a commendably balanced view of the racial prejudice exuded by Alf. It points out that the show's talented scriptwriter Johnny Speight, took an impeccable line in ensuring that viewers were able to laugh __at__ Alf, rather than commiserate with his prejudice. The programme suggests – quite rightly, in my opinion - that the show therefore did a good deal in helping to expose the ignorance and stupidity that lay behind the character's disagreeable attitudes.*

make-up to fulfil the producer's requirements. Irish jokes were particularly popular, and almost any European was fair game for sending up in a way which today might seem somewhat tasteless.

Attitudes to sexual orientation were also well represented, and the portrayal by John Inman of the gay Mr. Humphries in *'Are You Being Served?'* was a case in point. Even his catchphrase of *'I'm free!'* was a double entendre about as blunt as you are likely to get, and as if this was not enough, his uninhibited use of chiffon neck scarves and mincing walk was as subtle as a sledge hammer.

The same programme also played its part in underlining the general attitude to women; whereas the curvaceous Miss Brahms was seen as *a nice bit of crumpet* and actively – but unsuccessfully - pursued by the lad about town Mr. Lucas, her head of department, the stately Mrs.Slocombe, was an object of a different type of fun. To the delight of the audience, the dear lady's apparent naiveté concerning her lack of comprehension of the smutty alternative meanings of common words was an area to be ruthlessly exploited, and were alluded to at length. Of particular popularity was her frequent reference to her pet cat, and the almost inevitable references during the show to this domestic responsibility was a common source of the humour of the time. Thus *'Captain Peacock, I need to get home early this evening as my pussy needs a good brushing'* was pretty typical of the heavy handed humour and resulted in gales of laughter from the studio and home TV audience alike.

But then you have to realise that such portrayal was par for the course, and the even more blatant pigeon-holing of women as objects of lust probably reached a climax (perhaps an unfortunate turn of phrase) with another popular TV series from London Weekend Television entitled *'On The Buses'* which ran until the early seventies. The main theme seemed to revolve around the lascivious ambitions of the crew of a particular bus and this relatively simple theme was pursued with some enthusiasm by both scriptwriters and their viewers.

All a bit unseemly? The sexual exploitation of women who seemed happy with their lot as objects of leering affection? Well, yes, but of course, it was fiction, whereas TV shows such as *'Top of the Pops'* were not. At that time, mini dresses and hot pants were still in evidence, and it seemed to many an ardent male viewer that the studio direction went out of its way to get as many shots as possible of young women dancing – some from as low an angle as possible. Added to this, the studio group of professional dancers called *'Pan's People'* moved and grooved in what seemed to many a blatantly provocative way. Thus the scene was set for the *'The Kenny Everett Show'* where the semi erotic writhing of the dance group *Hot Gossip* left little to the imagination.

Something else that needs closer inspection, is the 1970's attitude of our generation to disability. You may remember from the introduction to my earlier book, my own reaction to the harmless Ben Parsons in his creaking self-propelled invalid carriage. Well, perhaps that was just a matter of a little boy being spooked by something a bit out of the ordinary, and an old man with a wobbly voice and a pair of glasses with one lens all milky. But also in that section, the description of the later motor driven invalid carriages appears to demonstrate that although an improvement in terms of propulsion, such vehicles did nothing at all to help people with disabilities to integrate as seamlessly as possible into society – in fact

the noisy and smoky engines associated with these ungainly little blue plastic vehicles - as well as the sign in the back window that said **'Caution: no hand signals'**- did the very opposite. Everyone knew when there was one about. The fact that they were limited to a low speed made such vehicles something to be overtaken with undue haste - and by association therefore, condemned their occupants as *the slow, the incapacitated, those deserving of sympathy...*

but not much else… 'So get out of my way!' The thought that such folk might, despite their physical limitations be a damned sight brighter than many an able-bodied person, and have the potential to contribute as much to society as everyone else never really entered our heads.

In retrospect, it all seemed to be about *segregation,* and in a way it was drilled into us. For example, the popular Saturday morning radio show *'Children's Favourites'* was hosted by the well known broadcaster Derek McCulloch, or *Uncle Mac* as he was known to his juvenile audience. The thing was, at the end of the programme he would always say *'So goodbye children everywhere – and a special goodbye to my little invalid friends'.* Now I have not a shadow of a doubt that this was kindly meant… but the subliminal message? *'Invalid children are a different group: they need separate and sensitive handling'.* You get my point I'm sure.

At the same time, this was the age of the institution: if you were long-term sick you went to a nursing home. If you were disabled to a degree that mobility, health maintenance, mental capacity or stability were in question, you were sent somewhere where such needs could be met – an institution. Whereas many of these became established as part of the new National Health Service, others were not, and this was particularly true of orphanages. Dr. Barnados remains, of course, very well known, but there were many others. I can remember that the Methodist Church was responsible for an organisation called *'The National Children's Home'* and that every year church members were invited to raise funds for this organisation by buying monochrome photographs of the orphaned children from a small catalogue entitled *'Sunny Smiles'.* That those purchasing the little pictures were expected to thumb through until they found one they liked, was seen as a normal and entirely expected part of the transaction. The lack of sensitivity such a process produced in terms of what could be seen as the *rejection* of those whose images were left in the last few pages of the mini album was not considered. As far as mainstream society was concerned, these were kids who had been dealt a hard start in life and needed a bit of support, and children's homes were the best place to provide it. Job done.

Or so we thought. The chilling revelations of the abuse suffered by so many in such institutions never entered our heads; that such crimes have now cast a shadow on the work of *all* children's homes is inevitable, but also a tragedy, for it is beyond doubt that many of these institutions did provide wonderful care and support for their children, and this important work continues to this day. Indeed, the National Children's Home is a case in point: under its new title *'Action for Children'* it still does great work in providing for vulnerable youngsters throughout the country, as does Barnados.

I suppose however, that the problem with all caring institutions set up after the war was that they became a salve to the collective conscience: the poor, sick and the disadvantaged were now provided for... they were *compartmentalised* into different caring organisations which were paid for out of our taxes and occasional flag days, weren't they? So there you are. Issue dealt with. Next?

Simplistic and insensitive remedies, you might say – but at least they *were* remedies. Prior to such provision, your chances of getting support from either the private or the public sector were at best patchy, and at worst highly remote. There was no real safety net – and so many went without the care they needed.

Even more apparently insensitive was the categorisation of some disabilities, and the one that always springs to mind is that of support for people born with cerebral palsy. They were known as *spastics,* and the organisation which specialised in their care the *Spastics' Society.* That such organisations had a title which underlined the nature of the debilitating condition in such a blunt and insensitive way says much about the age... but it is only part of the picture: disability seemed always to be characterised by what its victims could *not* do, rather than what they might achieve. Even in the 1970's, the term used for children at school who were severely under-achieving was ESN, which - believe it or not - stood for **Educationally Sub Normal.** Many of those so classified were then bundled off to a special school which was staffed and equipped to provide for the educational needs of these youngsters. So once again, the emphasis was on *segregation* rather than *integration*.

That is not to say that special schools did no good – of course they did, and the dedication of the many talented staff who made it their life's work to provide for such children and young people should never be underestimated. The problem was that such provision even into the 1980's tended to be a one-way street: once classified as needing support of this type, it was very difficult for a youngster to be reintegrated into main stream education should his/her situation make it a possibility.

Conditions such as autism were barely recognised and dyslexia and dyspraxia often remained undiagnosed. Children with ADHD (attention deficit hyperactive disorder) were just described as 'maladjusted'. As you might expect, the complexities of Obsessive Compulsive Disorder (OCD) and Aspergers syndrome were largely unexplored, and led many to describe such children as just unduly disruptive or overly introverted.

Consequently, expectation from society in general seemed to be that once categorised, that was it: there was little anticipation that those admitted to such institutions for whatever reason, would ever be able to contribute much, or could change their status once classified in this way. A tragedy indeed, both in terms of personal fulfilment for the people concerned, and the massive waste of unrecognised and unexplored talent from which the whole of society could have benefitted.

So, all of this requires me to repeat the question: did we, the uniquely blessed Baby Boomer generation get it wrong? Despite all the many advantages we had through being born just after the end of the greatest conflict ever experienced by man, did we oversee and accept racial intolerance, homophobia, misogyny, prejudice, discrimination and inequality?

Well, on the face of it, it seems yes, we did – and are therefore pretty much guilty on all counts. But I don't think so – and my main reason for this submission is that such a conclusion is not taking into account the highly significant factor I raised earlier – the ***context.*** So, to give a more rounded picture, let's examine the individual issues when set against the background of life as it was in those times.

Perhaps the most sensitive area to look at is the question of racial prejudice. By today's standards, the typical 1960's attitude to people from other cultures would appear very racist: after all, the terms 'coloured' and 'negro' were used quite openly as part of everyday speech – even the N word was freely used, although it must be said that in the vast majority of cases this was simply to describe a particular fabric colour. Even so, the term *'Nigger Minstrels'* was used without embarrassment until the mid sixties, although as mentioned before, there did seem to be an increasing unease with the term, especially in respect of the *'Black and White Minstrel Show'*.

'But just because such terminology was commonly used doesn't make it any better' I hear you say, and you'd be right... except that, in the fifties in particular, the majority of us had almost no experience whatever of dealing with *anyone* who could be regarded as a foreigner. Bear in mind that the most influential people in our lives - our parents - had just experienced a cataclysmic war when *any* foreigner was regarded with suspicion and could easily be seen as a potential enemy bent on blowing you to smithereens. OK, many foreign troops came to the UK to support the war effort – but as far as the civilian population was concerned, it was a matter of 'prove to us you're a friend before you are trusted'.

After the horrors of the war, the appalling details of the barbarities carried out by belligerents all over the world became known, and rightly or wrongly, there is good reason to believe that the nation almost turned inwards on itself and its closest allies (mainly the Yanks) as the only others who could be trusted. Now this sort of isolationism may be seen in retrospect as being unrealistic and counter-productive, but given the hideous experiences of the previous six years it is at least *understandable.* Thus the pattern was set whereby just about any foreign person was regarded with a certain amount of *caution* during the immediate post-war period. As events unfolded, and the effect of the war became less immediate, such a feeling ebbed away... but foreigners were still regarded as being, well... *different.*

And, what's more, they were also rare. Bearing in mind I lived in a naval city where lots of ships from foreign navies would visit, even this provided little experience of seeing people from other countries. You might get a glimpse of a sailor wearing a funny hat, but that was about it. As regards black people, in the early fifties at least, there appeared to be none at all in my city. I suspect that the first black man most of us kids ever saw would have been an Afro-American sailor from a US warship. It wasn't until probably quite late in the sixties that the first Caribbean immigrants started to settle in my town.

Furthermore, what needs to be understood is that the instant accessibility to contemporary information regarding the lives of other cultures right around the globe that we have today, was quite unknown throughout our formative years. Even in 1960, there were many homes that still did not have a television set, and were thus denied access to the 'living window' of documentary TV that at least gave an inkling of how life was for others. To some extent, therefore, we were not that different from previous generations, in that we were isolationist by default.

Accurate details about other cultures were scant, and informed only by access to dusty encyclopaedias from the local library, or by what we were told at school. And I suggest that I was not alone in not having any lessons which dealt with global cultural values. Yes, OK, at junior school we were told that some people in the Middle East still slept outside on the flat roofs of their houses because it was so hot, and that African villagers often used palm fronds with which to thatch their buildings. No mention that I can recall was made of the fact that millions of others from these countries lived in towns and cities not so very different from our own.

So, until documentary television started to make a real impact from the mid-sixties onwards, scant educational input, out of date publications and hearsay from those who had travelled abroad – and quite a lot more from people who had never been beyond the Isle of Wight but who had an opinion on everything - was about the extent of the input we had. That our knowledge of racial issues was skewed is therefore hardly surprising. Added to this was another aspect which scandalises the modern observer: how *all* foreign people were represented and depicted for our domestic consumption.

Enid Blyton was probably the most popular writer of children's books throughout the fifties and sixties. Ask any kid of the Baby Boomer generation to name a book of hers and they'll instantly recall stories from '*The Far Away Tree*' series and its like. But even more popular were her stories featuring *The Famous Five*. These tales were of a group of children (Julian, Anne, Dick, George and their dog Timmy) who went on adventures. That they came from a privileged background complete with Nanny, a cook and various other household servants, and had a mother whose specific role in life seemed to be baking yummy biscuits and creating her own home-made lemonade to lavish upon her children, only added to the attraction. It was escapism for ordinary kids, for heaven's sake. But in the context of contributing to opinions likely to have an effect upon impressionable minds – and perhaps of confirming certain prejudices - the stories were really quite powerful. You were left in no doubt at all about how things should be: the children in the stories were well off, secure, happy, and surrounded by thoroughly dependable adults whose sole purpose in life was to make them feel cheerful, and to ensure that all was right with the world. Any tradesman was of the 'stout artisan fellow' variety with rosy cheeks, eyes a-twinkle and prone to say *'Lord love you m'dear!'* at regular intervals.

Like I said, all good types… except, of course if they happened to be *foreign*. That was a different matter altogether. The adventures of the children (which always seemed to start on the first day of the summer holidays) seemed regularly to involve strangers who were up to no good. Often they would be espied behaving furtively around the entrance to secret caves in cliffs, carrying mysterious barrels and packages and behaving in a thoroughly suspicious way... not at all the type you would invite into your house and offer a plate of cucumber sandwiches to, that's for sure. And the point of all this? Well, such people were often described as 'looking like *foreigners'*. So, the implication that people of criminal intent were bound to be from abroad was not lost on young minds.

And that was not all. In the post-war years, BBC radio's *'Dick Barton Special Agent'* was very popular. The dramatisation of our hero's regular tussles with enemies of Great Britain, all of whom spoke with an accent which was distinctly mid-European, were something we all looked forward to. The sound recording of a fist-fight had, by its very nature to involve what can only be described as *interpretive narration*… otherwise all the listener got would be the squelchy sound of fist hitting stomach, or the occasional scream – not good radio, certainly. Thus the dialogue during such conflicts was frequently descriptive and would go along the lines of:

'There, take that you foreign swine!' (sound of a punch landing, followed by a compulsory ***'Ugh'*** in a German accent) then...***'And here's one from Uncle Charlie! Take that back to outer Mongolia!'*** ...with much the same result.

So, if our attitude to foreigners was biased, it's not really that surprising. With such an input it probably took considerably longer for youngsters to begin to realise that there were a lot of nice foreigners, and that not all of them were intent upon smuggling stuff via secret caves, or inventing deadly death-rays to wipe us all out.

But the context described above largely relates to attitudes towards our nearest continental neighbours, not specifically to those from completely different ethnic backgrounds. What little information there was about black people was limited, and occasionally completely bizarre.

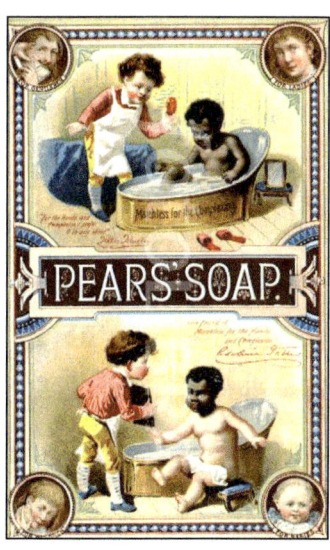

You may be aware of a Victorian advert for Pears Soap which shows a black baby being washed with the product… and in the process the natural skin pigment of the child being removed to be replaced by whiteness. Now, even pre-war this was seen as preposterous…but perhaps as much for its scientific inexactitude as for its racial implications. The reaction to such flagrant imagery, though not quite as outraged as it would be today, was nonetheless there. As time went on, that it was also an appalling example of racism in its crudest form was a sentiment that began to impinge more and more on society in general. The same could not, however, be said of a common childhood toy.

I suspect that throughout the late forties and early fifties, there was hardly a child in the country who did not own a golliwog. This doll-like toy was black, had spiky hair and red lips, and was a commonplace occupant of any pram or toy cupboard. I certainly had one, as did thousands of other children. Now, as we have already noted, I was a child imbued with a pretty low level of gorm. Nevertheless, I suspect that even I might have caught on to the fact that such representation was not acceptable, had that been the case. But it was not. Like me, I suggest that most kids did not even equate the cuddly black toy as being any other than that – and certainly had not the slightest notion that it would come to be regarded as a deliberately cruel racial lampoon.

The paper Golly stickers and an enamelled brooch. Many children – and some adults - became avid collectors. The all too obvious racial overtones were totally unrecognised by most… and ignored by others

Naïve? Unobservant? Yep. But just remember that throughout the post-war period, the famous jam manufacturer Robertson's continued to use the Golly as a powerful marketing tool. Purchasers of Robertson's products were encouraged to collect the paper Golly stickers attached to each label, and when a sufficient number had been accumulated, to send them off to the company to be exchanged for an enamel brooch. Not only that, the brooches depicted the Golly doing all sorts of interesting things such as playing a guitar, banging a drum and skiing which made them all the more desirable. But yet again, the collection of these stickers and brooches was not seen as having any racial implications. It was not even considered.

I suspect that the modern view of such an assertion is one of incredulity. All I can say is that the golliwog image was viewed by children (in particular) and society (in general) as simply a popular and desirable childhood toy – despite this being a time when racial prejudice was starting to become an issue brought to us with increasing regularity on our newly acquired TV sets.

At the domestic level, the previously mentioned *'Till Death Us Do Part'* pointing its finger at the absurdity of Alf Garnet's views, was playing it part* – but of much higher profile and increasing knowledge and great concern was what was happening on the international stage.

I speak of course, of the Civil Rights movement in the USA. The volatility of the actions which were brought about by the continuing – and often establishment sanctioned – conflict between those who sought to ignore the laws about racial discrimination and those who were subject to it, were very real, very urgent, and very disturbing to see. That a black woman could be arrested in Alabama for not giving up her bus seat to a white person seemed unbelievable in a country which had been our closest ally and friend during the war. How, for example, could some of the people of the USA – a country whose founding fathers had stated that all citizens had a right to *'life, liberty and the pursuit of happiness'* - be denied the right to attend a school of their choice? And how on earth could the men dressed in the fearsome apparel of the Ku Klux Klan be tolerated in what seemed to us to be the wealthy, democratic and well-ordered society to which we all aspired? Set against such violence and bitterness, our own problems seemed almost negligible.

But that's no reason to assume they did not exist. There were ugly incidents of race-related   prejudice – mainly in such matters as the provision of temporary accommodation, where signs in windows saying *'No Blacks, no Irish'* did appear from time to time. It is also a fact that some people were denied rights to particular services, just because they were *different* – an example being the refusal of a barman to serve a drink to a black customer. Although such incidents were far from being the norm and were nowhere near as extreme and violent as the indignities against which many fought in the USA, it does not excuse them. In my judgement, racism did exist but I think it would be fair – and I hope accurate – to describe the vast majority of it as *passive* rather than *active*. What we did, what we inadvertently sanctioned, was perhaps more to do with our own ignorance, rather than deliberate ill will.

* *It is interesting to note that in 1974, a year before 'Till Death' ended, ITV picked up the baton and covered issues of racial prejudice with its brilliant sitcom 'Rising Damp'. Again, the racial intolerance shown by the narrow-minded landlord Rigsby was a focus. Viewers were left in no doubt that the character's racist attitudes were based on his utter ignorance.*

In his excellent 2020 book *'Lancaster',* John Nichol relates the story of the great Cy Grant who was one of the relatively few black servicemen to be commissioned into the RAF in 1943. Although Cy did suffer from some racial prejudice, he is recorded as saying that such attitudes were more the product of *'ignorance and unfamiliarity'*. This view was also held by another commissioned officer from the West Indies, Lancaster pilot Billy Strachan. It is interesting to note that the title of Cy's own book *'A Member of the RAF of Indeterminate Race'* comes from his time as a German POW in the notorious Stalag Luft III, where he was thus described by his Nazi captors.

The stature of the man can be assessed when you consider that, after the war, Cy went on to train and qualify as a barrister. Failing to get a job in this career simply because of his skin colour, he decided to change direction and developed his acting and musical talents. He was so successful that he became a household name with his very popular *'Topical Calypsos'* screened every evening on the BBC's *'Tonight'* magazine programme. It would therefore be fair to say that Cy did a great deal to disperse the racial ignorance and unfamiliarity that underpinned the uninformed and blinkered views of many.

Whilst it would be foolish to claim that blatant, brutal and corrosive racism did not exist at that time, my view is that such extremism in the fifties and sixties was still mercifully rare. Indeed, it could be argued that it was a generation or so *later* that saw a rise in the number of such ugly incidents – perhaps epitomised by the ghastly cruelty of the Stephen Lawrence murder in 1993.

Like all generations, the Baby Boomers were in large part the product of the preceding one, and pre-formed views on social issues were inevitably part of this. However, things were changing and an example of this concerns a phrase used by some in those days. It sticks in my mind, as questioning its validity was an indicator of the way we were slowly becoming more sensitive to such racist issues. And the phrase? When being exhorted to do the right thing, to square our shoulders and stiffen our resolve, people would sometimes be encouraged to:

'Come on! Buck up! **Play the white man!***'*

I am glad to say however, that the most frequent use of this phrase by our own young generation was as a lampoon of our imperialist past. Indeed, it was used as a parody of our Colonel Blimp* type predecessors. For most of us its use had no overt meaning by way of racial prejudice… in fact it was quite the contrary.

One last reflection as regards our increasing awareness of racial issues. In 1965 I remember going to see a film called *'The Hill'*. It was set during the war, and starred Sean Connery - but this time in a role very different from his 007 character. The plot revolved around the appalling treatment meted out by the wartime military police to any soldier who had flagrantly disobeyed orders. Such men were sent to a camp in Libya where the regime to beat them back into shape did just that – in a brutal and violent way. The particular punishment from which the film got its name involved making men run up and down a small hill wearing full kit in the heat of the midday sun. Like I said, brutal. One of the film's characters was the overly stern Regimental Sergeant Major Wilson, played by Harry Andrews. The scene which remains with me to this day was one in which the outraged RSM was berating a black soldier played by Ossie Davis. At one point the row between them descended into a shouting match which suddenly came to an abrupt halt. At that point, the RSM stood up almost nose to nose with the soldier, and with every word individually stressed said:

'You black bastard!'

What struck me at the time was not the screen dialogue, though that was shocking enough…it was the reaction of the cinema audience. I can still hear in my mind the sharp intake of breath that went right around the auditorium. I kid you not – people were really shaken… and you could have heard a pin drop in the space that followed before the director cut to another scene. As an indication of what the public felt was right and what was wrong, it said a lot. Such blatant racism was becoming increasingly unacceptable - and a good job too.

The attitude of our generation to women was also a bit more complex than reference to *'On The Buses'* and the sauciness of the *'Carry On'*

' *Colonel Blimp was a press cartoon character parodied as possessing self-important stuffiness. Also, don't forget that the sixties was the dawn of the age of satire and as a consequence, we were getting pretty good at extracting the urine.*

films might imply. A quick flip back to Chapter 3 will provide a reminder that in terms of educational opportunity, gender equality in the fifties was what today would be seen as *a work in progress*. Girls got a pretty raw deal as regards the choices available to them, and whereas the education of both sexes was subject to a great deal of heavy-handed social engineering, girls came off worst. But there again, such a view needs to be seen within the context of what went before. Prior to the Second World War for example, a married woman would be expected to leave her job if she became pregnant. *'Fair enough'* I hear you say – but not fair enough when you realise that as far as society was concerned, her pregnancy was more or less the *end of her paid working life*. There was an expectation that once she was a mother, no woman would return to paid work… her husband would be the breadwinner, and she would be the housewife, no ifs, no buts.

The war changed all that. It is quite bizarre to note that it took a massive and deadly global conflict to change a nation's perspective of how accepted role models should be re-examined and changed, but that is how it was. Just as the First World War provided the momentum to force through women's suffrage, it took the next great conflict to introduce the notion that women could be independent, and could manage their own future quite as effectively as men. As you might expect, the change was neither instantaneous nor global – but the fact that it was just a part of the new post-war scene promoted by Clement Atlee's incoming Labour government saw it as an integral part of the brave new world rising out of the ashes of war.

As with so much else for the Baby Boomers, society's attitude to the role of women was changing. That this new departure in the post-war period took some time to gain momentum is not that surprising, but at least opportunities for women were opening up. And most important of all, the 1944 Education Act gave all the nation's children the right to be educated to a specific age, and to provide both sexes with a certain amount of vocation based education. OK, in girls' post-war Secondary Modern schools this might initially have been limited to skills which were also essentially home-based (mainly needlework and cookery) but as we have seen, the introduction of many secretarial and commercial skills also played an increasingly important part.

So too did our growing access to the media, and not just in terms of enabling all and sundry to see the young and beautiful strutting their stuff in front of the cameras. In 1965, the BBC's programme *'The Wednesday Play'* screened a powerful drama called *'Up the Junction'*. To a nation used to being cosseted with the cosy and unchallenging familiarity of variety shows and travelogues, this came as a shock. The play introduced such issues as abortion, social deprivation and the prejudices associated with those who had fallen upon difficult times. The dramatisation was so realistic that some viewers mistook it as part of the evening's news broadcast. The repercussions in the following days revealed that the play had been something of a wakeup call to the need for us all to re-examine our views on social issues in general, and our attitude to the plight of some women in particular.

In similar vein, Ken Loach's *'Cathy Come Home'* was another hard hitting play that in 1966 shook viewers into a greater awareness of the need to recognise the uncomfortable matter of homelessness, and the way in which some folk were condemned to an increasingly slippery slope of despair.

Whilst we are on this rather depressing analysis of some aspects of the values of the post-war years, let me drop another tiny bombshell. A recent news report focussed on the anguish suffered by many women who became unmarried mothers in the 1950s and 1960s. In those days, the policy of the authorities was to *remove the baby from its mother at birth* - and to offer the infant up for adoption: again, no ifs, no buts. Little wonder therefore, that the ladies interviewed in the programme have suffered a lifetime of aching sorrow through experiencing such trauma. In view of this the fact, that they now seek redress for all their pain and sorrow is hardly surprising.

But what you might be asking yourself is: *'How could any civilised society possibly endorse such a brutal and callous policy for children born out of wedlock?'* You would think that there is no excuse for such an outrageous policy, and you'd be right ... but again, at least some mitigation comes to light when you look more closely at the context.

Like it or not, to be an unmarried mother just a few decades ago, was considered absolutely taboo. It was a matter of shame, and as depicted in *'Up the Junction'* could all too frequently lead to the desperate measure of an illegal abortion. Society turned its back on unmarried girls who became pregnant, and single parent families - unless caused by the untimely death of either partner - were almost unheard of. With the introduction of the birth control pill in the 1960s this became less of a feature, but unwanted pregnancy was regarded as totally undesirable: it was a matter of shame, and a single mother – unless she was a widow – was often seen as being immoral.

Ugly, isn't it? You may also note that almost no condemnation fell upon the fellas, which is totally preposterous when you consider that in the 1950's, most young men expected their brides to be virgins!

From a modern perspective, there can be few who cannot understand the appalling hurt suffered by so many young women in those days, but putting the *'what'* of this dire policy into the context of the time – whilst not excusing it – does at least go a little way to provide clarity as to the *'why'*. Whilst contemporary opinion might be drawn into concluding that we Baby Boomers were born in repressive times, such a view fails to understand that the mid to late sixties - when we were coming of age - was the very time when society was at last struggling to break free of such subjugation.

It's also easy for the current generation to forget other pretty important contextual issues which circumscribed and moulded our views, the most significant amongst which was the fact that the Death Penalty for murder was still in place up until November 1965. Consequently, Baby Boomer formative years would sometimes acknowledge that someone had been sentenced to death, and would shortly be… *'taken to a place of execution and hung by the neck until dead'* as the sentencing judge was required to state. Blimey.

A little less severe but also deeply illustrative of the time is the fact that for most of the decade which saw the Summer of Love and all that trendy flower-filled stuff, *(letting it all hang out baby, you gotta do your own thing, man!)*… being a practising homosexual in the UK was **a criminal offence**. It was not until 1967 when the Sexual Offences Act was passed that such discrimination was finally eradicated – and then only in England and Wales *'between consenting males in private'*. As far as the youth of the sixties was concerned, men who were attracted to their own sex were called *homos*, and such behaviour was considered to be abhorrent. The term *'queer'* was frequently used and the thought that women too could be homosexual was rarely, if ever considered. If you had asked a typical teenager of the period what a *lesbian* was, I doubt whether more than a tiny percentage could have told you - and it almost goes without saying that the needs of the transgender members of society were not even *imagined*, let alone understood or supported. Same sex marriage? What are you? *A Martian or something?*

All very illiberal… but before you curl your lip in contempt at such reactionary views, please remember that prior to 1967 men could be – and were – *sent to prison for the full expression of their love and affection for a same sex partner*. So the fact that the BB generation was slow on the uptake as regards altering our attitudes to such fundamentals is hardly surprising, is it? Just because a law has changed doesn't mean that there is instantaneous acceptance of practices which you have been told - for all of your life so far - are *so wrong* that you can be banged up for doing them. So when characters in our TV shows demonstrated their gayness (and by the way, the term 'gay' was entirely new in the late sixties and early seventies) it was an indication of our coming to terms with such a change. Set against this background, that their depiction could now be described as blunt and unsophisticated is, again, hardly surprising.

And finally, forgive me if I labour the point, but may I remind you that even at a domestic day-to-day level, we Baby Boomers still had a long, long way to go before in any way resembling today's liberal standards. As noted before, the behaviour of some of the establishment left a lot to be desired. Recrimination for misdemeanours was often very physical – and getting thumped for bad behaviour was common at school, and especially for the boys. Less well recognised is the fact that our parents too, were quite likely to use physical punishment to discipline their wayward off-spring, and getting a clip round the ear, even in full public view, was usually seen by society as 'regrettable but necessary'. The phrase *'spare the rod and spoil the child'* was much used... most frequently by those in charge of the rod, we noted. And yet, whether beaten at home or at school, most felt hardly anything by way of resentment. It was just life's rich pattern, the way things had always been. It was not unknown that some of the most popular teachers in schools were also the most physically aggressive... getting beaten by some loony bloke wielding a gym shoe for all he was worth was just all part of the game, wasn't it?

Well, this is all pretty heavy stuff... but does it not contextualise the apparently flippant way our generation responded to such issues, views which are seen with such shock and horror by today's more enlightened critics? Given that perspective, does it not make the outraged reactions recorded by the celebrities featured in *'It Was All Right In The Seventies'* seem just a little OTT?

More to the point, it demonstrates that each generation needs to afford the preceding one the opportunity to be seen in the context of its own time, rather than simply being judged against contemporary views, opinions and standards. I think the BB generation stumbled along the path to greater enlightenment, but it took time: when you are on the foothills of a learning curve, you don't always recognise you are on it, however hard the going. I should also point out that the advice from the bible *'let he who is without sin cast the first stone'* seems particularly apposite – for is not *every* generation guilty of getting things wrong?... including us, right here and right now? With that thought in mind, it is quite easy to envisage in twenty years' time a programme entitled **'It Was All Right in the 2020's'** ...when outraged celebrities will be filmed as they watch in wide eyed amazement the excesses of our current lifestyle:

'What? They actually allowed trolling to go more or less unchecked? And cyber bullying was just a part of everyday life in the 2020's? Good grief!! And look at that! Animals being reared for slaughter and then eaten! Didn't they understand the concept of virtual meat? And just look at all that waste plastic fouling up the oceans for centuries to come…. And don't get me started on air pollution!!'

You get the point. In my view, it is very risky to take the moral high-ground when judging the behaviour of those in the past. From a current perspective, our contemporary generation has much to celebrate – but also a lot to feel guilty about. Take for example, the almost exponential growth in cyber crime and the ways in which criminals have infiltrated the internet and found myriad means by which this brilliant innovation can be put to antisocial ends. Look too at the lyrics of some of the songs now being blasted out 24/7 to all and sundry, but most of all directed at the young and impressionable.

Perhaps I'm being too hard on the *'It was All Right......'* programme which was, I have no doubt, highly entertaining for many. All I would say is – take a little extra time to see such presentations within their historical context, and don't forget, doing daft things, being illogical, thoughtlessly uncaring and downright gormless is all part of the human condition. It is therefore almost certain that the sort of issues which cause so much angst amongst the modern generation when looking at the Baby Boomers, will in twenty or thirty years' time be laid at its own door. In the fullness of time, accepted views and popular assertions have a habit of coming back to bite you. Perhaps we all need to learn that challenging the orthodoxy of a time gone by is a risky business!

So, to go back to the original question: did our blessed generation behave in a manner that reflected its unique advantages? In short, did we BB's get it right? As I think I have shown, the answer has to be:

'No, not completely ... but probably a bit more 'right' than that for which we are given credit'.

I would say that a fair proportion of received negative observations are at least substantially diluted when viewed in their unique historical context. That is not to say that we Baby Boomers are unaware of our generation's shortcomings: amidst all the sweetness of the things we enjoyed, there are also a number of uncomfortable reflections on what we really, really got wrong.

That's the thing with Acid Drops – they can be painfully refreshing.

8 So Far So Good

So, here we are – almost at the end of our amble through the Baby Boomer years, and before you interrupt by crying '*Hang on a minute! You've only got as far as the eighties, for heaven's sake! What about the rest?*' ... let me explain.

The trouble with the nineties and onward, is that we've been joined by another generation, the members of which have their own recollections and viewpoints. Now obviously, these are nearly always wrong, but that doesn't seem to deter such young upstarts from arguing the toss and contradicting their parents in a manner which I'm bound to say can frequently be described as *immoderate.*

So, if I were to continue in the same manner through the next decade or so, there is a good chance that it all might dissolve into a slanging match of the **'...it wasn't like that at all! We never played our music that loud, and in any case, it was a sleepover, and how was I to know the Tizer bottle was really full of vodka? And anyway you were supposed to be away in Benedorm...'** type, followed by the inevitable '*No we weren't, yes you were, no we weren't*' sort of conflict – all very unseemly. So I think it's getting very close to the time to throw out the anchor, to pull up the drawbridge, to call *'Time Gentlemen Please!'* - or any other suitable end-of-the-road platitude you can think of.

Let's not forget that the essence of the Baby Boomer generation was embodied in its germination and growth in the thirty five years following the end of the Second World War, and the circumstances and events that made up that period were utterly unique. The fantastic – and much underrated – resurgence of the fifties, together with the wholesale flamboyant explosion of the sixties were the epicentre of its breeding ground, the place where we Boomers took on our identity. The total joy and positivity of that era was our springboard – and we've been bowled along by its momentum ever since.

Those years were characterised by a generational confidence that saw *progress* and *improvement* in every area of life as a natural and pre-ordained expectation. Baby Boomers never had any doubt that each succeeding year would be better than its predecessor, however illogical and unrealistic this seems today. Self doubt was not a characteristic prevalent amongst the post-war generation, and the possibility of recession, hardship and decline was seldom considered. Now you might say well, that's just the natural over-exuberance of youth, and up to a point you'd be right – but in the case of the Baby Boomers, a goodly proportion of that expectation was *actually realised*.

That we were arguably the luckiest generation ever is perhaps a moot point for some, and a bone of contention for others. However, for many it remains the case and as mentioned before, the difficulty is to avoid the dangers of cloying self-satisfaction and smugness. Of course, there are some who might identify in this way – but in my opinion, not nearly as many as some observers might think. Once you can get us seniors to stop wittering on about what tablets we're currently taking, where you can get 2p off a litre provided you've got the coupons from last week's Independent, and important debating points such as *'have you seen the price of cous cous at Waitrose?'* …the vast majority of us agree that we have indeed been very fortunate, and have every reason to be grateful for living through a time when the welfare state - looking after all citizens *'from sperm to worm'* - became a governmental responsibility. It was also a time of massive opportunity, which combined with a growing measure of disposable wealth to be lavished on the output from thousands of factories, made for a heady mix.

In addition there is recognition that, despite being overtaken by the succeeding generation in so many things – like always being right and knowing all there is to know about anything electronic that needs you to press more than one button - we BB's are *still* having a remarkably good time. Take, for example, travel.

Now you may be surprised to learn that, despite not being the world's most attentive school kid, some odd snippets of the Humanities subjects still remain lodged in my memory. One such travel related item which springs readily to my mind concerns our Gallic pal, the Emperor Napoleon. Emerging from the inky depths comes this little jewel of knowledge concerning *le empereur*:

Evidently, after being thrashed yet again by the Royal Navy, the little bloke was in something of a bad mood, and was pacing up and down giving deep thought not only as to where the hell had Josephine got to, but the fact that Nelson and his lads always seemed to be hanging about whenever and wherever the French put to sea. And his generals were no help, just standing there wringing their hands, and wishing it was time for a croissant and a crafty Gitane behind *les sheds d' bicyclette*. All of a sudden Napoleon turned to them and yelled:

'Wherever wood will float, there you will find the English!'
Pretty profound, huh? I daresay one or two of the generals on his staff were thinking '*Hey mon empereur – lighten up, baby! We did pretty good at Austerlitz and Marengo, so why so gloomy?*'

Now I don't mean to lampoon the calibre of the French general staff (*who am I kidding? Of course I do!*) but I do think Napoleon hit the nail on the head. And his perceptive and pithy comment can so easily be adapted and applied to the Baby Boomers, paraphrased thus:

'Wherever in the world there is a holiday destination, there you will find a load of old Brits'

If you don't believe me, just ask anyone in their late sixties. You'll find loads of them tucking into a prawn and avocado baguette in any airport departure lounge. Once located, ask them if they've ever been to Kuala Lumpur or Virgin Gorda or Kathmandu. I guarantee they'll keep you pinned to the seat for the next hour or two explaining that, yes of course they had. In fact, the last time they were there was just before their third trip to Antarctica, and which they very much enjoyed… but not as much as two years before when they went paragliding over Iguassu Falls just before Geoffrey got his hernia, and they had to get a special Medicare flight back to Hemel Hempstead, with only a brief stopover in Bermuda for re-fuelling and the chance to top up with a two litre pack of duty free gin, one for us, and one for Mrs. Thompson who'd been looking after the dog.

I can tell you, us oldies have been absolutely EVERYWHERE. It seems there is not a square inch of the planet that has not been trodden on by the open-toed sandals (complete with grey hold-up socks – a fetching combination) of some old bloke, closely followed by his dear wife busily reminding him that he should use factor fifty on that bald spot, and *'you know what the doctor said about your legs'*.

And ships? Don't talk to me about ships. Cruising for some has become a way of life, and during every such venture you will find a number of *seventy-somethings* who have planned at least six or seven subsequent voyages, and seem therefore to live the majority of their lives bouncing around the high seas from one port to another like a demented seaborne pinball. I kid you not.

It is not difficult to understand that some of the next generation might harbour some resentment for such apparent extravagance, and I have little doubt that in some cases, it is a source of friction. At one extreme there is the *'well, we earned it, so we'll spend it'* view, and at the other *'we haven't got the opportunities you had, so help us out now'*.

As in most arguments there are aspects which hold true to both extremes, but my guess is that most potentially confrontational issues reach a compromise. For example, it might be worth reflecting on the assistance that is frequently supplied by the Bank of Mum and Dad … and on the other side of the argument, the support provided by the young for elderly folk whose health is failing. In the UK, we're pretty good at muddling along – it's a national characteristic of which we should be proud.

And as we ponder the future, there is reason to assert that at present, the world appears to be shrinking, does it not? Putting aside the huge issues imposed by the pandemic for a moment, international friction has meant that some parts of the globe well and truly on the tourist map less than a decade ago are now areas where you would have serious misgivings about venturing to at present. What a tragedy it is that some wonderful places are now virtually off limits for the conventional traveller, and as a result, there is increasing congestion in locations that remain free of any threat. I dare say such fluctuations in safe accessibility have been a feature of travel for many years, but it does seem particularly restrictive at the moment. Even the simplest travel overseas now requires you to stand in ever increasing queues with your shoes off, and belt, keys, loose change, laptop, smart phone and anything else remotely warlike removed from your pockets ready to be X-rayed. I guess I'm not alone in reflecting that this really does make the experience of international travel a lot less appealing.

And why is it always me that sets the damned alarm off? It's happened so many times that I'm almost getting to the stage of feeling ignored if I *don't* get frisked at the airport now ... and on the few occasions when this has happened I've felt this strange urge to turn round and ask the bloke with the rubber gloves *'Are you sure?'*

So travel ain't as easy as it used to be. But on the other hand it is still immensely popular: with modern cruise ships resembling floating blocks of flats and bigger airport terminals opening all over the place, the trend looks set to continue, rubber gloves or not.

Another 21st century problem upon which society quite rightly has to focus is the environment. Pollution, asbestos fibres, diesel particulates, the glut of plastic bags and even fluorocarbons from the humble domestic fridge are all matters of concern – and global warming is perhaps the biggest of them all. Now I have to say that up until about the nineties, the term 'environment' was seldom heard. Yes, there were concerns about the amount of plastic litter on the streets, and the growing need to find solutions for the rapidly accumulating mountains of waste country-wide, but it didn't have the high profile that the whole issue has today. And you could be forgiven for saying that it is a pity that the BB generation didn't have a more environmentally friendly outlook as the twentieth century drew to a close. Well, yes... but it's similar to the situation regarding recent identification of syndromes in the world of medicine: in days gone by, we didn't have to worry about a whole range of illnesses or environmental pollution... *because we didn't know we'd got them.* It's called blissful ignorance.

So the practices, processes, habits and fixations of each generation are full of complexities and apparently illogical thinking. Such is life, I suppose. I mean, ten years ago no one would have foreseen that by 2020, just about everyone under the age of forty would be spending hours every day on the phone to inform friends that they've just been down to Sainsbury's to get some oven chips, and are now on their way home because they want to wash their hair before *'Holby City'*. **'Love you Babe!'** And it's not just the young. Even we oldies are being drawn into the habit of telling all and sundry about the tablets we are taking, how the varicose veins are this morning and moving on to describe in some detail exciting plans we have for stewing some rhubarb in the afternoon, provided the post-lunch nap does not overrun. Strewth! And we thought Teletext was a bit time-consuming.

Now there's a case in point. Teletext was a real 1980's breakthrough in that it was probably the first step in making TV an interactive medium. Its only competitor was that table-tennis game where a little ball continually bounced around the screen, and you had to bash it back or suffer the inevitable censure and derision so freely dispensed by your six year-old who was *so* much better at it than you. And in the blink of an eye, bat, ball and Teletext itself vanished completely along with Yellow Pages, video tapes and Blackforest Gateaux.

Fortunately, there remains a rich diversity of simple pleasures, and I hope that the current generation is as good as seeking them out and exploiting them as we have been – for I really believe that Baby Boomers are expert in celebrating the ordinary. My proof? Just look at the fascination we hold for picking over the remnants of our past in TV programmes such as *'Antiques Roadshow'*, *'Cash in the Attic'* and *'Floggit'*. OK, there is a monetary interest there as well, but for many the pleasure of identifying objects from the past in an *'Oh, we had one of those'* sort of way is equally important. There has also been a recent succession of programmes showing what it was like to live in days gone by, and of these the Victorian period is most popular. Life below stairs for a scullery maid, or the daily experiences of a farm or factory worker spring to mind, as do the gruesome antics of Victorian cooks with their predilection for offal and boiled sheeps' heads... and so on. It seems that our love affair with social history - which had its first nationwide success in the 1960's with ITV's wonderful *'All Our Yesterdays'* - is alive and well. And why is this?

Well, its total fascination is a good starting point. As a nation, we all want to find out what our forebears were up to, let alone dig into the stories of love, lust, intrigue and other human frailties: there's nothing so attractive as a good bit of scandal ... plus, of course, you might find yourself a distant relative of Boudicca, which might explain your recurring lifelong dream which always seems to feature chariots with spiky bits attached. And the other reason for the enduring nature of such historical interest is that the wonders of the internet make it all so incredibly easy. Whereas twenty years ago you might have to trail off to Somerset House in London to get formal records, nowadays at the click of a button, you can view the census returns for 1911 and find out exactly where Mr. Zebediah Appleby was living. Not only that, but just a little extra reading will reveal his work, how many kids he had - and by comparing this entry with the next census in 1921, you could discover that in the meantime he had run off with his next door neighbour and was now living three streets away with two new kids and a part-time interest in bee-keeping.

Quite apart from the freedom of enquiry that the internet gives us, just look at all the retro stuff there is around. For those of us who have a habit of appearing pretty unkempt, the popularity of *shabby chic* has been an absolute godsend and the interest in, and availability of sweets from the past is another perfect example of how such ordinary things have immense attraction today. Exhibitions of 'Britain in the Fifties' and suchlike must be popular, because currently, there are so many of them. Memories of our domestic past, such as those on display at the National Trust's *Museum of Childhood* at Sudbury Hall in Derbyshire hold endless fascination for as many parents and grandparents as for their offspring.

If the expression *'happy is the man who takes pleasure in simple things'* is not already a phrase long used by the great thinkers of modern history, then it really ought to be, and the likes of Satre and Goethe must be kicking themselves that they didn't think of it first. Maybe they did – I don't know: I went to Highland Road Juniors, remember? Anyway, the expression is very true, but you have to be willing to look for interest where it may not be immediately obvious.

Let me give you an example: the humble bag of crisps. Believe it or not, this very ordinary commodity is a lot more interesting than the casual observer might think. The first and most obvious surprise with all crisp packets is that there are so few crisps within their shiny interior. Noshing your way through the sparse contents takes but a matter of seconds, and although *Pomegranate and Paprika* is indeed a totally new and must-have *taste explosion*, it doesn't really compensate for the depressing lack of bulk. And there the average person might leave it, and with a heavy sigh consign the empty bag to the correct recycling bin.

But whoa! Hold on! Those of us who spent our early years denied the wonders of instant entertainment and global communication, of a world completely devoid of computers, of a world where the introduction of sellotape was seen as an event of national emancipation – are not so easily disheartened. Surely the empty crisp bag must contain some hidden secret of interest, apart that is, from its apparently chromium plated interior and the fascinating description of how many kilojoules of energy each crisp contains written in both English and Japanese?

And yes! It does! If making entertainment from something as unprepossessing as an empty crisp bag doesn't impress you with the ability of old gits to wring out every last bit of value from a purchase, then I don't know what will. It really takes the biscuit – or in this case, the crisp. Now pay attention… flex your fingers and get ready for an exercise in what might be termed **'unexpected origami'**:

[219]

Now, if the ability to make a perfect pentagon from an empty crisp bag* doesn't leave you in a state of total gobsmackedness, then I'm a little worried about your sense of awe and wonder in the wider world. You have to bear in mind that of all the common geometric shapes, the pentagon is about the most awkward to recreate, and to do it from a container so mundane, so utilitarian… so *empty* as a crisp bag – well, surely there must be a Nobel prize for inventiveness hanging around somewhere, isn't there?

Now that reminds me… talking of interest generated from ordinary things, what could be more fascinating than sellotape, our old sticky-backed chum? Now I know it's been a chapter or two since I've banged on a bit about this most useful commodity, but I believe it's really only a matter of time before Social Studies at all schools will include the compulsory mantra:

'Look after your sellotape, and your sellotape will look after you'.
And it's still a matter of wonder, isn't it? For example, can you explain to me how it is that when you look at a brand new roll side on – i.e. looking at the collective edges of the tape - it appears yellow, but when you remove a piece for immediate use, *it is completely transparent?!* So where did the yellow go? Clearly, it's one of life's little mysteries.

Nevertheless, that's not to say that sellotape doesn't have its critics. There are a number of malcontents who grumble about the fact that they have probably spent what adds up to more than a complete decade of their lives trying to find the end of a part-used roll of sellotape - complaining bitterly that despite running their fingernail right around the roll in *both* directions at least fifteen times, they *still* cannot feel the little bump which gives an indication as to where the damn end is located. To these folk, all I can say is this - *that's because you haven't used the little dispenser which not only provides you with a handy place to store your reel, but also a serrated edge with which to cut the tape to just the right length – so you only have yourself to blame.* So there.

*Lest the manufacturers of Golden Wonder Crisps should be getting a little light-headed with the geometric properties of their packaging – perhaps considering it for the next Turner prize at the Tate Modern for example - I should point out that after extensive research I can reveal that this artistic miracle of folding works just as well with Walkers or Lidl's own brand.

And if you still don't believe me about the Baby Boomers' ability to recognise the power of the ordinary to fascinate, then I invite you to consider the following:

There cannot be many people who have never visited a fine country house or historic castle in this green and pleasant land. I bet even now you're instantly reflecting on the large slice of carrot cake and huge latte coffee you consumed with such relish at the conclusion your last visit, the only slight downside being the fact that the tenner you had in your pocket for the purchase of such delights failed to produce much – if anything - by way of change. Even so, I ask you to put such tedious monetary considerations to one side, and instead spend a moment or two reflecting upon your visit to the stately pile. In particular, give a thought as to where you spent the most time as you toured the dusty confines with its sinister suits of armour, its glowering portraits… and its steely custodians eyeing you warily lest you should put even one toe beyond the confines of the roped-off areas.

So, where did you spend most of your time? Was it gazing in awe at the sculptures which his lordship had collected from all over the world? Was it at the amazing collection of Charles II silverware? Did the fine portrait that a certain Mr. Rembrandt had spent a fair amount of time knocking out in the late sixteen fifties catch your eye and leave you suitably astounded at the superb brushwork for a good twenty minutes?

I doubt whether it was any of these. So, where did you and nearly everyone else spend most of the time? Go on – guess… well, it's in the *kitchen*, of course. If you don't believe me, next time you're in a stately house, just stand back and watch people going around on such visits.

The vast majority stand around the displays of fine *this*, or superb *that*, and usually make little comment. In fact total silence is not uncommon, although it may occasionally be interrupted by a rather tentative question directed to the steward for some point of further illumination. Once the answer has been given, the customary response rarely goes into the realms of wild excitement, and is more usually of the *'Well, fancy that… all right for some wasn't it?'* variety. Not so the kitchen. Here the response is much more vocal and lively, and often takes the form of *'My gran had one of those! I can see her now surrounded by clouds of steam every Monday morning!'* or *'Blimey! Fancy having to go down to a cave at the end of the west lawn to get some ice just because Milord wanted a lemon sorbet in the middle of July! Must have been a long time before Lyons Maid!'* And so on and so on. And why do you think that kitchen responses are so much more robust, lively and gleefully given? It is my contention that it is simply the fact that, unlike the rest of the displays, the kitchen houses the ones with which we can most easily identify – because they are *ordinary*, they are familiar, they are commonplace. They are the artefacts and experiences with which we have an immediate affinity, and to which we can all relate. We are comfortable with such ordinariness. The experiences of how preceding generations coped with the everyday problems which are the lot of humankind, are a source of magnetic fascination for us all. I guarantee that any child you take around on such a visit will probably have little recollection of the fine porcelain, the beautiful tapestries or the exquisite statuary. But what they will remember, and be busy bashing it out on Twitter to their mates the minute they get back in the car – will be along the lines of *'just been with the parents to this big house - soooooo boring. Loads of old stuff, but guess what? The scullery maid used to spit on this thing called a flat-iron to see if was hot enough yet to press his Lordship's long Johns! EVEN GROSSER, there were no en-suites in those days, and they used to do their number ones in a chamber pot under the bed ... and their number twos too!!'* Good to know that the power of the prosaic resonates well with the younger generation too, isn't it?

I suppose that when it comes down to it, such interest and enquiry for any generation is simply an expression of human nature – most of us just want to feel some association, some commonality with our forebears, and rightly so. Our common roots lie at the heart of family life, and the daily problems and triumphs experienced by our ancestors give us a sense of proportion and ownership with our own lives.

Well, this is all a long way from folded crisp bags, I'm bound to say. But the point I am making can be summed up by stating:

'Today's ordinary quickly becomes tomorrow's *extra*ordinary.'

You may quote me on that. Indeed, feel free to try it out on anyone sitting near you right this minute..... All done? How did it go? Well, OK. Perhaps it may have startled the lady on the checkout at Tesco's a little, but nevertheless, it was worth a try, wasn't it?

Which brings me neatly to J Cloths. If you think I'm now going to spend a page or two extolling the virtues of the packaging and in-built quality of this most useful of kitchen aids, then WELL DONE! Good guess! I mean, who wouldn't want to spend a moment or two rejoicing over the tall hexagonal packet whose top lid opens up with all the elegance and symmetry of a rose bud bursting into full bloom? Am I getting too misty-eyed and romantic for you? OK, enough said; you get the picture… so I'll bring you back to earth, and postpone detailing the virtues of these multi-coloured mopping marvels lest you become over-excited, and we all know that at your age, an attack of the vapours can have lasting side effects. So instead I'll turn your attention to something much less prepossessing – the common rat.

A number of health related programmes aired in recent years, have dwelt upon the fact that this adaptable and prolific rodent will always be a danger to worldwide health. Must be true I suppose – certainly the bubonic plague didn't do anyone much good did it? And as if such information is not unsettling enough, commentators then inform us that these dear little quadrupeds are increasing their number at a rate that can only be described as reckless. As a result, each and every one of us on the planet is **never more than fifteen metres from a rat!**

Well. That's a jolly thought, isn't it? You can imagine the broadsheet reaction of some folk: *'What? A rat? Living near me? In Eastbourne? Surely not…Worthing I could understand… but Eastbourne? Never!!'*

All a bit depressing really, so let me bring a little sunshine back into this gloomy landscape, because I can do better than the rats! Oh yes. I laugh in the face of your fifteen metres! I scorn your prolific output that can be counted in mere hundreds of thousands… for I can tell you, that after extensive research I can reveal that every man, woman and child across this most pleasant country, this green a sceptred isle, this jewel set among silver seas …etc etc …

… is never more than FIVE metres from a J Cloth!!

Think about it. I bet wherever you are sitting/standing/lying in a darkened room right now, you can pinpoint the location of at least a couple of nearby J Cloths. They might be lurking behind the wash basin in the bathroom, or be tucked down by the U-bend behind the loo. Of course, many will be adding their colourful presence by hanging languidly across the kitchen mixer tap… but don't forget the half dozen others that are screwed up in places as diverse as down the back seat of the car, or all squished up in the cupboard under the stairs where you had to mop up that burst bottle of home brew twelve years ago. And that's not to mention the girly pink one you used and in panic threw into the broom cupboard when the next door neighbour called to ask you if you knew how to replace the strimming line on his Flymo.

And J Cloths are so versatile. I once sent for a light-weight boiler suit, advertised as being great for those messy jobs in the warm weather, when traditional protective clothing will leave you all of a-lather. Imagine my surprise when I discovered that the said overall was none other than a full one-piece suit made out of J Cloth material. I daresay *wearing* this most useful of fabrics has produced a wide range of adaptations: I mean, for example, how about underwear? What could be better? It is brightly coloured and more importantly, absorbent! Perfect. And if worn to an orgy, an added bonus would be that you've got the instant wherewithal to do the mopping up afterwards!

And aren't J Cloths resilient? Despite the fact that after doing last night's dishes - when you threw yours carelessly across the mixer tap where it hung in a rather haphazard manner all screwed up, sopping wet and with a few bits of broccoli still stuck in the weave where you couldn't be bothered to rinse it properly – the following morning it is transformed! Overnight it had dried itself and become smooth and wrinkle free with no trace of errant vegetable remaining visible. I'm even coming round to the view that mine actually re-folds itself during the night in order that it might present an efficient and hygienic presence the following morning - which together with its *'ready for action and able to cope with a whole new day of thoughtless abuse'* attitude makes for a winning combination.

But of course, J Cloths and sellotape are not the only sources of intrigue and fascination for contemporary society. There are always other gritty little problems with which the inquisitive Baby Boomer can keep the grey cells occupied.

For example, is it not beyond the wit of man to discover a way of predicting which checkout at the supermarket is the best one to choose? Surely there must be some complex algorithm which will enable customers a reliable way of predicting which queue contains within its impatient membership the argumentative shopper who a) has selected an item whose bar code is missing and thus will require the services of another employee to walk the whole length of the store to find the correct charge for a bottle of *'thrice refined olive oil'* which is on special offer next to the Brillo pads; b) suddenly remembers the discount voucher lodged in a back pocket just *after* the final purchase has been swiped and the total calculated and c) is not entirely sure into which of the many little wallets and pockets he or she has secreted the credit card needed to complete the transaction.

There's got to be an answer somewhere, hasn't there? With mankind able to ascertain the most fundamental details of a person's genetic makeup through the close examination of the tiniest hair, or to send spacecraft to the outer-most reaches of the solar system to arrive in perfect orbit around Uranus on a particular Thursday afternoon at the end of October 2025, surely its only a matter of time before someone comes up with a reliable solution.

Now don't look at me! I don't know the answer! To be honest, I'm beginning to think that it's about time you took on a little bit more responsibility rather than leaving it all to me. So instead of putting your feet up and reaching for yet another chocolate digestive, you might at least *consider* the idea of wrenching yourself away from this terrific read and give a few moments' thought to the great questions of our time. After all, it's not as if you're unprepared for such a challenge is it? Over the past chapters I've done my best with you – given you tips on decimal coinage, provided suggestions on how to put four minutes to good use in case nuclear war should be declared, offered advice on dealing with a TV picture that keeps revolving round the screen - to name but a few. Armed with such a mass of useful facts, I feel it's really about time you had a go for yourself, and then give the nation your answer on Twitter or Facebook or any other of those things which we Baby Boomers don't understand.

And speaking of the BBs, I guess all of us in that august group are now more than a little aware of the fact that we have achieved septuagenarian status, and that the less than cheerful biblical estimation that any person reaching the old 'three score and ten' status ought not to book any holidays in anything but the immediate future, is a bit unnerving, to say the least. So perhaps I ought to stop now before I get into the '*but isn't seventy the new fifty?*' routine, or get all misty-eyed and noble, declaring that '*I've had a good innings*' or similar claptrap.

So let's just remind ourselves: we BB's are here for the long haul. Therefore, that we are also going to live *forever* is a taken as read, is it not? Besides, speaking personally, I've not yet fulfilled my lifelong ambition to be completely full of gorm, and submit the following as an example of the fact that even now, I still have some way to go to achieve my goal:

I was recently sent on an errand to a local supermarket to buy some odds and ends, one of which would enable my wife to replenish our bird table. Despite the fact that I had successfully managed to bypass the section of the shop which seriously tempted me to purchase a '*handy electric chain saw complete with tooth sharpener attachment*' for a very reasonable £79.99, I was unable to locate the required item which our blue tit chums were demanding. After a number of fruitless circuits of the supermarket aisles, I had to admit defeat and decided to ask a store employee where such an item might be found. This I did… and a few moments later I actually found myself asking the somewhat startled young man:

'Excuse me… do you have fat balls?'

And that, my friends, is absolutely true. I suppose it's just lucky I didn't go on to ask '…*and where can I find your ginger nuts?*'

So as you can see, a stack more gorm is still required before I shuffle off the old mortal coil, and I regret to say that the nearest and dearest still debate at immoderate length regarding my current level of feck, appearing fairly unanimous in their view that there is still room for a substantial top-up.

But am I disheartened? Like thousands of other Baby Boomers, don't I still watch University Challenge patiently awaiting a question regarding the number of tanners in half a crown in eager anticipation of scoring a first point over Jesus College Oxford? And with each morning's post do I not still cast aside with a merry *'Hah! Not for me matey!'* the endless succession of unsolicited pamphlets advertising solutions to incontinence problems, walk-in baths, discrete trusses and hearing aids so small that once inserted you'll probably never, ever see them again? And don't get me started on funeral plans! Is it me, or do the people featured look just *a little too cheery*? The impression given is that they're all speculating on how much loot they're going to get, and are even now wondering if there'll be enough for a new conservatory *and* an outdoor Jacuzzi.

Well, dream on. As far as all Baby Boomers are concerned, there's life in us old dogs yet, and despite being just ever so slightly aware of the grim reaper sharpening up his blade, there's still such a lot to do, so many people to irritate … so much sellotape to dispense.

9 'Hindsight's a Wonderful Thing'

Usually such a statement means:

'If only I'd known X at that time, then I wouldn't have done Y'

For example – during the heady days of home-made booze, my mate Steve wouldn't have decanted his Elderflower Champagne (*three florets of elderflowers, wine vinegar, two gallons of water... add yeast and withdraw to a safe distance – or better still a nuclear shelter*)... into glass screw-top bottles. Had he used the more usual plastic drum with a rubber bung, he and his wife would have been spared being woken by an enormous bang at 2am one morning... only to find that their utility room/downstairs loo where the bottles were stored had been eviscerated by thousands of tiny shards of glass ejected with enormous force when all of the bottles exploded. Still, picking the glass shards out of the wall, the ceiling, the laundry basket and the loo roll for the next fortnight did provide a diverting new hobby – plus time to reflect upon what might have been the outcome if the toilet had been occupied for its more usual purpose at the time of the explosion. Reeking of booze and trying to explain away your totally shredded underpants at A&E might have been awkward, to say the least.

I daresay each and every one of us could make a lengthy list of the *'things I would have done differently if I'd only known then what I know now'* type, and given some thought to how life might have been improved if such knowledge had been available at the time.

But making mistakes, choosing the wrong option, doing all sorts of stupid things is part of being human, isn't it? In some ways, being daft, illogical and irrational is an important ingredient: it's what makes us what we all are for varying proportions of time – whimsical, unreliable, credulous, capricious, unpredictable, contrary and arbitrary.

That being the case, I'm not saying that humankind is therefore totally hopeless and irretrievably flawed – far from it. A good dollop of *loopiness* is what has kept us going throughout history, and made our lives so much more interesting. To give a likely example:

It is 2500BC. You are sitting outside your cave in the Preseli Hills in

Pembrokeshire, and looking forward to the meal the wife is knocking up – likely to be her famous *'Tasty Bison Haunch with a side of shredded twigs'* recipe. Suddenly, the boss of the tribe comes up and says:

'Hi Bogga. Me and the lads have been having a think, and we reckon it will be just terrific to drag some really massive stones 125 miles to the south east, and then set them up on end to make a nice circle. Great idea or what?!!'

And of course, Stonehenge has been the subject of speculation, wonder and awe ever since. That no one really knows the why's and the wherefores doesn't really matter a jot. It's interesting... slightly bonkers but ***INTERESTING***, OK?!

And the range of human flaws listed on the previous page means that we need not be in the least afraid of being overcome by robots in the future. AI stands for Artificial Intelligence, and this very title describes its weak points, doesn't it? How can something so flawless, so logical, so *'utterly right all the bloody time'* ever replace the in-built irrational guile and unpredictable loopiness of us humans?

Of course, we've all done things we regret, and as pointed out in Chapter7, the Baby Boomer generation had been as guilty of loads of individual and group mistakes ... but probably no more than anyone else. What's more, those who would point the finger and offer criticism – however justified – might do well to reflect that irrationality and daftness is not time sensitive. It plays a part of life *all of the time*, so the self-appointed critics of times gone by might consider setting aside their self-righteous indignation for a moment or two in order to give some thought along the lines of ... **'and what are we cocking up right here, right now?** Because believe me, it's going on all the time.

Speaking of cock-ups brings me the great Denis Norden, whose TV show *'It'll Be Alright On The Night'* started its long and successful run in 1977. Based almost entirely on out-takes from a whole range of TV programmes, Denis was at pains to show that if anything can go wrong, in the world of TV, it almost certainly will. The hilarious results of such cock-ups proved so popular that the show and its derivatives lasted well into the new century, and such longevity speaks volumes for the huge public affection there is for mistakes, gaffs and avoidable errors. Like the song says: *'We're Only Human After All'* ... and all of this fun without a robot in sight. Or indeed, without *hindsight* - that much sought-after but apparently unattainable commodity which is at the centre of our current deliberations.

However, I would suggest that there is a different interpretation of the word, because from a different perspective we *all* have a fair dollop of hindsight, right here, right now. I am cautiously hopeful that this book has reawakened a number of memories that until recently remained forgotten in the dusty depths of your memory. If so, what more can a little gentle prodding and poking about in your own mental archive reveal? Rather like a dusty article retrieved from a seldom visited cupboard, what forgotten jewels only need a little concentrated polishing to bring them back into sharp focus and Technicolor glory?

Like many of my age group, I'm quite a fan of BBC's *'The Repair Shop'* and enjoy seeing how the old bits and pieces, many of them apparently far beyond redemption can be re-born in such startling ways. So before the analogy becomes overwhelmingly obvious, let me just say that a delve back into your own past – your own hindsight- can be well worth the effort. If you're not sure how to start, just drag out a few old photos, or listen to music from four or five decades ago. If you identify as a Baby Boomer, I encourage you to Google a tune called *'Puffing Billy'*. If this doesn't conjure up a flood of memories and put you on the path to re-investigate your own hindsight, I'd be mighty surprised. What's more, each re-visited memory will produce others, and like a blossoming plant will produce a prodigious array. Human nature being what it is, such recollection will more often than not be both stimulating and happy.

Worth the effort? Absolutely!

Postscript

Along with the first book in this series – *'The Time of Our Lives'* - my aim has been to write an affectionate commentary on the age of the Baby Boomers as seen through the eyes of one very ordinary bloke – a sort of essay in gratitude for the good fortune and opportunities which fate has dealt our post war generation and to put these firmly within the context of the time. I hope that both have given detail and perspective to our experiences.

No doubt our successors will go on to witness and participate in stuff which is beyond our imagination. I just hope they all have as much fun. No doubt things will be very different – for example, banning the sale of new petrol and diesel cars from 2030 means that transport will be totally transformed in no time at all… and probably makes my generation the last to live its whole existence surrounded by the throaty roar of straight-through exhausts and the screech of tyres as the local souped-up Ford Fiesta leaves a number of interesting scrape marks over the local speed bumps. I can't really see electric cars having such a dramatic presence, can you? And what will become of the roar of the big motorbikes? Will future Hells Angels still have quite the same aggressive presence all dressed up in black leather complete with white skull and crossbones, sitting astride their mighty machines, and twisting up the old throttle to *a mild electric hum*? Don't think so.

On the other hand, there will no doubt be other experiences of dynamism and excitement which at present are not even thought of – especially by us oldies, most of whom are still having problems finding the defrost button on the microwave. Whatever happens, and as is always the case, the future will be set against and circumscribed by the backdrop of what is happening on the international stage. At present this is all looking just a shade less stable than for the last few decades. That which we Baby Boomers considered immovable and the very bedrock of our society is no longer quite so certain, either at home or abroad. But if you look back in history, *'twas ever thus*. The argument that the apparent stability with which the post-war generation has lived is the *exception,* rather than the rule, does hold some merit. Turbulence at home and abroad is very much a feature of human existence, and it may be that the world is reverting to type. However mysterious and unpredictable this might be, let us hope that what emerges will be a new age of discovery, hopefulness and cooperation - and one in which mutual respect plays a significant role.

We Baby Boomers can only look on – but for whatever uncertainties and challenges that lie before succeeding generations, we have but one word of advice. It comes from a certain bus conductor we met in the pages of Book 1, and now seems particularly apt: it is, of course,

*Odetetnyaah!**

****

What Next?

For many of us, the generational bungee jump of excitement and possibility still continues, and the final book in this *'All In Good Time'* series entitled *'Third Time Lucky!'* is in its embryonic stage. Being perhaps a little more reflective than its predecessors, Book 3 will take a headlong dive into important questions of the time including:

Why does my garden never look like Monty Donn's?
What is the point of a Tricorn hat?
Why are the subtitles on my TV getting smaller?
Is 'disposable time' now more of an issue than 'disposable income'?
Who on earth was Barbara of Seville?
Is the fact that there's an S in the word 'lisp' an unnecessary cruelty?

Join me on the final uplifting bounces of our bungee jump through the exciting Baby Boomer years.

* *Odetetnyaah!* interprets as *'Hold Tight Now!'*

Acknowledgements

Any book of detailed reflections requires a lot of corroboration, and as with the first volume of the series, I have spent a large amount of time diligently seeking well-informed and thoughtful views from a whole range of contemporaries. Sound a bit pompous? Er yes…you're right. OK, I admit it – what I mean is, I chatted to loads of people, all of whom were full of amazing details, pithy stories and hilarious anecdotes usually accompanied by loads of laughter. It only takes a little prodding to get the old mental archives fired up again with half-forgotten stories tumbling forth and blinking in the sudden light of re-discovery. So to you all, I offer my sincere and heart-felt thanks – and this includes my old SGS friends Paul Knox, Derek Buckle and Peter Higgins whose reflections and encouragement have been much appreciated.

Those who kindly offered their specialist knowledge include:
- David Higginson of the Vintage Wireless Society for the images and information related to TV, radios, music centres and test cards;
- Bruce Hunt at Saltash Heritage Museum for all images and information about cameras, typewriters and telephones;
- Steve Harrison for GPO memories of Bletchley Park in the 1960's;
- Dorset Vintage & Classic Auction for 1960's car images;
- Ivan Bell at MokeInternational.com for all Mini Moke images;
- Gail and Steve Edginton for 8mm movie info…and home-brew;
- Phil Ashton for image and details of his GPO Telegram motor bike;
- Paul Bunce for images and information concerning the last Mini

Other picture credits

Title page: WikiHow and IMGBIN.com

Chapter 1: *Two Tin Cans a Piece of String*
Banda machine: courtesy of Graham Yapp
Adding machine: Science & Society Picture Library, Science Museum

Chapter 2: *A dedicated Follower of Fission*
HMS Vanguard: courtesy of *The News,* Portsmouth
Winkle Picker shoes; courtesy of *Madcap England*

Chapter 3: *Sky Hooks and Elbow Grease*
Cyclemaster moped: courtesy of Studio 434
Lambretta Mk 2: courtesy of Stephen Robertson
Lambretta: *Smart Alec Scooter Boys,* Juno Records

Chapter 4: *Two Thirds of Sex, Drugs and Rock 'n' Roll*
1960's traffic jam: Wikimedia Commons
The Flowerpot Men: Alamy.com
Che Guevara image: Wikimedia Commons
E Type: courtesy of Studio 434
Twiggy: Alamy .com

Chapter 5: *Vertical Hold*
Vision On: Wikimedia Commons
Bruce Forsyth at the London Palladium: Mirrorpix .com
Earthrise photo by Bill Anders. NASA:Rawpixel.com
Buzz Aldrin: Unsplash, photo by Neil Armstrong

Chapter 6: *Shell Suits, Vertical Artex and Other Mistakes*
Ford Gran Torino: Wikimedia Commons
The two Davids: The Times

Chapter 7: *Acid Drops*
Invalid carriage: Imperial War Museum
Invacar: Elvis Payne at www.3-wheelers.com

I have made good use of Wikimedia Commons, and thank the Wiki organisation for its generosity in sharing information around the globe.

Most of the images not mentioned above come from my own collection. However, I say *'most'* because there are still a tiny number of photos that, despite my best efforts, I have been unable to track down. So, if you are an owner of an image not recorded above, please accept my apologies and rest assured that any omissions or mistakes that are brought to my attention will be corrected in future editions.

Finally, my thanks to Neil Jones at Archangel Design for his graphic skills, and to my sister Daphne Rex for her patient proof reading.

****

Any polite queries and comments to: jballingoodtime@gmail.com

… and in case you missed it:

Printed in Great Britain
by Amazon